Demagogues in American Politics

Demagogues in American Politics

CHARLES U. ZUG

OXFORD
UNIVERSITY PRESS

OXFORD
UNIVERSITY PRESS

Oxford University Press is a department of the University of Oxford. It furthers the University's objective of excellence in research, scholarship, and education by publishing worldwide. Oxford is a registered trade mark of Oxford University Press in the UK and certain other countries.

Published in the United States of America by Oxford University Press
198 Madison Avenue, New York, NY 10016, United States of America.

Library of Congress Control Number: 2022943200

ISBN 978–0–19–765195–7 (pbk.)
ISBN 978–0–19–765194–0 (hbk.)

DOI: 10.1093/oso/9780197651940.001.0001

1 3 5 7 9 8 6 4 2

Paperback printed by Lakeside Book Company, United States of America
Hardback printed by Bridgeport National Bindery, Inc., United States of America

For Mimi Zug, Grant and Cynthia Witherspoon, and Jeffrey Tulis

This country, with its institutions, belongs to the people who inhabit it. Whenever they shall grow weary of the existing government, they can exercise their constitutional right of amending it, or exercise their revolutionary right to overthrow it.

—Abraham Lincoln

Vox populi, vox humbug.

—William Tecumseh Sherman

CONTENTS

ACKNOWLEDGMENTS

A modified version of Chapter 3 of this book appeared in *American Political Thought* 10, no. 4 (Fall 2021). Material from Chapters 1 and 5 has appeared, respectively, in *The Constitutionalist* (February 18, 2021) and *Interpretation: A Journal of Political Philosophy* 47, no. 1 (Fall 2020). Permission to incorporate is gratefully acknowledged.

This project has benefitted from countless conversations with friends and colleagues, particularly Kyle Shen, Thomas Bell, Corey Herndon, and Zac McGee. I thank my editor at Oxford University Press, David McBride, for his guidance and expertise, and the two reviewers who provided thoughtful comments on the manuscript. I also thank The University of Texas–Austin and my colleagues at the University of Colorado–Colorado Springs for financial and professional support.

Above all, I am indebted to my teachers. Russ Muirhead has been exceedingly generous with encouragement and feedback. Rob Goldberg, my friend and mentor, introduced me to political theory, and Devin Stauffer helped me mature in my understanding of it as I have tried to apply its insights to American politics. I thank Gary Jacobsohn for all of the opportunities he has given me, for his generosity and care, and for teaching me the fundamental importance of constitutionalism. I owe my greatest debt of gratitude to Jeff Tulis, my model for scholarly and intellectual excellence, without whose guidance, support, and friendship I would not have completed this book.

1

Demagogues in American Politics

On December 10, 2019, eight days before President Donald Trump's first impeachment by the United States House of Representatives, the *New York Times* ran an op-ed that equated Trump's notoriously aggressive rhetoric with the rhetoric of numerous presidents before him.[1] The article's author, Philip Terzian, endeavored to refute the view that Trump's rhetoric is unprecedented in American presidential history. To substantiate his position, Terzian compared Trump's enormities—including his allegation that House Intelligence Committee chairman "Adam 'Pencil-Neck' Schiff's impeachment proceedings [were] illegal, invalid, and unconstitutional"—with public statements by Theodore Roosevelt in his capacity as president.[2] "[Trump's] impulsiveness," asserted Terzian, "is nearly as habitual as Theodore Roosevelt's."[3]

One might reasonably question the equivalence Terzian sought to draw between these particular presidents. After all, given Trump's notorious and well-documented aversion to reading, it hardly seems like an exaggeration to speculate that President Roosevelt—the author of at least thirty-five monographs—had, at the time of his death at age sixty, written more books than Trump has read.[4]

At the same time, and lest we mistake the forest for the trees, there is an important theoretical puzzle underlying Terzian's otherwise misguided article. In trying to establish that an identifiable form of aggressive and disruptive rhetorical leadership has been deployed for different purposes by different presidents in the course of American history, Terzian was provoking his readers to look beyond the mere *accusation* of demagoguery—which tends to end interesting conversations rather than start them—and to reflect on the range of meanings that demagoguery can have when deployed in different ways, by different political figures, for the sake of different political ends.

Despite a renaissance in the study of demagoguery and related concepts like populism in recent years, this question has received surprisingly little attention. Indeed, almost all discussions of demagoguery describe a form of rhetorical leadership that is essentially bad. In this view, demagoguery is defined at the outset

Demagogues in American Politics. Charles U. Zug, Oxford University Press. © Oxford University Press 2022.
DOI: 10.1093/oso/9780197651940.003.0001

of the discussion as a divisive and destabilizing practice that appeals to what is worst in an audience at the expense of what is best for the sake of the leader's own aggrandizement.[5] As a consequence, writers and politicians laboring under these assumptions have closed themselves off from the more interesting possibilities that a less vehemently moralistic approach to the subject opens up.

Curiously, these same possibilities seem to be intuitive for most people who have reflected on demagoguery, even though the implications of these possibilities have not been explored. The same authors who argue that demagoguery is bad in all cases will also concede that rhetorical tactics we traditionally associate with demagoguery, like appeals to the passions and prejudices of one's audience, can be legitimate in certain instances and when executed in a responsible way for the sake of a publicly beneficial end.[6] For example, as Erwin Hargrove concedes in his masterly account of presidential leadership, Franklin Roosevelt was "the exemplar of the good leader of the polity."[7] Accordingly, Roosevelt "was not a demagogue or an abuser of power"—even though Hargrove admits that he "used artifice and demagoguery at times."[8]

What are the factors and considerations that could make the use of demagogic tactics legitimate, even though many cases are acknowledged to be bad? Looking to the basic principles of constitutional democracy, I suggest a way to distinguish instances in American politics where demagogic rhetorical tactics are justifiable from those in which they are not.[9] My goal is to help us see the good in rhetorical leadership that we have previously dismissed as mere demagoguery, and to see what is harmful in rhetoric that we currently lack the tools to understand.

Contending with traditional approaches to the subject, I suggest that studies that define demagoguery in procedural terms (i.e., as rhetoric delivered in an impassioned or divisive way) as well as studies that define it in terms of outcomes (i.e., as rhetoric that provokes an emotional reaction in an audience) are both misguided. Though these behaviors—emotional public speaking and emotional audience reactions—can and often do signal that demagoguery is being practiced, describing demagoguery in such broad strokes results in a definition far too inclusive to provide meaningful descriptive and analytical leverage. Indeed, as many have observed, American political discourse and democratic discourse in general tend to be so replete with emotional appeals that any concept of demagoguery based simply on passion and emotion will be all but useless. A more exclusive and theoretically robust understanding is therefore needed.

As I will argue at length in the following chapters, demagoguery in the American context is best understood as a form of public rhetoric, employed by governing officials, that attempts to induce one's audience to see the political universe through a distinctive interpretive lens. This demagogic worldview envisions a part of the public that comprises the community as an authoritative "people" whose unified will constitutes the common good, and whose collective judgments about all aspects of policy therefore cannot be scrutinized.

In important respects, my account of demagoguery as sketched here borrows from work by scholars of populism such as Jan-Werner Müller, Nadia Urbinati, Margaret Canovan, and Kas Mudde and Cristobal Rivera Kaltwasser.[10] These authors have suggested that populism is at heart a worldview (or what Mudde and Kaltwasser call a "thin-centered ideology") that *anyone*—private citizen, political party, or public official—can adopt, and that can be held or expressed publicly or privately. Further, populism in this perspective threatens and sometimes actively violates liberal and pluralistic norms, both by invoking the goals and concerns of a part of the community, often of a particular race or ethnicity, as the true embodiment of the community and therefore unchallengeable, and by dismissing the goals and concerns of other groups, often peripheral and marginalized, as illegitimate and subversive. Relatedly, Patricia Roberts-Miller in her work on demagogic rhetoric contends that demagoguery is neither inherently political nor necessarily a form of public speech.[11] For her, demagoguery is "discourse" that demonizes and scapegoats an out-group while celebrating an in-group; accordingly, anonymous posts on an internet forum are just as demagogic as, say, a president's speech, so long as both demonize an out-group and celebrate an in-group.[12]

My account of demagoguery differs from approaches like these in two significant ways. First, instead of arguing that demagoguery is fundamentally incompatible with liberal pluralism and constitutional democracy, I suggest that it can be compatible with—and, further, that it can even improve—these forms of government. As I will argue, modern pluralism and constitutionalism are complex in that they seek to vindicate different and often competing normative aspirations, such as majoritarianism, individual liberties, and effective execution and administration.[13] Within this framework, constitutional processes and political institutions are created to structure, normalize, and moderate political conduct; but they also exist to realize the community's substantive goals and aspirations. And as scholars have begun to show, dysfunctional processes and institutions can thwart the community's goals as much as they can help to achieve them.[14]

With these insights in mind, I propose here to modify and correct the conventional wisdom about demagogues in American politics. Demagoguery cannot *simply* be proscribed from our politics on the grounds that it disrupts our institutions, because American politics is not *simply* institutional. Rather, our institutions themselves are ultimately instrumental; they exist for the sake of accomplishing goals that are of greater value than themselves.[15] Within this picture, demagoguery can become a resource for improving and circumventing defective institutions and, in the most remarkable cases, for proposing and creating new ones.

My second intervention in the literature is that in a constitutional democracy like the United States, where individual rights (and free speech, specifically) are constitutionally prioritized, demagoguery is best understood as a form of public rhetoric employed by governing officials, as opposed to private, non-office-holding citizens. As I will describe in Chapters 2 and 3, traditional and authoritarian regimes invariably regard critical political speech by private citizens not as a legitimately exercised liberty but as a threat to the established government. Much like the terms "faction" and "party," "demagoguery" as it is traditionally invoked therefore describes a fundamentally subversive phenomenon that cannot be tolerated or accepted as a normal part of political practice by the state. Indeed, like factions that seek to form political organizations apart from, perhaps in opposition to, the established regime, popular leaders or "demagogues" who do not belong to the official governing apparatus but who nonetheless employ rhetoric to appeal directly to popular audiences are regarded as presenting a direct challenge to the political order.[16]

Things are, or at least ought to be, different in modern constitutional democracy, where citizens enjoy the freedom to speak about politics in whatever manner they find appropriate.[17] For this reason, just like the term "party," the term "demagoguery" takes on a meaning in the American context that differs significantly from its meaning in the contexts of traditional and authoritarian politics. Because public political speech by private citizens is afforded significant license in the United States—just as political parties are afforded constitutional sanction by the First Amendment's "freedom of assembly" clause—the concept of demagoguery must be reconstructed on a different normative foundation in order to make sense and remain relevant in the context of American politics, and in modern liberal politics in general. Indeed, as I will contend, modern liberal government shifts the burden of speaking publicly in politically suitable ways from the general public to officers of the state itself. In stark contrast with private citizens, public officials who derive their authority from the Constitution are, by virtue of their place within the normative framework of the constitutional order, obligated to live up to the constitutional responsibilities of their institution. One of these responsibilities, I will argue, is to speak publicly in constitutionally appropriate ways. Therefore, whether or not constitutional officers are using demagoguery in a way that accords with the particular responsibilities of their office is a question of serious interest to public officials and the general public alike.

What is the first step toward answering this question? In a constitutional democracy, the demagogic worldview is politically problematic for both leaders and the public because it frames political disagreement in terms of claims that cannot be adjudicated by a community of free and equal human beings assumed capable of employing their rational faculties; these claims therefore cannot contribute to a transparent and deliberative political process, itself a requisite for free, non-authoritarian governments.[18] At the same time—and this is the more provocative claim I will be making in this book—it is also conceivable that the very elements that make demagoguery dangerous can also make it justifiable (indeed, even an exceptional form of constitutional statesmanship) when deployed in specific ways. To speak analogically, demagoguery is like a weapon: though it is easy to abuse, and we would prefer to proscribe it in our everyday lives, it is also invaluable in the service of a just cause and when faced with fanaticism or outright violence. How might this be the case?

For now, consider two brief examples. In the lead-up to the Second World War, as Fascist Germany began to rearm itself in defiance of international law, Winston Churchill, then a member of the British Parliament, believed that his government's policy of appeasement was generating an existential threat, and that the Nazi regime needed to be opposed with aggressive military action. And yet, the substantive debate over whether to go to war with Germany was far from clear-cut; it involved questions of justice (e.g., what Britain owed to the nations of concern) as well as strategic questions regarding the nature of the threat and the possibility of lasting peace in Europe. For these reasons, the British Parliament was far from convinced that Germany constituted the grave danger Churchill alleged it did. Retrospectively, then, we might conclude that Churchill had at least a plausible argument for waging a rhetorical campaign on the basis of severely exaggerated, perhaps even falsified, evidence of German aggression toward Great Britain.

And to some extent, Churchill did just that. As he himself later admitted, in the years leading up to the war "I strove my utmost to galvanize the Government into vehement and extraordinary preparation, even at the cost of world alarm. In these endeavors no doubt I painted the picture even darker than it was."[19] Whatever distortions he may have advanced during those years, he nevertheless maintained they were justified by both the severity of the threat and the intractability of the Parliament: "I remain convinced . . . that it was right to spur the Government by every means."[20] This is a theme Churchill discusses in greater detail elsewhere:

> My mind was obsessed by the impression of the terrific Germany I had seen and felt in action during the years 1914 to 1918 suddenly becoming again possessed of all her martial power, while the Allies, who had so narrowly survived, gaped idle and bewildered. Therefore, I continued by every means and on every occasion to use what influence I had with the House of Commons . . . to urge forward our military preparations.[21]

Every means? Generalized as a principle of rhetoric, Churchill's assertion would seem to authorize any number of demagogic extremes given the prospect of a bad outcome, even in the face of a general denial by the legislature and perhaps a majority of the public that such an outcome was likely. Indeed, a major theme of Churchill's war memoirs is that presenting the facts and merits of an issue (in his case, why Germany ought to be confronted) can be insufficient to persuade a legislature—even if they ought to be persuaded. Accordingly, a "gaping, idle, and bewildered" legislature cannot be trusted to register arguments as a functioning legislature ought to; in the case of the British Parliament, "unwisdom, carelessness, and good nature allowed the wicked to rearm."[22]

A second and more recent example carries a similar lesson. In 2009, with the global financial crisis about to send the world's economies into a death spiral, newly elected President Barack Obama was agonizing over passage of the American Recovery and Reinvestment Act (ARRA), legislation that was needed to stabilize the American economy and prevent the recession from becoming a second—and possibly worse—Great Depression. Yet the ARRA was following on the heels of the previous administration's immense Troubled Asset Relief Program (TARP), which originally authorized expenditures amounting to $700 billion. This law, the so-called bailout, was seen by many as an unjust reward for bankers whose irresponsible investment decisions had precipitated the financial crisis in the first place. And while Obama himself sympathized with these sentiments, he also understood the need for action that would arrest the crisis' metastasization. As he records in his memoirs:

> Despite the horrific headlines of early 2009, nobody—not the public, not Congress, not the press, and (as I'd soon discover) not even the experts—really understood just how much worse things were about to get. . . . [W]e were about to ask the American public to spend close to a trillion dollars on sandbags for a once-in-a-generation hurricane that only we knew was coming.[23]

In the president's view, the knowledge that had persuaded him and his advisors that the ARRA was needed to stem the tide of economic disaster could not be persuasively communicated to other policymakers and the public at large. Like Churchill, Obama believed he faced a political situation in which normal modes of political persuasion and negotiation were inadequate to meet an existential crisis faced by the community.

What additional rhetorical modes might have been required under such circumstances? The Churchill and Obama cases confirm an inescapable fact about demagoguery that we all, on some level, know to be true, even though our customary use of language prevents us from recognizing it. Indeed, as I will suggest, we inhabit a semantic maze around demagoguery that hinders our ability to recognize our own best understanding of democratic politics. Though many uses of demagoguery are bad, some are good, and a few are truly exceptional, because there are imaginable situations in which the prejudices of one's audience are so firmly settled on an erroneous conception of the common good as to render them closed to arguments about the need for desperately needed political change. When routine negotiation and deliberation fail to produce an outcome that the public interest urgently demands, rhetoric is needed to enlist additional sources of human motivation in a cause that the common good depends on, thereby bridging the gap between the ordinary political process and the country's true needs. Alexander Hamilton, one of the Constitution's principal architects, sketches the logic of this understanding of constitutionalism in *Federalist* #31. Describing different sources of resistance to the (then) proposed Constitution, Hamilton writes:

> In disquisitions of every kind, there are certain primary truths, or first principles, upon which all subsequent reasonings must depend. These contain an internal evidence which, antecedent to all reflection or combination, commands the assent of the mind. Where it produces not this effect, it must proceed either from some defect or disorder in the organs of perception, or from the influence of some strong interest, or passion, or prejudice.... [T]his untractableness may be carried too far, and may degenerate into obstinacy, perverseness, or disingenuity.

For a leader, what is the proper response to such "untractableness" when the Constitution's own goals and aspirations are at stake? Hamilton answers clearly later on in the same paper: "A government ought to contain in itself every power requisite to the full accomplishment of the objects committed to its care, and to the complete execution of the trusts for which it is responsible." Though demagoguery—like other extreme political tactics—is undesirable in much of ordinary politics, as one of the "powers" that Hamilton speaks of, its utility for accomplishing the objects committed to the care of the United States government renders it a necessary and legitimate tactic when circumstances demand it.

In this perspective, it is the legitimacy of democracy itself that bleeds into the potential legitimacy of demagoguery. Demagoguery is therefore politically necessary to the extent that it is self-consciously integrated into a broader political strategy, one that is based on a diagnosis of political dysfunction and a rationale for change that are themselves derived from a plausible, contestable conception of what the community requires in order to function and succeed.[24] Politicians using this kind of rhetoric, which I call good demagoguery, will deploy demagogic tactics to amplify a strong argument, one that the orator in question has reason—supported by evidence—to believe is not being heard or adequately engaged with by the public, elites, or both. In contrast, bad demagoguery uses demagogic tactics to compensate for the incoherence and overall weakness of an argument.

In the chapters that follow, I furnish a set of analytical tools for discerning which of these is taking place in any given instance of demagoguery. Such tools are necessary because, strategically, a politician who traffics in bad demagoguery has the political incentive to claim that their rhetoric is being deployed in the service of a strong argument—after all, no orator will readily admit to being an ignoramus and a fraud. Relatedly, those who use bad demagoguery tend to invoke shared communal knowledge: the notion that an explicitly articulated rationale is unnecessary because everyone already knows and agrees with that rationale in their conscience. Thus, according to the logic of bad demagoguery, only those arguing in bad faith will demand an explicit rationale from the demagogue; such people, for subversive, perhaps even treasonous reasons, are denying what they know to be true. Accordingly, demagogic tactics must be analyzed alongside the actual depth and quality of the rationale that the orator develops to justify those tactics. In my analysis, it is therefore the internal quality of that rationale that is central, not an external signifier or variable such as the frequency of certain words or phrases, or the pitch of the speaker's voice.

As a consequence, good-versus-bad demagoguery is not a binary classification in my framework. Rather, as I describe at length in my case studies, instances of demagogic rhetoric exist on a normative spectrum of good and bad. Where these instances fall on that spectrum must be determined through a holistic assessment of both the arguments deployed by the demagogue in question (their sophistication, logical coherence, empirical accuracy, etc.) and the way in which those arguments are bolstered by strategic, instrumental uses of demagogic rhetoric. Accordingly, I by no means claim to offer definitive assessments of particular historical uses of demagoguery in this book. Because each conclusion I reach is qualitative and requires political judgment, where I place a given orator on the spectrum of good and bad demagoguery is necessarily contestable; a different scholar using the same evaluative framework I propose here might reach conclusions that differ from my own, and yet this fact would not render the enterprise of evaluation and classification itself any less worthwhile. Broadly stated, my burden is not to execute a falsifiable research design that produces replicable outcomes, but to illustrate a transparent, open-ended mode of assessment that will establish the terms for a new kind of political debate around demagoguery without seeking to establish in advance the correct conclusion to that debate.[25]

Demagoguery and Constitutional Office

The seven cases I have chosen to illustrate my approach to demagoguery (Chapters 6–8) are drawn from American political history dating to the founding era, and all of them involve officeholders under the United States Constitution. Why does it make sense to concentrate on constitutional officials and not, say, state and local officials and private citizens?

For the reasons that I sketched above and which I will elaborate in the following pages, a citizen of the American regime cannot truly (or at least fully) be a demagogue without having some kind of formal political power at his or her disposal. To understand the ground of this intuition, we need to understand the relation between free speech, political rhetoric, and constitutional office. A helpful way of approaching this subject is by inquiring whether constitutional officers in their official capacities—as presidents, judges, and members of Congress—should be afforded the same First Amendment free-speech protections as are afforded to private citizens.

On January 13, 2021, the House of Representatives voted to indict President Donald Trump with inciting an insurrection at the United States Capitol. In their January 8 brief responding to the House impeachment managers' memorandum, the former president's lawyers argued that efforts to punish Trump for his role in the events of January 6 must meet the exceedingly high burden of proof the Supreme Court has articulated regarding what kinds of pure political speech are punishable by law.[26] For their part, the House managers had averred that public officials holding "sensitive policy positions" should be held to a higher standard when it comes to their public utterances, and that the same permissive First Amendment standards that apply to private citizens do not apply to those who hold the public trust. In stark contrast, Trump's lawyers concluded that the First Amendment protects sitting presidents who would engage in any kind of conduct the Court has deemed protected as "political speech." Among other things, this kind of speech includes flag burning (*Texas v. Johnson*), protesting the deaths of American soldiers killed in battle (*Snyder v. Phelps*), racist cross-burning (*RAV v. St. Paul*), and protesting at rallies of the Ku Klux Klan (*Brandenburg v. Ohio*). Is it true, as Trump's counsel evidently believed, that a sitting U.S. president could picket a fallen soldier's funeral, or yell racist chants at a Klan gathering, and all the Constitution allows Congress to do is wring its hands in frustration?

The obscene ludicrousness of this conclusion—which Trump's lawyers neglected to spell out in their brief, perhaps sensing its ludicrousness—should provoke us to ask why exactly it is that outrageous and offensive speech acts perpetrated by private citizens seem to take on a different significance when perpetrated by presidents and other constitutional officers. What is the basis of our intuition that a president's words matter for the Constitution—indeed, matter more than perhaps anyone else's? This intuition is rooted in the commonsense understanding that different jobs require different kinds of speech. Words that are appropriate at an athletic event or a political protest, for example, would be disruptive or even damaging at a legal proceeding or a funeral, because these different shared activities exist for the sake of different social ends. More broadly, the ways in which we communicate our thoughts affect the ability of ourselves and others to perform the tasks and honor the responsibilities that make up our daily lives.

In my account, the Constitution applies this insight at the societal level. As the generative principle of the American political community, the Constitution creates offices that require different kinds of speech on the part of officeholders in order to function properly. A president's words matter, as do those of all our political leaders, and their speech must be taken seriously if the Constitution is to realize its own fundamental aspirations.

As their defense of the former president in his impeachment trial made clear, Trump's lawyers object to this view of the Constitution, insisting that the president's words on and leading up to January 6—regarding the allegedly "stolen election" and the need to "fight like hell" to preserve the country—should not be understood as impeachable offenses, or "high Crimes and Misdemeanors" in the language of Article 2, section 4. For this reason, they also insist that the only element of the constitutional order that is empowered to judge a president's speech is not Congress but the voting public, who decides whether the president should be elected or reelected: "Mr. Trump, having been elected nationally, was elected to be the voice for his national constituency." This statement implies that, except for violating criminal statutes for which anyone might be punished, a president is permitted to behave in whatever manner he desires, and to say whatever he thinks is fit, so long as the public has voted to put him in office. The principle on which this understanding of the presidency is based is that the president is responsible to the portion of the public that voted for him, and to no one else.

This view is plainly at odds with the text of the Constitution, which makes no mention of the president's own "national constituency." Rather, it admonishes the president to "preserve, protect, and defend the Constitution." The crucial consideration for determining whether a president deserves to hold the public trust is not whether his national constituency supports him but whether he is "faithfully execut[ing] the Office of President of the United States" in accordance with his constitutionally mandated oath of office.

Can a president's words count as a breach of this faith? Some scholars, including Bob Bauer, have suggested they can, arguing that the particular class of punishable acts referred to in Article 2, section 4 of the Constitution is different from ordinary statutory crimes for which a private citizen could be convicted.[27]

Such acts, wrote Hamilton in *Federalist* #65, "are those offenses which proceed from the misconduct of public men, or, in other words, from the abuse or violation of some public trust. They are of a nature which may with peculiar propriety be denominated POLITICAL, as they relate chiefly to injuries done immediately to the society itself." In other words, public officials are forbidden from doing certain things *as public officials* that they might be at perfect liberty to do as private citizens, in the same way that private individuals are forbidden to perform many acts that we entrust public officials to perform on our behalf, such as voting in Congress, serving as judges, and punishing criminals. Representing the interests of the community and not just themselves, officials have responsibilities that the rest of us do not, and the process by which disputes about those particular responsibilities should be adjudicated is not criminal litigation but impeachment.

Is speech one of these responsibilities? Or, as Trump's lawyers contend, does the principle of free speech protect ordinary citizens and officeholders equally? The First Amendment says "Congress shall make no law . . . abridging the freedom of speech," and Trump's lawyers have inferred from this prohibition that Congress is forbidden from abridging the president's speech by means of impeachment and removal.

To think through this question, it is helpful to notice that the impeachment process is not a part of the ordinary legislative process outlined in Article 1, section 7. Under the Constitution, all "laws" must pass by simple majority in each house of Congress before being signed into law by the president or vetoed. In turn, Congress can override a veto with a two-thirds supermajority in both houses. By contrast, impeachment requires a majority in the House and a two-thirds supermajority in the Senate and, for obvious reasons, does not require the president's signature to become authoritative.

The reason for this design feature of the Constitution would seem to be that the First Amendment protects a class of activity that is distinct from the class of activity that impeachment exists to regulate. The five liberties that constitute the First Amendment—freedom of speech, free exercise of religion, freedom from established religion, freedom to peaceably assemble, freedom of the press—are means for protecting the public from abuses of power by the state. Such protections are necessary in a constitutional democracy, where citizens are presumed free and equal and therefore entitled to debate the worthiness of leaders and merits of public policies in a free and open manner.

In contrast, impeachment concerns the conduct not of members of the public but of officers of the government. The rationale behind impeachment is that officeholders must meet standards of conduct above and beyond those that apply to private citizens because officeholders have powers and responsibilities that private citizens do not.[28] Because officials can be removed for improper conduct other than violations of the criminal code (which applies to everyone), impeachment is a power of Congress, not of the courts. Further, and contrary to the arguments of Trump's lawyers, the voting public is not the only judge of a president's conduct. Congress is empowered by the Constitution to decide whether presidents and other officials have lived up to their constitutional responsibilities.

What do these responsibilities entail in terms of public speech, written and spoken? Put slightly differently, can we infer and elaborate rhetorical standards for constitutional officeholders, standards that members of Congress might look to in deciding cases of impeachment? I will discuss these questions in greater detail in the following chapters. For now, let me sketch the framework I have in mind with reference to a handful of recent examples drawn from U.S. national politics.

In some ways, it is easier to think about rhetorical standards and constitutional office by examining the conduct of judges than by looking at presidents and members of Congress. The federal judiciary is one institution in which speech norms are easy to identify and, for the most part, strictly enforced. Unlike in the case of presidents, there seems to be a broad consensus that judges should speak publicly in a way that befits their particular constitutional duty. When the late Justice Ruth Bader Ginsburg publicly criticized then-candidate Trump in 2016, for example, the editorial board of the left-leaning *Washington Post* rebuked the left-leaning justice in a lengthy article.[29] The substance of their rebuke was that by weighing in on a partisan debate, Ginsburg had abdicated the particular responsibilities of her constitutional office. The editors of the *Post* were elaborating their constitutionally rooted intuition that judges are obligated to speak to the public in a way that honors the deliberative, impartial character of the judicial office and, by the same token, to eschew forms of demagoguery that are (more) permissible for other officials. More generally, we might say that the Constitution expects *elected* officials to weigh in on ordinary political matters and to take partisan stands because part of what it means to be a good elected representative is to advocate for one's constituents. By constitutional design, members of Congress (for example) represent a part of the whole community, and they are supposed to communicate the needs of that part to the whole—as well as the needs of the whole to their respective part—in a way that conduces to harmony between the two.

Presidents, too, are elected officials, and they play a fundamental role in national policymaking, so it makes sense for them to be permitted to weigh in on matters of political discussion, defending the views that they and their party support and criticizing alternatives. At the same time, because presidents are elected to a constitutional office that represents the entire country (and not just one electoral constituency), they have rhetorical responsibilities that members of

Congress do not.[30] Constitutionally, presidents play a significant role in the legislative process, which inevitably makes them partisans of particular measures and policy outcomes. But they are also in charge of enforcing the law, which means there is a limit to how much political discretion they can ultimately exercise: they are administrators as well as legislators. What is more, presidents have the solemn duty to command the nation's armed forces, a duty that should temper their speech and conduct. For this reason, Americans in the nineteenth century for the most part expected presidents to keep out of everyday politics, and to stay above the partisan fray in their spoken utterances to the public. Presidents who did not, such as Martin Van Buren and Andrew Johnson, were punished for their indiscretions. And though Woodrow Wilson changed these expectations through his new interpretation of the constitutional order, until Trump presidents still felt compelled to toggle between a rhetorically activist mode à la Wilson and the more dignified and reserved posture of their nineteenth-century predecessors.[31]

In contrast with presidents and members of Congress, judges represent no popular electoral constituency, and their role is to adjudicate cases arising under the Constitution in an impartial manner. Accordingly, the way they speak to the public must reflect the particular burden that the Constitution places on them. What is that burden?

As I will discuss in greater detail in Chapter 6, on the federal judiciary, officials in the early republic were forced to grapple with this question when Associate Justice Samuel Chase, a vehement Federalist, litigated a series of demagogic harangues against the Jefferson administration directly from his judicial bench. In one instance, Chase publicly instructed a Baltimore jury as to how they should vote in a particular case—a clear violation of the constitutional principle (from Amendment VI) that juries should be "impartial," that is, that they should use their own independent judgment in deciding cases. A heated debate then ensued over whether Chase's speeches were impeachable, and in 1805 the House brought charges of impeachment against him. Chase was successfully impeached by the House, but the Senate vote to remove him on the eighth count was 19–15, falling short of the two-thirds supermajority needed. Accordingly, the precedent set by Chase's acquittal helped construct judicial autonomy in the political sphere by establishing a relatively high burden of proof for what counted as impeachable conduct by judges.

Nevertheless, what scholars tend to overlook in the Chase impeachment are the robust notions of official responsibility that officials of the early republic held and were capable of debating—notions that contrast with the thin (indeed, impoverished) conception of official responsibility espoused by Trump's lawyers. Of the eight articles of Chase's impeachment, the eighth, which concerned the justice's rhetoric, garnered the most support in favor of removal.

Furthermore, debates in the *Annals of Congress* show members of both houses putting a great deal of thought into why judges should be held to a different set of rhetorical standards from other public officials. And even though the Senate failed to reach the two-thirds supermajority needed to remove Chase, the capaciousness of their debates over judicial speech should give us food for thought in trying to make sense of what constitutes an impeachable offense and, by the same token, what kind of public speech we should expect from judges and political officers generally.

A more recent example of judicial demagoguery is that of Justice Samuel Alito, who on November 13, 2020, delivered a Zoom address to the Federalist Society that, among other things, criticized the COVID protocols of individual states and singled out those of Nevada.[32] With a relevant case (*Roman Catholic Diocese of Brooklyn, New York v. Cuomo*) still pending before the Supreme Court, Alito vehemently expressed his partiality for overturning such regulations. Stated Alito:

> The COVID crisis has served as a sort of constitutional stress test and in doing so, it has highlighted disturbing trends that were already present before the virus struck. One of these is the dominance of lawmaking by executive fiat, rather than legislation. The vision of early 20th century progressives and the New Dealers of the 1930s was that policymaking would shift from narrow-minded, elected legislators to an elite group of appointed experts. In a word, that policymaking would become more scientific. That dream has been realized to a large extent. Every year administrative agencies, acting under broad delegations of authority, churn out huge volumes of regulations that dwarfed the statutes enacted by the people's elected representatives. And what have we seen in the pandemic? Sweeping restrictions imposed, for the most part, under statutes that confer enormous executive discretion.

Statements like these made it clear that Alito viewed many or all of the measures taken by states to ensure public health during an unprecedented pandemic as illegitimate, even as he was preparing to hear arguments for and against those very measures.

How should we think about this kind of speech in light of a judge's particular rhetorical responsibilities? Alito's assertions about "disturbing trends" in administrative regulations do not seriously engage with constitutional interpretation or political thought. They do not seriously engage with past Supreme Court opinions that defend the administrative state on constitutional grounds, or with scholarship that shows how modern American bureaucracy and the welfare state are supported by the best understanding of the Constitution itself.[33] Rather, they are a kind of demagogic shorthand for familiar Republican Party talking points about the evils of progressivism and government regulations of any kind, clearly intended to prejudice his audience in favor of a particular outcome in the very cases he himself was in the process of deciding.

None of this is to say Alito should be impeached for this speech, or that what he said comes close to Trump's speeches and tweets on and preceding January 6. Rather, negative reactions to politically charged utterances by Chase, Ginsburg, and Alito are illustrative of a partially buried though nonetheless vital intuition that the Constitution has embedded in our political culture and which continues to shape our political judgments in ways that we are only dimly aware of.

Demagoguery in the Modern Perspective

How does the Constitution shape our judgments, and what is the best rationale for choosing a constitution that works the way ours does? These are the questions I take up in Chapters 2–5. In my account, the American constitutional regime purposely sets in motion a political dynamic animated by tension between deliberation and procedure, on the one hand, and justice and the common good (or "general Welfare"), on the other.[34] The offices of the Constitution—the institutions created by its three branches—are designed to bring these competing concerns to bear on politics, so that it is more likely that desirable political outcomes will not simply be forced upon citizens without their consent but will be achieved *deliberately*—that is, through rational judgments about the common good. So understood, the Constitution contains implicit criteria for evaluating the public speech of officeholders; it is a template for thinking about what kinds of rhetoric are a healthy part of American politics and how demagogic tactics as I have defined them might be deployed in better and worse ways.

Taking what might be called a constitutional approach to the study of demagoguery (and to rhetoric in general) is by no means novel. What is novel about my approach is the understanding of demagoguery that I argue can be inferred from the American Constitution's structure and aspirations. Many have argued that the framers of the Constitution wanted its institutions to stimulate reasoned debate and, by the same token, to constrain demagogic appeals.[35] At the same time, as I contend, the Constitution is not committed to deliberation simply for its own sake; as the language of the Preamble indicates, the Constitution is purposive (as opposed to merely formal and procedural) in that it wants deliberation to issue in better political and legislative outcomes. The Constitution thus provokes us to make principled judgments about those situations where deliberation is unable to realize the common good, and where demagogic tactics might be necessary to bridge the gap. To this end, I highlight the choices that went into the Constitution's design (choices that concern rhetoric, discourse, and demagoguery) and then elucidate the arguments that should persuade a reasonable person to commit to those choices today.[36] The American founders—Hamilton and Madison, in particular—believed that, historically, republics had tended to oscillate between the extremes of oligarchy and radical democracy, and that neither political system had been able to make deliberative judgments about the common good a constitutive part of its politics.[37] Rather, by alienating most of the public, oligarchies perpetuated injustice and tended to provoke democratic revolts led by demagogues. For this reason, the founders saw most instances of popular leadership as dangerous insofar as they tended to lead to precipitous decisions by the community, decisions it would not have made had its "deliberate sense" been consulted.[38] The founders' dilemma, then, was to navigate the Scylla of reactionary oligarchy, which alienated the public by demonizing all demonstrations of popular leadership, and the Charybdis of radical democracy, in which political actions were provoked by demagogues who appealed to the public's passions and prejudices, thereby stifling deliberative, consent-based decision-making.

For the founders, resolving this dilemma required a decisive break with the classical approach to demagoguery as developed by ancient republican theorists such as Plato, Aristotle, and Cicero. These thinkers had insisted that demagoguery could be constrained and elevated in a republic through rigorous civic education that formed the character of the citizenry. For the ancients, demagoguery was significant because it reflected an ethical defect: demagogues were characterized as rhetorical leaders willing to say whatever was necessary to gain public favor, leaders lacking internal moral constraints based on considerations of justice and the common good. In light of this conception, the solution the ancients proposed was to teach leaders to make the right rhetorical decisions (and audiences to follow the right leaders) because it was the right thing to do.

The American founders were unimpressed by the actual results ancient republicanism had delivered, however. In their view, the ancient republicans had failed because individual virtue—that is, voluntarily imposed self-restraint—is too fragile to function as a foundation for public order and good government. In this perspective, the ancients had been overly moralistic in their approach to politics; they had focused too much on the personal ethics of citizens and politicians and not enough on how to incentivize public officials to act in a way that contributes to the public interest, regardless of their personal ethics. In contrast with the ancients, these founders saw demagoguery as significant insofar as it affected the ability of the public and its government to make political decisions thoughtfully and responsibly. For them, demagoguery was a distinctive form of rhetorical leadership that could interact with politics in different ways, not an internal disposition that had to be managed through education and exhortation. Accordingly, if the founders could design a political order to incentivize rhetoric that would make better political outcomes more likely, they were relatively unconcerned with the personal ethics of citizens and office holders.[39] Thus, whereas the ancients had made moral character—making the right choice for the right reason—the foundation of government, the American founders tried to design a system that would incentivize political officeholders to make publicly beneficial choices regardless of their personal reasons for doing so.

As I demonstrate through a historical reinterpretation, the events that have come to be known as Shays' Rebellion vindicate the founders in their repudiation of the classical republican approach to demagoguery. Indeed, those events are a case study in the virtues of the founders' non-moralistic approach to political leadership. As I show, the Massachusetts farmer Daniel Shays was erroneously blamed for being the demagogue who provoked the Massachusetts farmers' insurgency of 1786–1787. In fact, founders like Hamilton and Madison recognized that Daniel Shays was merely a product of the oligarchic regime of Massachusetts at the time, and that he was saddled with the reputation of demagogue by elites looking to deflect blame from their own politically disastrous decisions. The problem, in their view, was not the vice of Daniel Shays but rather what Madison called "the vices of political system of the United States" under the state governments and the Articles of Confederation. And what was needed was not civic education—the remedy proposed by Anti-Federalists who followed classical republicanism—but a new political system that would minister to the general welfare through a framework of offices designed to stimulate thoughtful judgments on public policy.

Broadly, I contend that the Constitution the founders went on to design in the summer of 1787 displaces a classical conception of demagoguery, which is "moralistic" in the sense that it situates responsibility for demagoguery in the character and choices of a particular speaker. In the Constitution's modern conception, by contrast, the origins of demagoguery lie not in individual choice but in the incentives provided by the social and political order one happens to inhabit. In this interpretation, for example, Daniel Shays was not the archetypical demagogue; he was a farmer recruited into his role by conditions that were so punishing that someone would have been recruited to the role even if Shays had been on another continent. Accordingly, the true origin of demagoguery was not in the decisions or character of Shays but rather in the oligarchic structure of John Adams' 1780 Massachusetts Constitution, and the social conditions—a combination of inequality and financial power of the few—that it facilitated and cemented.[40]

To this end, the founders sought to reduce the threat of bad demagoguery by creating a Constitution that diminishes the occasion for it while also leaving room for the use of good demagoguery in exceptional situations. One might say that the Constitution creates a new kind of popular leadership by reconstituting the American demos. Rather than leave the demos assembled in the agora, akin to ancient Greece, and rather than convene it annually on an election day when every office is filled, as in the 1776 Pennsylvania constitution, the Constitution creates a network of national offices that are tethered to "the people," but never to the whole people all at once, and almost never to even a part of the people directly.[41]

The Constitution thus invites those who are ambitious, who seek power and fame, to become leaders. But to succeed, to gratify their ambition, they need to please the Constitution, and the modes that an ambitious power-seeker employs to do this—to become and successfully wield power as a member of Congress, a senator, a president, a Supreme Court jurist—are not the same as those employed by the demagogues of classical democracy, or even of the states between 1776 and 1786. One does not enact the procedures and directives of the Constitution by inspiring people to come together in a crowd and then investing the crowd with turbulent and powerful passions. Attaining power in a constitutional mode requires a different set of skills.

What are these particular skills? In the American constitutional order, the destructive modes of demagoguery—appealing to powerful passions like fear and anger that interrupt reflection and deliberation, that turn people against each other, in contrast to passions like hope and love—remain relevant for political leaders insofar as they are necessary for obtaining power and keeping it. (The examples I discuss in Chapters 6, 7, and 8, which treat the Court, Congress, and the presidency, all show how demagoguery can be relevant in American politics.) More to the point, demagoguery can be permissible. What is particularly modern about the form of constitutional democracy embodied in the U.S. Constitution is not that demagoguery has to be excluded from it entirely. Rather, it is that demagogic rhetoric should no longer be the object of moralistic judgment—it is no longer coded as "bad," but instead, is understood as a morally neutral technique that may be used for good or for ill, depending on the purpose to which it is applied. The U.S. Constitution wants to recruit demagoguery for constitutionally enjoined ends, by directing popular leaders to use their powers to serve "the permanent and aggregate interests of the community" and to protect the rights of individuals.[42]

Road Map of the Argument

In Chapter 2, I sketch the principles of the traditional understanding of demagoguery, which the American founders inherited from Greco-Roman antiquity.

I then discuss writings from the American founding in order to explicate the arguments with which the Constitution's most sophisticated framers rejected, both implicitly and explicitly, the traditional understanding. My aim in this chapter is not to tabulate the range of perspectives on demagoguery that existed either during classical antiquity or at the time of the American founding, but rather to use the founders' most thoughtful and coherent utterances—both about demagoguery and about how their constitution was designed to interact with it—as aids for understanding the nature of the Constitution itself.

In Chapter 3, I turn to a historical event from the founding era—the so-called Shays' Rebellion of 1786—that helps confirm the validity of the founders' novel understanding of demagoguery. Daniel Shays is frequently described by historians and political scientists as a malevolent demagogue who tried to overthrow the early republic for the sake of his own political and economic gain. I reject this traditional interpretation of Shays' Rebellion, arguing instead that Daniel Shays was an unlucky farmer who was arbitrarily branded with that reputation (which scholars today unwittingly perpetuate) by reactionary Massachusetts elites, elites who were attempting to deflect blame away from inegalitarian state institutions that benefitted them personally, and from their own mismanagement of the post-Revolutionary economy. Shays was subsequently rendered a villain, an archetypal bad demagogue, because the figures who villainized him succeeded in deploying the moralistic traditional understanding of demagoguery that they had inherited from antiquity and which—decisive for my broader argument—astute founders like Hamilton and Madison had rejected in building the Constitution of 1787. Broadly, the Shays case helps to discredit moralistic approaches to demagoguery by illustrating the ways in which they distract public attention from genuine political problems touching on the common good. Accordingly, for founders like Hamilton and Madison, Shays' Rebellion did not so much expose the threat of demagoguery as reveal the need for a better constitutional response to demagoguery.

In Chapters 4 and 5, I describe the ways in which the Constitution the American founders went on to design and defend in 1787–1789 was meant to function as just such a response. Classical regimes were meant to form the characters of would-be leaders in publicly desirable ways, which included restraining or suppressing the impulse to use demagoguery. In contrast, the offices of the U.S. Constitution create incentive structures meant to extract publicly desirable conduct from officeholders—conduct that may include demagoguery—without necessarily changing their characters. Accordingly, Chapter 4 explicates the design choices that produced the institutions of the American regime. Yet ascertaining whether the Constitution is living up to the standards it is designed to attain—whether leaders are conducting themselves in publicly desirable ways *as defined by the Constitution*—presupposes a comprehensive picture of constitutional health, including a picture of what it means for the different officers of the Constitution to be living up to their respective institutional responsibilities. To this end, Chapter 5 elaborates the different rhetorical responsibilities of members of each branch of the United States government, deriving these responsibilities from the different constitutional ends these institutions are designed to realize and the kinds of conduct that make realizing those ends more probable.

Chapters 6–8 contain in-depth case studies of leaders from each of the Constitution's three branches. Each case I examine used demagoguery in a different way and for the sake of a different political cause, and it is the burden of these chapters to leverage the normative framework proposed in Chapters 4 and 5 to produce a holistic assessment of each leader's rhetorical choices from a constitutional standpoint. The cases examined are Samuel Chase and Antonin Scalia (Chapter 6: Supreme Court), Joseph McCarthy, Adam Clayton Powell Jr., and Huey Long (Chapter 7: Congress), and Franklin Roosevelt and Donald Trump (Chapter 8: the presidency). Taken together, the cases I examine and contrast in each chapter are meant to illustrate the spectrum of constitutionally good and bad demagoguery I describe in Chapters 4 and 5.

I conclude the book in Chapter 9 by suggesting that, paradoxically, a moralistic understanding of democratic politics that regards demagoguery as necessarily evil—as a practice to be castigated wherever it occurs and ultimately banished from the community—becomes the cause of the very thing it wishes to obliterate, because it deprives the public of the ability to distinguish between better and worse uses of demagogic leadership. Demagoguery is an American pathology, and we have become a community of demagogues because we claim to hate demagogues.

* * *

The argument I have sketched here occasions the twin interventions I make in this book: namely, articulating the reasons we all admit—albeit unwittingly—that demagoguery as such is not good or bad, but rather can be used in better and worse ways, and then developing a way to analyze and evaluate the use of demagoguery within the American political context. As I have tried to indicate, my aim is not primarily to say what causes demagoguery or to describe its political effects, though I do consider these points when appropriate. Rather, it is to provide us with a lens that enriches our view of what we are already looking at, and that equips us with the means to make better judgments about those we have chosen to lead our country.

2

Demagoguery in the Founding Perspective

The story of demagoguery in American politics begins with the understanding of that concept that was developed and articulated by the principal designers of the American constitutional system. While many have described the ways in which the founders' political theory differed from—indeed, rested on a rejection of—classical conceptions of democracy and republicanism, few have observed that their rejection also entailed a reconceptualization of demagoguery and, more broadly, a new understanding of the role of leadership in a constitutional regime. Hence, scholars commonly read the American founders as embracing an understanding of demagoguery that is more or less identical to the classical understanding as elaborated by authors such as Plato, Aristotle, and Plutarch.[1] According to this interpretation, the founders conceived of demagogues as viciously motivated popular leaders who lack internal restraints and who are willing to say whatever is necessary to acquire political power, irrespective of justice and the common good. Further, the founders designed the American Constitution with this conception of demagogues in mind and expected it to function as a successful response to demagoguery so understood.

There is something to be said for this interpretation, because the founders did frequently use the word "demagogue" and its cognates in decidedly pejorative ways. Their use of language gives the impression of ideational continuity from the classical period through the American founding. Yet the founders' nominal agreement with the ancients serves to obscure an emphatic conceptual disagreement about the nature of demagoguery that some of the Constitution's most sophisticated originators were aware of and addressed in their writings.[2] In turn, this disagreement is a function of the more comprehensive rejection of classical conceptions of politics and government that these founders had committed themselves to. Broadly, these founders contended that politics in a modern regime should be structured by offices that incentivize publicly desirable behaviors

Demagogues in American Politics. Charles U. Zug, Oxford University Press. © Oxford University Press 2022.
DOI: 10.1093/oso/9780197651940.003.0002

through institutional punishments and rewards, rather than by civic educations that shape and develop the characters of leaders in politically desirable ways (as the ancient republican theorists had held). They saw demagoguery not as a consequence of moral depravity that only education can remedy, but rather as one form of rhetoric out of many upon which the politically ambitious can seize. To be sure, demagoguery can still be harmful in this perspective; but it can also be rendered beneficial if tethered to constitutionally enjoined ends. This chapter sketches the theory of demagoguery that these founders developed, and uses that theory as a guide for understanding the constitution we actually got in 1787—a constitution that contains none of the resources we would need to deal with demagoguery if we understood it in a classical manner.

The Ancient Democratic Assembly

What were the essential contours of the traditional understanding of demagoguery with which the American founders had to contend, and in opposition to which they developed their own? The ancient political philosophers regarded demagoguery as a problem confronting all regimes, and especially those in which popular participation constituted a normal part of governance. But they also taught that the sources of demagoguery within human nature could be shaped and refined by subjecting citizens and political leaders to an edifying civic education that would make them morally better, educations in which traditional religion would play an important role.[3] This kind of education would craft citizens' characters so as to render them fit for republican self-government. Because true republicanism required robust civic participation by all citizens, the hope was that everyone in the community would be equipped with the ability both to speak publicly in a responsible way and to discern among the many orators who rose to speak who was worthy of leadership.[4]

The classical republican situation as regards political rhetoric is vividly on display in an episode recounted by Xenophon, the ancient Athenian general and writer, in his book *Memorabilia*:

> When Glaucon, the son of Ariston, attempted to be a popular leader [*epexeirei demegorein*] out of a desire to preside over the city although he was not yet twenty years old, none of his other relatives or friends was able to stop him from being dragged from the speaker's stand and making himself ridiculous.[5]

The obvious point in the passage is that Glaucon, an overconfident and inexperienced adolescent, made a fool of himself before the Athenian legislative assembly. Less obvious—though of interest for us—is that as immature and inexperienced as Glaucon clearly was, it was still possible for him to have an audience with the city's lawmaking body in the first place. Indeed, there appear to have been no formal or legal impediments to influential young men like Glaucon trying to hold sway in the city's legislature through rhetorical expertise. The required age was minimal, and every adult male had the right to attend and address the assembly, so Glaucon would not have had to comply with any of the rigid constitutional forms characteristic of a modern constitutional democracy.[6] Rather, as the unhappy result of Glaucon's attempt confirms, the impediments or constraints on rhetorical practice were decidedly informal—how was his speech received by his immediate audience in the assembly?—and Glaucon was free to make his attempt and just as free to fail miserably.

From a more contemporary standpoint, the informal character of Athens' legislative norms is quite remarkable. Insofar as Glaucon was able to make his "attempt at demagoguery" at all, the Athenian assembly was at least in principle open to being led by him. Only once it became clear that he lacked the requisite rhetorical capacities did the Athenians drag him from the podium. Thus, from the standpoint of Xenophon's classical audience, the Glaucon passage likely would have been significant less because Glaucon attempted to become a demagogue and more because—unlike more successful orators such as Pericles, and Cleon after him—Glaucon did such a bad job of it and failed utterly when given the chance.

For our purposes, the fact that Glaucon was given a chance to speak before and sway policy in Athens' sovereign lawmaking body in the first place indicates something of core importance for the classical perspective. To be sure, the assembly was quick to dismiss Glaucon as unworthy of being their popular leader, as his unceremonious withdrawal by Socrates indicates. What their dismissal implies, however, is that the Athenians placed a premium on provocative and emotionally enticing speech. One glimpses how seriously the ancient republicans in general took rhetoric by considering the cultural and educational expectations with which young men seeking entry into politics tended to meet. For the Athenians, this meant that one's audience possessed refined rhetorical tastes—tastes that can be inferred from the sophisticated style of Athenian oratory on display in Thucydides' speeches, as well as the speeches of the Athenian logographers like Lysias, Aeschines, and Demosthenes. Given these political demands, there would appear to have been immense pressure on actual and would-be leaders to distinguish themselves in the popular assembly. And to the extent that the Athenian legislature was relatively informal in how it came to decisions, it ratcheted up the rhetorical demands on orators. Influence in and dominance over the ancient assembly was, in principle, within the grasp of any ambitious man charismatic enough to assert himself and hold sway. Accordingly, as the Athenian obsession with—not to say mania for—sophistry and other forms of rhetorical training suggests, young Greeks were willing to go to great lengths to acquire the ability to move a political audience in the direction of one's own choosing.[7] And the Greek sophists, for their part, echoed and flattered this view by celebrating the omnipotence of rhetoric. Indeed, many sophists seem to have taught that almost any political obstacle could be surmounted through public speaking.[8] By the same token, the obsession with rhetoric points to a shared understanding among leaders of the time that popular government required perhaps above all the ability to lead in the assembly through speech. Nothing, in other words, could be relied upon to get done in governance if it did not have a powerful rhetorical advocate.

Classical Rhetorical Doctrines

As the above snapshot suggests, the classical political philosophers had included rhetorical teachings as part of their broader political theory precisely because the role of rhetoric in public affairs was so central—because the community's fate hinged both on the ability of ordinary citizens to distinguish good rhetorical leaders from those who would lead the city to ruin, and on the ability of good leaders to use charismatic displays to keep power away from potential tyrants. As the community's well-being depended on the emergence of good orators and the restraint of bad ones in the assembly, rhetorical sophistication was deemed to be a matter not merely of private but of public concern.[9] Specifically, rhetoric was understood to be the means by which the passions of the soul were guided, and so in the ancient republic, where unity of vision and sentiment were imposed on the citizenry directly by the state, it was also seen as playing a foundational role in shaping the community's shared opinions about justice.[10] Hence, the classical philosophers in their capacities as civic educators endeavored to shape political rhetoric, not by designing offices that would manipulate political discourse indirectly but by meeting orators on their own terms and educating them to a more civically responsible form of rhetorical leadership.[11]

The classical concern with rhetoric goes deeper, though. For the ancients—Plato and Aristotle in particular—rhetoric, like all other human arts, must ultimately be seen in light not of political effectiveness but rather of individual human perfection, or virtue.[12] The classical philosophers appreciated the dignity of politics, but they also saw it as instrumental to the individual human being's fullest perfection as set by nature; this goal, rather than politics itself, was of the deepest concern in their teachings.[13] As a consequence, for the ancients, rhetoric (like politics) was to be viewed insofar as it played a foundational albeit instrumental role in the formation of moral character and the realization of wisdom and happiness by individual human beings.[14]

For this reason, the classical philosophers sought to elevate rhetoric in part because they recognized it as a competitor with philosophy for preeminence among the city's most promising students. Unmoored from the concern for virtue, happiness, and wisdom, rhetoric would become little more than a means for unreflective self-advancement. Worse yet, it would pose as a better means to what philosophy itself promised. As Devin Stauffer has suggested, Plato's *Gorgias* shows Socrates trying to enlist one of Athens' greatest teachers of rhetoric in a project to make the study of rhetoric more philosophical—that is, less concerned with creating the impression of knowledge for the sake of political gain and more concerned with acquiring genuine knowledge and communicating it in a politically responsible way.[15] In so doing, Socrates indicates what it would mean to evaluate rhetoric from the highest epistemic viewpoint, that of philosophic knowledge. He does this by sketching the principles of a "noble" or "beautiful" rhetoric that would serve as a paradigm for future students of the art of rhetoric.[16] Judged in light of this ideal, anything less than a philosophic use of rhetoric would seem like a perversion of the art and a betrayal of the orator's highest responsibility. Through dialogues like the *Gorgias* that teach readers to look at rhetoric from such an awesome height, Plato evidently sought to engender both a sense of shame and a sense of yearning in students who were attracted to rhetoric and the gain that it seemed to promise. He wished to moralize rhetoric—that is, to teach that its use entailed duties and responsibilities and that it was not merely a tool for political ambition—so students would recognize that rhetoric could not be haphazardly used without also abandoning what is central to their true happiness and humanity.[17]

The classical text that gives Socrates' approach to rhetoric its most comprehensive and systematic treatment would seem to be Aristotle's *On the Art of Rhetoric*. For Aristotle, full human development depends on the perfection of reason, and the goal of the rhetorical art—rarely achieved in practice, though its ideal nonetheless—should therefore be related to the development of this capacity.[18] On this basis, Aristotle contends that rhetoric properly understood is a subdivision of science or knowledge, and rhetoric is the art by which the discursive means for moving an audience from the apparent truth to the truth itself, and thereby cultivating the reasoning part of their souls, are discerned: "What is true and what resembles the true are seen by the same capacity [of the human soul]."[19] By the same token, the ultimate measure of perfection in rhetoric according to Aristotle is not success in persuading an audience, since such success can be achieved through misleading one's audience.[20] Rather, it is getting one's audience as close to the truth as the rhetorical situation—that is, audience and venue—allows. Aristotle likens the rhetorician to a doctor, who has not failed but rather has done well if he makes a permanently ill patient as healthy as his condition will admit, even if that condition is less than perfect.[21] The perfection of the patient's physical condition is the standard of medicine, whereas the perfection of the audience's moral condition is that of rhetoric.[22] Just as one practices medicine to the extent that one uses knowledge of health to bring one's patient to a healthful condition in their body, one practices the rhetorical art to the extent that one leads an audience to the truth and thereby achieves order or perfection in their souls.[23]

It is important to see that, for Aristotle, rhetoric and science are not the same, because science trades in syllogisms or deductions from universal principles: "The aim or end of the syllogism is truth; the syllogism is the form of strict demonstration, of demonstration which is meant to be true and which is concerned only to serve the truth." Aristotle recognizes that "the rhetorical syllogism," by contrast, "is something other than" the syllogism of dialectics. It "is not concerned with 'truth' but rather with what is 'similar to truth.'" One might say that rhetoric is the approximation of the truth in the context of politics, whose subject matter consists of what ought to be done about particular persons, groups, and events. The rhetorician's concern is with "proving that the fact is or isn't so, that it happened or didn't happen"—a proof that cannot be demonstrated with the syllogistic rigor of dialectics.[24] Consequently, "rhetorical demonstration rests . . . on particular facts which do not, as such, partake of the intelligible necessity of the universal propositions of dialectic; whereas syllogistic demonstration is strictly true, rhetorical demonstration, by the very nature of its subject matter, is only *probably* true." Still, "this does not appear to mean that the end of the rhetorical syllogism or of rhetorical art altogether is anything other than the truth. The rhetorician must state the truth insofar as it lies in him to do so."[25]

Importantly for our purposes here, failing to state the truth is not merely a matter of misinformation to be rectified in the "marketplace of ideas." It implicates the very character of the orator who misleads. Aristotle's rhetorical doctrine is based on, and issues in, an *ethical* distinction between expert orators and sophists: "The sophist is not defined by the power (*dunamis*) but by the moral choice (*proairēsis*)" to use rhetoric irrespective of the truth.[26] Aristotle seeks to provide orators and their audiences with an ethical standard for rhetorical excellence (what change was brought about in the souls of the audience as a result of the orator's character?) rather than a standard based on political efficacy (how many were persuaded and how quickly?). This contrasts decisively with the rhetorical doctrine of sophists like Gorgias, who placed effectiveness over morality:

> I call [rhetoric] the ability to persuade with speeches either judges in the law courts or statesmen in the council-chamber or the commons in the Assembly or an audience at any other meeting that may be held on public affairs. And I tell you that by virtue of this power you will have

> the doctor as your slave, and the trainer as your slave; your money-getter will turn out to be making money not for himself, but for another,—in fact for you, who are able to speak and persuade the multitude.[27]

This means that the core consideration in the Aristotelian framework is an internal one (moral choice in the orator and condition of soul in the audience) rather than an external one (e.g., political success). It is the orator's moral choice to lead or mislead the audience, and it is a corruption of orator's art to attempt to lead to the extent that the orator is uncertain of the truth of their goals. A true rhetorical education would therefore consist in leading the would-be orator to understand why their own perfection or virtue consists, in part, in developing the moderation necessary to use rhetoric in a way that accords with their own understanding. In this perspective, whether rhetoric is good or bad, statesmanlike or demagogic, hinges ultimately on the moral education of the orator—whether they know why it is choice-worthy to persuade their audience in a just rather than an unjust way.

Evaluating rhetoric within this framework does not rest satisfied with weighing the merits of the orator's arguments, then. It asks to what extent the orator has actually thought through and understood the arguments he or she is making and whether those arguments harmonize with the orator's own best understanding of the demands of justice. A demagogue makes speeches with a view to bringing about a desired outcome, heedless of what he or she believes to be right, whereas a true orator imposes self-restraint insofar as he or she lacks knowledge of what justice truly demands.

Broadly, we might conclude that the classical political philosophers set a high bar for rhetoric in part because it was so central to politics as they experienced it. Rather than let uninstructed citizens choose indiscriminately between irresponsible and ambitious demagogues, they tried to condition citizens so they might discriminate between better and worse popular leaders when they invariably appeared in the public assembly. Further, they addressed their works directly to aspiring orators so as to shape their conduct in public. But they also saw it from the even higher standpoint of ethical formation and philosophy and so tried to conceptualize the rhetorical art in a way that would prevent it from becoming the mere servant of political ambition. Politics and rhetoric were ultimately subservient to human perfection.

Rhetoric in Ancient and Modern Political Thought

The movement from classical rhetoric to rhetoric as conceived by modern constitutional democracy was part of a larger movement from classical to modern political philosophy. Starting with Machiavelli's rejection of the best regime as the normative standard of politics, political theorists began to conceptualize the nature and purpose of politics in wholly new terms.[28] For the ancient philosophers, politics was to be analyzed from the standpoint of individual human perfection as set by nature. For characteristically modern thinkers, by contrast, the purpose of politics was to be limited to administering humankind's basic, less controversial needs, particularly peace and material prosperity. As part of this shift, modern philosophers appropriated ideas and institutions from classical philosophy and redeployed them for purposes that accorded with their own goals, as opposed to the goals of the classics. Hobbes, for example, retained many of the moral and political virtues core to ancient thought, but unlike Plato and Aristotle who saw those virtues as ends in themselves, Hobbes justified them on the *political* basis that they contributed to peace and public order.[29] Similarly, Montesquieu defended republicanism not in terms of its ability to generate human excellence and patriotism but in terms of its commitment to equality.[30] And Locke defended versions of natural law and biblical interpretation that differed from their original conceptions by ancient and medieval authorities.[31]

One feature of classical thought that was not thus redeployed—at least initially—was political rhetoric. Machiavelli appears to have initiated its demotion when he reconceived political philosophy as the study of what human beings do as opposed to what they say.[32] His rationale for this demotion appears to have been that human beings always offer "professions of good"—that is, they assert their good or virtuous intentions—as evidence for why what they want done should be done.[33] For the ancients, these professions of good were core to the analysis of political life because they reflected competing legitimate claims to rule by competing regimes, claims that in turn pointed toward the best regime as the normative standard for politics and human life.[34] By contrast, for Machiavelli (for whom the standards of politics were lower and less tinged by normative questions—i.e., wealth, security, and glory) the uprightness or virtuousness of the politician's motives should be replaced with virtue reconceived as the ability to realize desirable political outcomes.[35] In this analysis, rhetoric was at best a means for gaining the compliance of peoples and individuals whose support was in some way necessary for political success, and at worst a means by which incompetent politicians could acquire power and influence that would be dangerous for the community.[36] Because human beings are overwhelmingly hypocritical—and, more importantly, because even those who *do* intend well are not necessarily good at getting the job done or choosing what the job should be in the first place—rhetoric as the vehicle for professions of good should cease to be a meaningful consideration in politics.

As Bryan Garsten has shown, the modern philosophers for the most part retained Machiavelli's suspicion of political rhetoric. Hobbes, in particular, saw it as a source of mischief and tried to proscribe it from politics. In general, modern political theory lacked a place for rhetoric.[37] This story began to change, however, with the emergence of modern constitutionalism, with the authors of *The Federalist* evolving a defense of political speech and rhetoric on characteristically modern grounds. Their defense is based on the insight that, done properly, political rhetoric can actually serve to advance the goals to which modern politics is committed. For his part, Machiavelli was suspicious of rhetoric because it seemed to him to consist primarily in vapid reassurances of the orator's moral purity, a consideration he did not care about because it was irrelevant to what really mattered in politics. For their part, founders like Hamilton were cognizant of and sympathetic to Machiavelli's critique. As Hamilton himself notes in describing interactions between the states and the national government under the Articles of Confederation:

> It was presumed that a sense of their true interests, and a regard to the dictates of good faith, would be found sufficient pledges for the punctual performance of the duty of the members to the federal head. The experiment has, however, demonstrated that this expectation was ill-founded and illusory.

For these founders as well as Machiavelli, professions of good are inadequate as a basis for good government and political accountability.

And yet, Machiavelli's argument about rhetoric reflects only one perspective on the subject. As their own rhetorical efforts in *The Federalist*—a series of pamphlets actually intended to sway public opinion—suggest, American founders such as Hamilton, Madison, and Jay recognized that elements of political rhetoric that actually concern topics of public concern, if developed into arguments about the common good, can furnish the public and the government with better resources for choosing between a superior range of political alternatives—alternatives of which they would have been unaware, or only dimly aware, otherwise.[38] In addition, by involving the public in that decision-making process, political rhetoric can enhance the regime's political legitimacy by assuring citizens that they are owed an explanation by their rulers and that their opinions therefore matter for political decision-making. Finally, along Machiavelli's lines, rhetoric is but one of many tactics that power seekers will invariably enlist as they attempt to gain and consolidate political support. For this reason, it is naive to think that rhetoric could ever be effectively suppressed, especially in a regime where the public is involved in the political process.

The task before the founders was to construct a system that would harness the natural propensity to use rhetoric to advance the Constitution's own goals. The way they did this, as I will suggest, was by designing and then defending a Constitution that was silent regarding the virtue and ethics of officeholders, a Constitution committed instead to the idea of general welfare understood as an objective state of affairs that could be legitimately and profitably debated by all citizens, regardless of their personal motives.[39] By withholding the cognitive resources citizens and public officials would need to make judgments about the virtue of orators, and instead creating institutions whose differing designs reflect the competing normative commitments of democracy itself, the Constitution indicates a framework for the analysis of political rhetoric in which argumentative merit is core and personal ethics are ultimately peripheral.

The Founders' Alternative

The commitments underlying this framework can be glimpsed at the outset of *The Federalist*, where Hamilton warns against orators who indulge the public's enthusiasms:

> A dangerous ambition more often lurks behind the specious mask of zeal for the rights of the people than under the forbidden appearance of zeal for the firmness and efficiency of government. History will teach us that the former has been found a much more certain road to the introduction of despotism than the latter, and that of those men who have overturned the liberties of republics, the greatest number have begun their career by paying an obsequious court to the people; commencing demagogues, and ending tyrants.[40]

At first glance, Hamilton appears to share the ancient view we have just outlined. He speaks of demagoguery as if it were a moral defect, pointing to inauthentic public-spiritedness and ambition as the things that are to be feared by the public. Yet on closer view, Hamilton's perspective turns out to reflect a different set of priorities. He emphasizes that it is reasonable to assume that *all* who present themselves as zealous for the rights of the people are in fact plotting tyranny—a conclusion that would appear too sweeping and indiscriminate in the classical perspective. Because the classical republicans were deeply concerned with the development of moral character, regarding virtue as the final cause of political life, they would never have endorsed reducing all leaders enthusiastic about popular rights to the category of potential tyrants. Rather, they would have viewed such enthusiasm or public-spiritedness as in need of refinement through rigorous and prolonged civic education. By the same token, they would have seen Hamilton's willingness to write off popular leadership without engaging it in education as evidence of a conflation of means with ends.

Whereas the classical republicans saw political flourishing as a means to the perfection of individual character, Hamilton views individual political leadership from the standpoint of the communal aspirations staked out in the Constitution's Preamble: domestic tranquility, common defense, and general welfare. In Hamilton's frame of reference, political speech and action ought therefore to be evaluated in terms of whether it makes a plausible contribution to the public good. To this end, Hamilton proceeds in the same *Federalist* paper to articulate the way he believes political rhetoric ought to be evaluated:

> I frankly acknowledge to you my convictions, and I will freely lay before you the reasons on which they are founded. The consciousness of good intentions disdains ambiguity. I shall not, however, multiply professions on this head. My motives must remain in the depository of my own breast. My arguments will be open to all, and may be judged of by all.[41]

Hamilton's position is illustrative of the deepest theoretical argument of the American founders regarding political rhetoric and demagoguery. Central to this argument is the understanding that it is profoundly difficult if not impossible to distinguish good and bad leadership on the basis of personal ethics alone, because the purity of one's moral commitments is difficult (if not impossible) to know except for the individual whose commitments are in question. On the other hand, the arguments that a public official makes in defense of what they have done or propose to do can be evaluated and contested by all who are capable of reasoning through the assessment of internal coherence and empirical validity—assessments that can, in principle, be undertaken by everyone in the community.

This view can be glimpsed in Hamilton's remarks on Daniel Shays in The *Federalist.* Unlike other elites who sought to demonize Daniel Shays as a demagogue on moralistic grounds, Hamilton saw a structural defect at the root of the rebellion of which Shays was a part. "If Shays had not been a DESPERATE DEBTOR," wrote Hamilton in *The Federalist #6*, "it is much to be doubted whether Massachusetts would have been plunged into a civil war."[42] Though this remark occurs within a discussion of how individuals can destabilize political systems, the thrust of Hamilton's remark is a rebuke of the traditional view that demagogues are the causes of social unrest in democracies and an accompanying diagnosis of the political and economic defects of the political order set up by the Articles of Confederation. What is more, Hamilton is contesting an argument common among elites at the time of the founding. Reflecting the ancients' moralistic view of demagoguery, this argument held that demagogues had been the *cause* of political dysfunction under the Article of Confederation, rather than one of its effects. As Elbridge Gerry maintained in the federal convention, for example, "Demagogues are the great pests of our government, and have occasioned most of our distresses."[43] In Hamilton's telling, by contrast, what matters most is not Shays' moral character and the virtue of the community but rather the political and economic conditions bearing responsibility for his desperation as a debtor. Hamilton thus shifts focus from what a moralistic conception of demagoguery would seize on—the character of the popular leader and of the public at large—to the question that Hamilton regards as central to an analysis of politics under the constitution being proposed and defended. That question is whether government can assimilate information relevant to the public and then deliberate on that information by means of institutions designed to bring a range of alternative perspectives, rooted in multiple and often competing interests, to bear on questions of public policy. The general welfare, not the uprightness of individual leaders, thus becomes the core criterion in the analysis of political rhetoric in the American political order.

3

Shays' Rebellion and the Collapse of Discourse

> In high party times, a vanquished reformer is most likely to be branded by the victors as an incendiary and a demagogue.
>
> —John Adams, 1787

The Constitution's designers formed their ideas about demagoguery not solely through critical dialogue with the classical political philosophers. They also looked to contemporary experiences as sources of insight, one of which was the so-called Shays' Rebellion of 1786–1787.[1] Countless scholars have argued that Shays' Rebellion convinced the founders that the country required a Constitution that would serve primarily to constrain demagogues such as Daniel Shays—so many that this particular interpretation of the events of 1786–1787 has entered more or less unquestioned into American political discourse and vernacular. What these scholars have overlooked is the deeper insight that *certain* of the founders were afforded by Shays' Rebellion. In that event, founders like Madison and Hamilton discerned the destructive consequences not of a vicious demagogue who had manipulated a foolish public for his own ends but of a political regime that had tried to cement its authority through a system of repressive and retrograde political institutions that founders like Hamilton and Madison had come to reject. For these founders, Shays' Rebellion was actually a case study in the inadequacies of the classical approach to government generally, and to demagoguery, in particular. It also provided the justification for their distinctive solution to these two problems, which took tangible form in the Constitution they led the design of in 1787.

One clue that the founders did not accept the conventional explanation of Shays' Rebellion—the explanation that has come down to us through the centuries—is the basic fact that, upon inspection, the individual man Daniel Shays turns out not to have led his namesake rebellion in the first place. Indeed,

Demagogues in American Politics. Charles U. Zug, Oxford University Press. © Oxford University Press 2022.
DOI: 10.1093/oso/9780197651940.003.0003

as I will argue in this chapter, though Shays has long been regarded as America's first great demagogue, we have no good reason to believe he actually exhibited any of the attributes of demagoguery that he was alleged to have. Rather, because Massachusetts elites needed a "demagogue" to hold responsible for the 1786–1787 Massachusetts insurgency, lest they take responsibility for the systemic factors that were actually at that movement's root, attributes of demagoguery were ascribed to Shays *ex post* through a fictive narrative that vindicated those elites' classical republican conception of demagoguery and politics.

Relatedly, rather than elevating the political and economic conflicts that precipitated the insurgency in a way that might have made a successful and deliberative resolution of those conflicts possible, state officials attempting to enforce the Massachusetts State Constitution of 1780 had tried to tamp down demagoguery by means of a state-backed civic and religious education meant to instill public-spiritedness and civic virtue in the citizenry, an education that bore the hallmarks of the classical understanding of civic republicanism and demagoguery.[2] As a result, the society created by the Massachusetts constitution precipitated precisely the kind of classical republican factional conflict that the American founders associated with the flawed classical understanding of politics.[3] Specifically, the Massachusetts insurgency witnessed politically marginalized factions—farmers unable to repay their debts as a result of dramatic fluctuations in credit—staging an insurgency and justifying it on the grounds that the state at all levels had failed to acknowledge their most basic concerns, needs, and goals. For their part, state officials were insulated from grappling with these concerns, both *institutionally*, by virtue of the 1780 Constitution which imposed steep property requirements on officeholders and disenfranchised many voters, and *ideationally*, by virtue of their moralistic classical understanding of democracy and demagoguery. Instead of meeting the challenges that provoked the movement head-on, they demonized the movement itself as the product of morally corrupt demagoguery. They did this by saddling Daniel Shays—a relatively minor and moderating figure in the insurgency—with a reputation as a depraved demagogue.

The Conventional Interpretation of Shays' Rebellion

Because it is known today as "*Shays'* Rebellion," many take for granted that Daniel Shays, "the nominal leader and namesake of the rebellion," originated as well as executed the popular movement.[4] Michael Signer begins his account of "Demagoguery in America" with a discussion of Shays' leadership:[5]

> An unlikely demagogue—a Revolutionary War veteran and farmer who had never before been involved in politics—rose on the tide of the people's fury. With Daniel Shays as their leader, a group of farmers soon resolved to strike against the judges who met periodically in each town to imprison debtors. Through his identity as an anti-elite farmer, his passionate relationship with the common people, and his ambition to create a political force, Shays revealed himself as a demagogue to be reckoned with.[6]

Such statements echo a centuries-old tradition of historical and political science scholarship. When Louis Hartz analyzed the events of 1786–1787 in *The Liberal Tradition in America,* he referred not to the insurgents, or even to the "Shaysites," but specifically to the leadership of the individual demagogue, Daniel Shays, and more broadly, to "the problem of Daniel Shays."[7] Leonard D. White, in his foundational study of public administration, alleged that "the farmers of western Massachusetts took up arms under Captain Daniel Shays."[8] In his aptly titled volume *Homage to Daniel Shays,* Gore Vidal wrote that "property is power, as those Massachusetts veterans of the revolution discovered when they joined Captain Daniel Shays in his resistance to the landed gentry," concluding with an exhortation to his radical egalitarian contemporaries in twentieth-century America: "Here now exists a potential American majority willing to see its best interests served not through the restrictive Constitution of the elite but through the egalitarian vision of Daniel Shays and his road not taken—yet."[9] Joseph Bessette, in his discussion of the "critical period" of American history, attributes a decisive leadership role to Shays: "Not able to gain control over the government [of Massachusetts], the paper money forces took to arms under the leadership of Daniel Shays."[10] Historians specializing in early American politics and Shays' Rebellion contend, in a collaborative account of the latter, that in 1786 "Daniel Shays emerged as one of the local leaders of the protest movement."[11] Similarly, *The Emerging Nation*—a documentary history of the Confederation, edited by the National Historical Publications and Record Commission—states that Shays "emerged as leader of insurgents who prevented [Massachusetts] courts from sitting."[12] Jeffrey Tulis in *The Rhetorical Presidency* contends that "the founders were made more acutely aware of the problem [of demagoguery] by the presence in their own midst of popular leaders such as Daniel Shays, who led an insurrection in Massachusetts."[13]

This view is by no means confined to scholars. On January 13, 1987—the rebellion's bicentennial year—President Ronald Reagan gave constitutional sustenance to the idea of Shays' importance by announcing Proclamation 5598: "Shays' Rebellion Week and Day."[14] The purpose of the proclamation was to "celebrate the bicentennial of many events relating to the drafting of our

Constitution. One of those events was Shays' Rebellion." According to the president, "Shays' Rebellion was to have a profound and lasting effect on the framing of our Constitution and on our subsequent history." President Reagan's proclamation turns out to have been only one of numerous similar efforts. A century before in 1897, in the midst of the agricultural crisis that spawned popular leaders like William Jennings Bryan, writer George R. R. Rivers published *Captain Shays: A Populist of 1786*:

> From the close of the Revolution until 1787–88 the agricultural classes, especially in New England, were in very much the same frame of mind as that in which we find the farmers of the Western States to-day. . . . In each case the results have been much the same. The aggrieved have arrayed themselves against the aggressors, and, led by demagogues, who set the masses against the classes, have lost sight of the real evil and the true remedy in their desire to punish those whom they blame for all their misfortunes. . . . *[H]ad it not been for the evil and selfish leadership of Daniel Shays and his lieutenants, much suffering might have been prevented.* [My italics][15]

By drawing a parallel between contemporary politics and the historical crisis of 1786–1787, the novel *Captain Shays* drew on, and articulated further, the existing narrative and normative understanding of the place of Daniel Shays in particular and demagoguery in general in American constitutional identity: "The spirit of Daniel Shays still lives in the hearts of some of those leaders who are showing the farmers the wrong path, and who have nothing in view but their own selfish ends." Indeed, as historian Leonard Richards states, writing a century later in his authoritative account of the rebellion:

> Daniel Shays has become a folk hero, and the rebellion that bears his name has inspired novels, plays, ballads, films, folk-singing groups, and even websites. Tributes have come from men and women of all political persuasions. One came from the novelist Gore Vidal, another from President Ronald Reagan.[16]

As accounts like these suggest, the story of American demagoguery and Shays' role in that story might be said to constitute a subnarrative within the broader "story" of American politics and constitutionalism that gets told today: "All narratives of early United States history include accounts of an uprising labeled Shays' Rebellion."[17]

Yet closer scrutiny reveals a gulf between contemporary understandings of Shays' role as demagogue, on the one hand, and the set of facts concerning

Shays' role about which historians actually agree, on the other. This gulf, between political "interpretation" and political "text," was explicitly pointed out in 1954 by the American historian Robert J. Taylor, who insisted that the contemporary understanding of Daniel Shays' role as a demagogue is an embellishment of what is actually known.[18] Not only have the empirical details of Shays' role in the Massachusetts insurgency been massively distorted, but the normative principles on which the popular movement was based have been subsequently twisted and mischaracterized.

Though several thorough studies have been made of the insurgency, none treats the role of Shays himself in a thematic way. Instead, historians view the movement with which he was associated as a historical entity, making only occasional references to Shays' particular role in it.[19] This contrasts strikingly with popular views as well as the views of political scientists, who, as we saw previously, assume that Shays' role was a foundational and decisive one.

Through minimal speculation about Shays' internal motives, and on the basis of facts about which there is a reasonable historical consensus, what kind of role can we say Shays had? Only by achieving some clarity on this question can we gauge the disparity in magnitude between Shays' actual involvement and the role of demagoguery that was retrospectively attributed to him. Moreover, we can adequately assess differing views among the Constitution's originators regarding the nature of the rebellion and the lessons that could be derived from it for political foundings.

The Case of Shays, Part 1: Shays in Action

In the years preceding the Constitutional Convention of 1787, Massachusetts, like many states in the Confederation, was experiencing dramatic economic problems rooted in a debt crisis not unlike the Great Recession of 2008. A sudden contraction in credit caused ordinary citizens, many of them farmers, to lose property they had financed during a period when credit had been artificially inflated.[20] For these defaulting borrowers, the situation in Massachusetts was particularly egregious because that state's constitution—designed by John Adams—excluded lower-income citizens, many of whom had been affected by the economic downturn, from the political process entirely by preventing them from voting. The constitution also imposed steep property requirements on those who would seek elected office.[21] In the wake of the American Revolution, the Massachusetts constitution created a thoroughgoing oligarchy.

As a consequence, "during the summer of 1786" in western Massachusetts, "conventions were the order of the day."[22] Municipal leaders began assembling in their respective towns for the purpose of drafting petitions to the state government (or General Court) in Boston. These petitions concerned state economic policy.[23] "In addition, the legitimacy of the 1780 state constitution [was being] questioned. So too [was] the legitimacy of the state's rulers."[24] Though several petitions drafted at town meetings were received by the General Court, that institution voted on July 8 to adjourn until January 31, 1787—roughly six months later.[25] It had taken no action with respect to the state's economic vicissitudes or constitutional concerns.

In response to the Court's adjournment, the town leaders or "selectmen" of Pelham—a small municipality in Hampshire County—held a meeting at Conkey's Tavern.[26] Pelham was the residence of Daniel and Abigail Shays. Daniel was "active on the Pelham Committee of Safety"; he was also a warden, a delegate at Hampshire County meetings, and a drill instructor of the local militia.[27] He appears not to have been present for the meeting at the tavern, after which the meeting participants drafted a letter urging twelve Hampshire County towns to assemble a subsequent meeting of selectmen at Amherst on July 31. The latter meeting materialized as planned, and a countywide meeting was planned for August 22. At this meeting, the largest and most comprehensive so far, "yeomen in fifty of the sixty towns of Hampshire County attended."[28] Again, Shays' presence was not noticed—a fact that scholars have paid insufficient attention to. Some, perhaps puzzled by his absence, insist on maintaining the legacy that has been assigned to him.[29] For her part, Starkey contends that Shays "had taken no part" in the meetings of the Pelham selectmen.[30] And Richards makes no mention of any role played by Shays at these initial meetings, focusing instead on the figure of Dr. Nehemiah Hines, a leading man at Pelham.[31]

On August 22, fifty Hampshire towns were represented at the home of Colonel Seth Murray, where a petition of twenty-five articles was drawn up.[32] Shays appears either not to have made any impression at this crucial meeting or not to have been present at all.[33] This fact is of particular interest, as (according to Richards) it was at this meeting that the town representatives decided to "break up the [Northampton] Court"—thereby initiating the series of court closures that would come to characterize the whole insurgency.[34] How this decision was reached and whether it was achieved through the leadership of a particular representative are not answered in the literature. At most, we can say that Shays was either silent at or absent from the insurgency's formative meetings.

Since Shays had achieved the rank of captain in the Revolution and had subsequently become a drill instructor in Pelham, it is unsurprising that members of the Pelham group initially turned to him to lead their contingent to Northampton. "The town fathers of Pelham had wanted Daniel Shays to lead the Pelham men, but he had refused and the task had fallen to Deacon John Thompson."[35] Thus on August 29, a force of roughly fifteen hundred Hampshire insurgents prevented the Court of Common Pleas at Northampton from sitting.[36] Yet Shays "assuredly had not gone with [the insurgents], for the Pelham men arrived under the command of Captain Hinds of Greenwich, and Sheriff Porter, taking careful note of names, could not have missed Shays had he been present."[37] Why might Shays have refused to lead? Starkey quotes him answering this question: "I told them it was inconsistent after we had agreed to petition."[38] On the basis of this statement, she infers that Shays in August 1786 felt the soon-to-be insurgents were "going about it the wrong way."[39] Since they had yet to receive a response to their petition, justice required that they take no action until receiving one.[40]

Insurgents from other counties continued to close Massachusetts courthouses in the weeks following the events at Northampton. Shays appears to have been absent from all of these. Notably, the insurgents closed the Worcester courthouse on September 5. In response,

> state authorities took notice. To them, it was evident that the rebels were doing far more than just disrupting debt cases and harassing judges. They were attacking the most visible symbol of state authority in the west, the state judicial system that had been sanctioned by the Constitution of 1780, thus challenging the very legitimacy of the new state government. The authorities' first instinct, therefore, was to suppress the rebellion.[41]

On September 7, Governor James Bowdoin began what would become several days' worth of meetings with his executive council and closest advisors, as well as with "William Phillips, the president of the state's only bank," and "other financiers"—an assembly of the oligarchs, indeed.[42]

It was shortly after this meeting that Bowdoin, in a proclamation published in the *Hampshire Gazette* on September 13, 1786, struck the tone that the reactionary forces would take in the months to come.[43] The governor did not know of Daniel Shays, as the latter had yet to take any part in the insurgency. Nevertheless, Bowdoin had already begun to articulate the government's narrative of the insurgency, a narrative in which Shays would soon find a place. The happy people of Massachusetts—alleges that narrative—had been "misguided by the machinations of internal real enemies," whose ambitions had led them to create "anarchy and confusion" ultimately with a view to making themselves "absolute" despots. Accordingly, Bowdoin and his executive council had already decided that some demagogue was responsible for the events.[44] As Bowdoin himself contended in his address to the emergency plenary session on September 28,

> many of the good people of those Counties have been unhappily and incautiously induced to support, or not oppose, the destructive measures,

> which artful and wicked men have, for some time past, been pursuing; and which, with indefatigable industry, they are still pursuing.[45]

A demagogue was needed to blame because Bowdoin and the state government generally "argued that no matter what the causes [of the rebellion] were, the disturbances themselves could not be justified."[46] Even if the rebellion could be traced at least in part to systemic factors, like underrepresentation of farmers and mismanagement of state debt, Bowdoin felt that such factors could not be acknowledged publicly. Instead, agency for the disturbances had to be attributed to certain "wicked and artful men." Bowdoin thus announced in his September 13 proclamation that "the Attorney-General is hereby directed to prosecute, and to bring to condign punishment the Ringleaders and Abettors of the aforesaid atrocious violation of law and government; and also the Ringleaders and Abettors of any similar violations in future." What was needed on September 13, 1786, was a particular face to put the label of demagogue to.

Governor Bowdoin soon had two contenders—neither of whom was Shays. On September 12, the day before Bowdoin's proclamation, a town meeting was held in Concord to discuss closing the court. County sheriff Loammi Baldwin arrived that morning, and noted Nathan Smith of Shirley, Job Shattuck of Groton, and Captain Adam Wheeler of Hubbardston attempting to rouse the assembly against the court. Baldwin wrote to Bowdoin that day, disclosing the names of all three men.[47] In addition, members of the town meeting wrote to the governor condemning the actions of those who attempted to close the court.[48] Thus, when the Supreme Judicial Court of Massachusetts met at Worcester five days later, on September 19, it indicated eleven men suspected of involvement in court closings.[49]

At this point, the Supreme Court was set to meet next at Springfield on Tuesday, September 26, and it was suspected by many that the previous indictments would go forward and additional indictments against insurgent leaders, including Luke Day, would be brought.[50] "The insurgents," explains Warren,

> feared that in the Supreme Court indictments of treason would be returned against them. Consequently, they assembled in sufficient numbers to completely paralyze the proceedings of that court. . . . Till the following March the Supreme Court was seen no more in Western Massachusetts.[51]

Shays arrived the morning of Tuesday, September 26.[52] It was determined at this meeting that Shays would be permitted to march the insurgents in front of the courthouse.[53] Afterward, Shays was also on the committee of seven men charged with negotiating with the Supreme Court judges. The petition was signed: "The people collected now in Springfield . . . for the purpose of moderating government."[54] It drew no particular attention to Shays.

Why did Shays wait until this juncture to participate? And what did his participation amount to? Rufus Putnam, in his January 8 "interview," reports that Shays claimed "the sole motive with me in taking the command at Springfield [on September 24–26], was to prevent the shedding of blood, which would have absolutely been the case, if I had not."[55] This suggests that Shays had in mind to resist popular sentiments, which if unchecked might have precipitated acts of violence.[56] In contrast, Starkey contends that even though Shays had been reluctant to participate at first, "the current was too strong; there was in his town a passion for unity that was beyond him to withstand."[57] Rather than attempting to moderate popular sentiments, Shays was overtaken by them. To that end, Starkey suggests that Shays felt strongly the trials of those who had led the movement so far, like Adam Wheeler and Luke Day, should not go forward.[58] Crucially, neither of these plausible interpretations holds Shays responsible for the closing itself.

As of October 1786, halfway through "Shays' Rebellion," Shays himself was still neither popular nor, at least in any palpable way, a leader.[59] His name appears in only one major correspondence:[60] that of John Adams, to whom Samuel Osgood wrote a letter containing the following remark:

> The Leader of the Insurgents in Massachusetts is entitled to the Ribbon & Eagle—He left the Army in the Fall of 1780 being then a Captain of good Reputation; his name is Shays.—A Man without Education—but not without abilities.—He is privately involved—which may be the reason why he has adopted such violent Measures—It is generally supposed that he cannot Retreat.[61]

On September 28, Governor Bowdoin addressed a special joint session of the General Court, stating that "artful and wicked men," the "Ringleaders and Abettors of such attrocious violations of law and Government," were responsible for the "tumults and disorders, which have lately taken place in several Counties within [Massachusetts]." Though he was evidently sure they existed, the governor did not name who these leaders were. While the special legislative session was taking place, insurgents continued to assemble in cities and to produce petitions to the government.[62] Shays appears not to have been present at any of these closings.[63] Starkey claims that after Springfield, Shays "went back to Pelham and husked his corn."[64]

The one crucial, albeit indirect, appearance Shays seems to have made at this time was through a circular letter in Hampshire County, instructing households to prepare themselves for government suppression of insurgent activity. The letter, quoting the governor's September 13 proclamation, reads as follows:

> Pelham, October 16, 1786
> Gentlemen, Information having been received that the General Court are about adopting measures to bring the leaders of the late risings of the people to *condign* punishment, you are requested to assemble immediately all the inhabitants of your town, and provide that the town is furnished with ammunition, the militia with arms, and organized with officers agreeable to law.
> I am your's, signed
> DANIEL SHAYS[65]

In response, the governor on November 6 delivered the following brief address to a joint session of the General Court:

> I have just had delivered to me, a letter from the County of Hampshire, dated a few days ago: which, as it gives information of measures the insurgents are taking there, that are very dangerous to the peace & safety of the Commonwealth, I think it highly necessary should be immediately communicated to you. — It appears by it, that circular letters are sent to many towns in that County, directed to the Selectmen, & requiring them to assemble immediately the inhabitants of their respective Towns; & to see that they are furnished with ammunition & arms, & are organized with officers according to law; and that some of those letters have this addition, that the Militia be furnished with sixty rounds of Cartridges, & stand ready to march at a minute's warning. . . . These proceedings, Gentlemen, are of a very alarming nature, & require your immediate attention.[66]

Bowdoin makes no mention of the fact that the letter was signed by Daniel Shays, suggesting that, in November, Shays' name still had no significance for the government forces. At this stage in the insurgency, he was to them just another agitated yeoman, not yet an "artful and wicked" demagogue.

In the course of the next ten days, the General Court suspended the writ of habeas corpus (November 9) and passed an act of indemnity (November 15). The latter promised the "many deluded persons" who had taken part in the insurgency between June and the date of the act that they would not be prosecuted if they took an oath and ceased taking part in protests.[67] In addition, the General Court on November 14 issued an "address" to the people clarifying and defending its position vis-à-vis the insurgency. Crucially, the legislature reiterated the governor's view, articulated in his address and proclamation, that certain demagogues must be responsible for deceiving the people: "We have no doubt, that endeavours are used by evil & designing men, to alienate the affections of the people in general, from those who are concerned in the administration of Government." However, the legislature went even further than the governor had gone, positing that "a great part of the uneasiness in the State has arisen from *misinformation*."[68]

On November 28, they succeeded. Oliver Prescott, a selectman from Groton, sent a letter to the governor containing a list of the men he believed to be the insurgency's key demagogues: Job Shattuck, Oliver Parker, Benjamin Page, Nathan Smith, and John Kelsey—he reported—"have been active in the late rebellion & stirring up the people to oppose government, are therefore dangerous persons & May a Warrant be issued to restrain them of their personal Liberty."[69] The letter made no mention of Daniel Shays. Governor Bowdoin responded by dispatching a cavalry squadron, which succeeded in capturing Parker, Page, and Shattuck, with Shattuck resisting arrest and being injured in the process.[70]

Historians agree that it was in response to these arrests and acts of intimidation by government that the insurgency greatly intensified:

> More than thirty towns formally protested against the state's action. Held directly responsible was the governor, who had ordered the arrest and had power to pardon and recall troops. His behavior, along with the decisions of the legislature, were likened to "British tyranny," and denounced as "dangerous, if not absolutely destructive to a Republican government." The state's action also caused some men to publicly endorse the rebellion.[71]

The insurgents retaliated by closing the Worcester court on December 5. Additionally, the leaders of the insurgents drew up a petition to the governor. Importantly, Shays led a contingent of men to the Worcester closing, as well as participated in the petition drafting committee. Historians know little concerning the details of his participation, however. Minot claims Shays arrived from the Revolutionary War barracks at Rutland.[72] This view is confirmed by a contemporaneous report in the December 7 issue of *Worcester Magazine*: "We learn [Shays] issued orders to many towns in Hampshire and this county [Worcester], to turn out and join him at Rutland."[73] That Shays came to Worcester from Rutland, having begun to consolidate his forces there, suggests that Shays had been preparing for action since before the Worcester closing.

The December 20 issue of the *New Hampshire Mercury*, for example, published a copy of the petition that was drafted by petition committee at Worcester.[74] According to the *Mercury*, the petition was sent in a letter by mail from Worcester; the newspaper does not report the name of the sender. The petition is preceded by the following prologue, which contains the only mention of Shays in the petition:

> *The petition of a committee from several towns in the county of* Worcester; *together with a committee from a body of men from the counties of* Worcester, Hampshire, *and* Berkshire, *all convened at* Worcester, *under the command of capt.* Shays *and capt.* Wheeler, *who, on the 4th inst, did obstruct the sitting of the Court of Common Pleas.*[75]

Crucially, the letter to the *Mercury* containing the petition states: "I am told their leaders, and about 300 men, are now at Rutland. Of this intelligence respecting the number of men at Rutland, I am not certain." According to Minot and Condon, the contingent of men referred to here would have been led by Shays. Yet the author of the letter, who was evidently present at the Worcester closing, appears to be ignorant of the role played by Shays in leading the Rutland contingent. The author refers to the "leaders" of the Rutland contingent, as if it were headed by a committee and not by Shays himself. Shays would appear, then, not to have made himself known as a leader, despite actually having led men at court closings, as well as having signed his name to official petitions. To this end, none of the accounts of the court closings at this time—contemporaneous or historical—indicate that Shays gave orations or in any way drew attention to himself in a public way. Even the Worcester petition is ascribed to joint committees "under the command of capt. Shays *and* capt. Wheeler," rather than to Shays himself.

Shays' understated role continued in the days immediately following the Worcester closing. On December 9, "regulators in Hampshire County organized themselves into six regiments led by a 'Committee of Seventeen' . . . the fourth regiment was to be led by Captain Daniel Shays of Pelham," together with two other Revolutionary War captains.[76] Nothing appears to be known about Shays' role in this committee. The news that Shays had become one of the participants was only gradually becoming known to those well informed as to matters of state. On December 14, General Lincoln sent Governor Bowdoin intelligence regarding "the Number of Rebels that would march under the direction of Shays in the County of Hampshire, should the contest be in said county, and the towns where they belong."[77] Lincoln estimated 970 insurgents—a number historian Richard Beeman regards as "wildly exaggerated."[78] On December 16, Artemas Ward, a judge from Shrewsbury, wrote a letter to the governor advising him to send troops to Worcester to ensure the opening of the court there on January 23.[79] The same day, later Massachusetts attorney general and governor James Sullivan wrote to John Adams in London that "some of the ring leaders [of the insurgency] have been taken by Coup D[e] main but the Government has neither learning ability energy or honesty."[80] Major General William Shepherd wrote a similar letter to the governor a day later, on December 17.[81] None of these letters mentions Shays.

The Springfield Court was set to open on Monday, December 25. On Monday morning, roughly three hundred insurgents arrived before the judges. As Eleazar Porter reported to Governor Bowdoin, in a letter dated December 26,

> a committee from the insurgents . . . presented a paper signed by themselves to the Justices, of which the following is a copy, "Springfield, Decemr 25th, 1786. We Request the Honble. Judges of this Court not to open said Court at this Term, nor do any kind of business whatever, but all kind of business to remain as tho no such Court had been appointed. Luke Day. Daniel Shays. Thomas Grover."[82]

In a letter dated December 27, Samuel Lyman reported to Samuel Breck that "Shays & Luke Day & one Grover of Montague headed this party of mad men" in Springfield.[83] Though he lists Day and Grover in addition to Shays, Lyman draws particular attention to the last, noting that "a spirit of energy in [the Massachusetts] government . . . has appeard in the capture of three of these rebels"—Parker, Page, and Shattuck—"and I hope it will appear in the capture of three or four more of them, at least of *Shays*" (italics in original).[84] In response to reports like those of Ward and Shepherd, Governor Bowdoin in late December and early January assembled a militia force of 4,400 men to oppose the insurgents.[85] After the second Springfield closing, a contingent of insurgents reencamped at the Rutland barracks, remaining there for most of January. It was at Rutland that Putnam interviewed Shays on January 9; he subsequently sent the interview to Governor Bowdoin as intelligence concerning the rebellion.[86]

On January 19, General William Shepherd occupied the federal arsenal at Springfield with a thousand troops. On the same day, General Lincoln arrived at Worcester—where government forces anticipated another court closing—with four thousand men. "As the regulators became aware of the size of the force headed to Worcester to defend the court, they eventually decided not to go to Worcester, but rather to converge on Springfield."[87] Eli Parsons arrived at Chicopee, just north of Springfield, with three hundred men from the Berkshires. At the same time, a thousand insurgents under Luke Day gathered at West Springfield. Daniel Shays gathered a thousand insurgents at Palmer, to the east of Springfield.[88] Correspondence between the three does not indicate that one of them was acknowledged by the others as holding supreme command.[89] In fact, "the initial plan was for a three-pronged assault on January 25. But just before the scheduled attack, Luke Day unilaterally changed the plan." Day actually sent

Shepherd a twenty-four-hour ultimatum in which he claimed to represent "the body of the people assembled in arms."[90] Additionally, in contrast with Day's ultimatum, Shays sent Shepherd a letter in which he promised to disband the insurgents if Governor Bowdoin would pardon those who had participated in previous court closings, release the two protestors who were currently in prison, and disband the militia under Lincoln until the state election in the spring.[91] As Shepherd did not respond, Shays and Parsons decided to seize the arsenal as planned (they had not received Day's injunction to delay the attack, which had been intercepted by Shepherd's forces). On January 26, Shays and Parsons marched with their united forces toward the occupied arsenal. Shepherd fired several warning shots from the arsenal's artillery pieces before spraying the insurgents with grapeshot. The insurgents reportedly scattered without firing a single shot. Shepherd did not give chase, though General Lincoln, who had been marching from Worcester to Springfield, did. In the days that followed, Lincoln pursued the insurgents to the town of Petersham, where he captured 150 of them on February 4. Shays, Day, and other insurgent leaders escaped to Vermont, and the insurgency officially concluded.[92]

The Case of Shays, Part 2: Creating a Demagogue

Because Shays' role in the rebellion was so understated, he was not immediately raised to the status that he would subsequently attain. As late as January 5, 1787, a few weeks before the end of the insurgency, a statesman as well connected as future Chief Justice John Marshall admitted in a letter to James Wilkinson that "we have contradictory accounts of the motives and views of the insurgents," and made no mention of Shays.[93] Similarly, an article in the January 12 edition of the *American Recorder and Charlestown Advertiser,* a Boston newspaper, reports that the insurgents at the second Springfield closing "were headed by the noted captain Shays, and Luke Day and his brother"—evidently unable to settle on who the true leader was.[94] While it was not at all clear to government forces who or what group was primarily responsible for the insurgency while it was still underway, figures like Bowdoin were still confident that there *were* demagogues responsible. Hence, Governor Bowdoin's address as published in the January 17, 1787, *Massachusetts Centinel* assures the public that

> success on the part of the insurgents . . . must be destructive of civil liberty, and of the important blessings derived from it; and as it would be the result of force, undirected by any moral principle, it must finally terminate in despotism—despotism in the worst of its forms.[95]

The idea that a demagogue seeking to annihilate republican government and to establish himself as tyrant must have been responsible for the insurgency thus preceded the "discovery" that Shays was the demagogue responsible for the insurgency. It created the political space with which elites filled Shays *ex post.* According to Leonard Richards, Shays' Rebellion

> resulted in only a handful of court closings and skirmishes [and] failed as a revolution. [Yet] long after the rebels fled the battlefield, the insurrection [nonetheless] reverberated through American society. Much of the backlash was due to the Boston elite. Had they treated Daniel Shays as simply a small-town rebel leader, the aftermath might have been different. But they portrayed him instead as a major villain, a threat to the entire nation, an archetype for anarchy. He thus became memorable, hailed and damned long after they were forgotten.[96]

Similarly, Szatmary remarks that "Shays' Rebellion . . . marked an important point in the social development of the United States, as evidenced by the reaction of the dominant commercial elite to it on the regional and national levels."[97] Such public fears and sentiments as were nurtured by political elites created the political space in which to construct a demagogue who had been "responsible" for the insurrection. As Abigail Adams explained in a letter to her son (and future president), John Adams had begun work on his *Defense of the Constitutions* in part to demonstrate that those responsible for the Massachusetts insurrection must have been "the real Enemies of freedom" rather than legitimate reformers:

> The seditions in Massachusetts induce your Pappa to give to the World a Book which at first he designed only for a few Friends. He thought it was a critical moment and that it might prove usefull to his Countryman and tend to convince them . . . that those who from a turbulent restless disposition endeavor to throw of[f] every species of coercion, are the real Enemies of freedom, and forge chains for themselves and posterity.[98]

In short, Adams had begun work on his anti-Shays tract before it was discovered that Shays was the man to blame.

Accordingly, in the months and years immediately following the insurgency, elites in turn came to settle on Shays as the demagogue who was primarily responsible. "The authorities insisted that the entire rebellion was . . . under [Shays'] direction, that he was the commander-in-chief, the 'generalissimo,' as the attorney general put it. Some saw him as a potential dictator . . . the authorities would continue to depict him as the man in charge and eventually label the entire uprising

'Shays' Rebellion.'"[99] The narrative these elites developed fit squarely into the mold of demagoguery that had been prepared for it. In the weeks following the Worcester closing of December 3, alleged reports of and interviews with Shays began appearing in Boston newspapers. Most of these were editorials, or were penned by anonymous or pseudonymous authors. They were part of a propaganda effort on the part of state elites to plant the idea in the public mind that it was Shays who had been responsible for the protest movement. Rather than provide verifiable evidence to this effect, however, these writings begin with the premise that Shays was responsible before proceeding to develop a series of moralistic attacks on his character. An editorial in the December 22 *Salem Mercury* entitled "Anecdotes of Daniel Shays, Leader of the Insurgents" amounts to little more than a slanderous, unsubstantiated diatribe.[100] "From his youth," asserts the author, Shays "was remarkable for subtility and duplicity, which, notwithstanding his want of education, was conjectured would one day or other make him famous." Yet "he probably would have continued," speculates the editorial, in "his original obscurity, had not the tumult of the times given him an opportunity to display his activity, by joining a mistaken multitude." The article ends by confessing its ignorance as to Shays' goals, but forecasts the worst: "What his real designs are, time must bring to light—this much is certain, his ambition is unbounded."

Similarly, a pseudonymous article published in the January 17 edition of the *Massachusetts Centinel* alleges to be reporting a conversation between the author and the author's friend, a New Yorker who was in the Continental Army during the Revolution and who recently had an encounter with Shays.[101] This unnamed friend, the article claims, was at the time of the Revolution a fellow officer of Shays, the "mushroom General" and "infamous and ignorant leader of the insurgents in the western counties." The article claims that the unnamed friend and former officer recently sought out Shays because the latter owed the former money. On visiting Shays' house—"or rather, *stye*, it having much more the appearance of a den of brutes, than a habitation for men"—the unnamed friend is told by Shays that ten thousand insurgents are ready to fight government forces in a minute's notice. What is more, after closing the Worcester court,[102] he intended to

> march directly to Boston, plunder it, and then, in order as he expressed, "*to destroy the nest of devils, who by their influence, make the Court enact what laws they please*" . . . [Shays] swore he would take possession of the heights round the town, and fire red-hot shot into it. . . . [H]e also said . . . that it was in his power to overthrow the present Constitution, and that he would do it.

According to the article, the unnamed friend then asked Shays how he anticipated the Confederation government would respond and what government he planned to replace the Massachusetts Constitution with. Shays "replied, that as to the former his ideas never extended so far as to think of it, and touching the latter, he knew no more what government to set up, than he knew *of the dimensions of eternity*." Though it concludes with a statement that "you may depend on the above been authentick, as the person from whom I received it is a gentleman of the strictest veracity," the piece would seem to be a piece of fear-mongering, demagogic propaganda. Likely written by a pro-Bowdoin editor at the *Centinel*, its hyperbole renders it almost satirical, and paints an incongruous picture of Shays that is at once frightening and laughable, ambitious and improvident, depraved and subhuman. It is clearly calculated to appeal to an audience that wishes simultaneously to lambast Shays as an ignorant plebeian, and at the same time to vilify him as constituting a genuine threat.

The change in public attitudes toward Shays can also be glimpsed in a shift in the language of the Massachusetts government's official records, the "Acts and Resolves." The March 10, 1787, entry announces a general pardon, extended by Governor Bowdoin to Massachusetts citizens involved in the insurgency. The pardon contains the condition that "the Commissioners" who have been assigned to carry out the pardon "shall not be empowered to promise indemnity, in any manner whatever, to Daniel Shays, Adam Wheeler, Eli Parsons, or Luke Day." Roughly a month after the insurgency, the government has yet to settle on a single leader, instead listing all four men it knew to have been involved in the organization. In a letter from London dated January 27, John Adams echoes this uncertainty, asking (rhetorically) "Is not a Shattuck & a Chase [Shays] as great a tyrant, when he would pluck up Law & Justice by the roots?"[103] Similarly, the entry for June 15, 1787—three months after the first—states that

> nothing in these resolutions shall extend to, or in any manner avail Daniel Shays, of Pelham, in the County of Hampshire, Gentleman, Luke Day, of West Springfield, in the same County, Gentleman . . . but they and each of them shall be liable to be tried, convicted and punished for any of the offences aforesaid, in the same manner as if these resolutions had not been made.

All those known to have exercised some leadership role are mentioned. A year later, however, the records simplify things. The March 31, 1788, entry makes no mention of the other insurgent leaders, referring instead to "Daniel Shays and others."[104]

A notice in the *Massachusetts Centinel* of December 27 mentions a "prose-poetick parallel between Erostratus, Jack Cade, and Daniel Shays."[105] Erostratus (*hērostratos*) was a fourth-century BCE arsonist who sought fame by burning down the temple of Artemis at Ephesus; "the Ephesians passed a decree condemning his name to oblivion."[106] Jack Cade was a demagogue who led a popular revolt against Henry VI of England in 1450. "Cade was defeated," writes one historian, "and his name lies buried beneath the rubbish of nations. But his example did not die."[107] Similar writings continued to appear in newspapers in the months and years following the insurgency. A satirical poem in the July 5, 1787, version of the same paper, entitled "Shays to Shattuck," uses clumsy couplets to depict Shays as half-insane with guilt and regret:

> Guilt clotted with blood, leads to Horror and Fear,
> And rueful Repentance comes slow in the rear,
> My conscience breaks out in the blaze of the sun,
> Upbraids and exposes the crimes I have done,
> With knav'ries and vices presents me so foul,
> That I fly from the face of the day like an owl.[108]

Shays was depicted as repentant because, according to the narrative that was being developed about him, his ambitions were tyrannical and utterly devoid of public spirit. Accordingly, "the mercantile elite," writes Szatmary, had "predicted a short-term dictatorship for Daniel Shays." According to Szatmary, William Shepherd, commander of the Massachusetts militia, predicted that Shays had hoped to " 'erect a military government for the coercion of the state, and by setting up his standard' in Massachusetts *expected 'to be supported by great numbers from all the states, and be able to declare himself dictator of the whole union.'* " Similarly, "William Williams, wealthy Berkshire County creditor, also *charged Shays with designs to 'conquer' Massachusetts and eventually become 'the tyrant of America.'* "[109] The same note was struck by Henry Lee, who in a speech at the Virginia Ratifying Convention on June 9, 1788, states with remarkable confidence that the course of the insurgency came down to the leadership exercised by Daniel Shays himself:

> The insurrection in Massachusetts . . . I was then in Congress, and had a proper opportunity to know the circumstances of this event. *Had Shays been possessed of abilities,* he might have established . . . King, Lords, Commons. *Nothing was wanting to bring about a revolution, but a great man to head the insurgents; but fortunately he was a worthless captain . . . he wanted design and knowledge.* [My italics][110]

Shays is depicted by Lee as having been responsible for leading a movement that posed a genuine threat to the entire nation. At the same time, Shays is slandered as vicious, depraved, and incompetent. It seems implausible that a "worthless captain" could really bear responsibility for such an achievement as leading a mass movement. Either Shays was incompetent, in which case he cannot be said to have led the movement so much as to have ridden on top of it, or he was *highly* competent, in which case he would not merit Lee's insults. Lee seeks to hold Shays responsible for the insurgency—thereby making him blameworthy—while at the same time denigrating him and depriving him of precisely the military virtue that Shays would have needed to possess in order to have led the movement in the first place.

As Lee's rhetorical flourishes suggest, ratification provided the ideal opportunity for proponents of the Constitution to brand their opponents as aiders and abettors of the great demagogue, Daniel Shays. As Richards contends, "Shays' Rebellion gave the nationalists the edge they needed. It provoked the spark on which to advance the nationalist cause and play on the fears of others."[111] A Federalist political cartoon, entitled "The Looking Glass for 1787," depicts a mob dragging an enchained state of Connecticut to a raging bonfire, from above which a thunderstorm lowers and hurls lightning bolts (see Figure 1). One of the

Figure 1 A piece of Federalist propaganda, "The Looking Glass of 1787" shows a group of Anti-Federalists (top right) pulling the state of Connecticut (then debating whether to ratify the proposed Constitution) toward fire and brimstone. The Anti-Federalists are shouting, "Success to Shays."

mob members shouts: "Success to Shays." The cartoon's subtitle confirms its hyperbolic message: "A house divided against itself cannot stand. Mat. chap. 13th verse 26." The biblical implication of this piece of propaganda is that following demagogues like Shays is tantamount to consigning oneself to perdition.[112]

Several years later, on May 17, 1796, and well after ratification, elites were still developing the notion of Shays as the archetypal demagogue. A writer styled "Lucius," writing in the *Aurora General Advertiser* (Philadelphia), asserted that "Shays' rebellion . . . struck at the existence of government." Similarly, Mathew Carey in a letter to James Madison, June 26, 1821, wrote, "A little more talent and good fortune might have rendered Shays a Caesar, a Cromwell, or a Bonaparte."[113] Carey would seem to have been drawing on Hamilton's formulation from *Federalist* #21, originally published shortly after the insurgency, on December 12, 1787:

> A successful faction may erect a tyranny on the ruins of order and law. . . . The tempestuous situation, from which Massachusetts has scarcely emerged, evinces that dangers of this kind are not merely speculative. Who can determine what might have been the issue of her late convulsions, if the mal-contents had been headed by a Caesar or by a Cromwell?

According to the dominant narrative, the insurgency's goal was not legitimate democratic reform of the Massachusetts political system—reform in accordance with the aspirations of the Revolution itself. Rather, Shays is saddled with the legacy of a depraved demagogue endeavoring to reestablish European-style ascriptivism and despotism.

Shays' reputation was truly cemented in the years and decades following the constitutional convention, *after* the public writings and private correspondences of notable founders had begun to be absorbed in the public mind. The conception of demagoguery held by elites, many of whom were involved in framing the 1787 Constitution, would seem to bear responsibility for Shays' subsequent reputation. Nevertheless, this conception is not reflected in the design of the Constitution nor in its most theoretically sophisticated defense by the authors of *The Federalist*. In fact, the collapse of discourse witnessed in the entire Shays ordeal vindicates the Constitution by revealing how a moralistic conception of demagoguery obfuscates and distracts from genuine political dysfunction in favor of scapegoating and demonization.

The moralistic conception is reflected in remarks like Elbridge Gerry's to the effect that those who participate in protests and insurgencies are merely "dupes of demagogues."[114] As Gerry proceeds to explain, "The people do not want virtue. . . . In Massts. it has been fully confirmed by experience that they are daily misled into the most baneful measures and opinions by the false reports circulated by designing men, and which no one on the spot can refute." Most of those who participate in protests are, according to this view, not really aware of what they are doing, having been misled by the truly knowing and vicious among them. Only a people out of their wits, insists John Adams, could have been so taken in by the leaders of the insurgency: "If the good People of our State, are not disposed to surrender their Liberties and Safety and the Rights of Posterity into the hands of a few drunken Horse Jockeys, they will think it time to support a Government which is worthy of them."[115]

Arguments like these are designed to discredit and delegitimize a protest movement that, like Shays' Rebellion, involves a significant portion of the community's population. A large portion of the community in protest might well be interpreted as a sign that the protestors have a legitimate complaint, and that the government should listen to rather than suppress them. If, however, it can be persuasively argued that most of those involved in the protests are acting under false information diffused by demagogues who knew better, and that they would not have joined the protests had they not been so deceived, then the protest in question can be discredited and delegitimized. This was the view of most leaders who opposed the Massachusetts insurgents. Governor Bowdoin insisted that the people of Massachusetts had been "misguided by the machinations of internal real enemies," as well as "unhappily and incautiously induced to support . . . artful and wicked men."[116] James Iredell held that "in the state of Massachusetts, where very lately there was so formidable an insurrection . . . I believe a great majority of the insurgents were drawn into it by false artifices. They at length saw their error, and were willing to disband."[117] According to George Minot, who wrote the first history of the insurgency, "One principal cause of the disturbances among the people, was the misrepresentation of designing men, by which they had been led to believe the grossest falsehoods."[118] An author with the pseudonym "Truth," writing for the *Hampshire Federalist* on March 22, 1810, described how "the unfortunate insurrection, commonly called Shays' Rebellion, was quelled, and the honest, though deceived and deluded, insurgents had laid down their arms."[119] In the preface to an act of indemnification, John Hancock extended pardon "to those unhappy offenders who are the objects of [the pardon], and who have been deceived by wicked and designing men."[120] The most complete summary of this view, however, would seem to be an anonymous January 20, 1787, article in the *Massachusetts Centinel*:

> That men, having no more principle or knowledge than Shays . . . both *civill* and military, possess[es], should have influence enough to lead from the duty they owe to their God and country, large numbers of the yeomanry of this State, is really astonishing—*it could not have been*

> *effected but by the circulation of the blackest lies, and the obstruction of the rays of political knowledge from the minds of adherents* . . . when . . . coercive measures shall have been adopted . . . we shall see their reign shall be short.[121] [My italics]

The article closes with the prediction that "we shall see . . . the people who now follow them, their eyes been opened by right information, execrate the authors of their infatuation, and hand down to society with infamy, the detestable names of Shays, Chapman, Wheeler, Day, and Willard, as enemies to the rights of mankind."[122]

Shays and the American Founding, Revisited

The case of Shays thus complicates the story of those who would interpret the Constitution as an elite backlash fearful of demagogues like Shays. A more nuanced interpretation would say that the elite backlash against Shays was itself symptomatic of the demagogic pre-modern politics described in *The Federalist*, which the new Constitution was designed to replace.

We can begin to glimpse the Constitution's new vision of politics in some of the founders' own utterances regarding Shays' Rebellion. In *Federalist* #74, Hamilton defends the pardon power in Article II of the Constitution with reference to the insurgency in Massachusetts, advancing a Machiavellian argument about how suppressing insurgencies can actually serve a beneficial political role.[123] As he explains, "terror," perhaps even brutal punishment of "the condemned person"—that is, the person held responsible for the movement—is politically "necessary." In the context of this argument, Hamilton marshals Shays' Rebellion as an example that illustrates his broader point:

> Treason will often be connected with seditions, which embrace a large proportion of the community; as lately happened in Massachusetts. In every such case, we might expect to see the representation of the people tainted with the same spirit, which had given birth to the offence. And when parties were pretty equally matched, *the secret sympathy of the friends and favorers of the condemned person, availing itself of the good nature and weakness of others, might frequently bestow impunity where the terror of an example was necessary.* [My italics][124]

Hamilton's statement is remarkable for what it implicitly concedes to the Massachusetts insurgents, and to popular movements in general. In such movements, a substantial portion of the community, perhaps even the government of the community itself, will likely be moved by the cause of rebels, and will therefore be inclined to pardon them, or at least not to punish them. This—as Hamilton evidently knew—is precisely what transpired in Massachusetts, where the state government chose not to punish the major "leaders" of the rebellion because they knew how far and wide support was for them among the people. But instead of ceding ground, Hamilton contends, the government should use insurgencies as an opportunity to re-exert authority for the sake of the public good. Like Machiavelli, Hamilton justifies the "terror of an example," not on moralistic or retributive grounds, but on basis of domestic tranquility and the common good: "Indeed, [in the modern as opposed to classical perspective] it is human ambition and insolence that need to be restrained and managed rather than actual violations punished."[125] Hence, in *Federalist* #25, Hamilton views popular movements from the standpoint of natural human recalcitrance, and therefore the state's need to impose public order, rather than from a more elevated standpoint of civic education and moral character:

> The conduct of Massachusetts afford a lesson . . . that cases are likely to occur under our governments, as well as under those of other nations, which will sometimes render a military force in times of peace essential to the security of society. . . . [I]t also teaches us, in its application to the United States, how little the rights of a feeble government are likely to be respected, even by its own constituents.[126]

Implicitly rejecting the more elevated yet precarious rhetorical doctrines of antiquity that were based on moral and civic education and devotion to the common good, the Constitution as Hamilton elucidates it both urges and enables us to analyze popular leadership and demagoguery in terms of the low but solid standard of peace, security, and economic prosperity. Hamilton evinces a similar view in a private letter to George Washington dated August 8, 1792: "Massachusetts threw her Citizens into rebellion by heavier taxes than were paid in any other State."[127]

In this interpretation, rather than embracing the moralistic conception of demagoguery espoused by the elites who were responsible for Shays' erroneous reputation, the Constitution was instead designed to address the *structural* factors that were deemed responsible for that very insurgency. Accordingly, the 1787 Convention produced a constitution without property requirements for voters or for officeholders, one that extended suffrage in a way that the 1780 Massachusetts Constitution emphatically did not. Agreeing with Hamilton's Machiavellian view of the intractability of human nature, which we discussed in Chapter 2, these writers all reflect the view that no best regime could ever educate the public to the extent of being able to eliminate the threat of demagoguery.

4

Constitutional Design

> There are men who could neither be distressed nor won into a sacrifice of their duty; but this stern virtue is the growth of few soils; and in the main it will be found that a power over a man's support is a power over his will.
>
> —Alexander Hamilton, *Federalist* #73

How can the founder of a constitutional system make it as likely as possible that the community's problems will be addressed and debated in a way that is attentive to the different parts and interests of the community, thereby surmounting the pitfalls on display in Shays' Rebellion? More specifically, how does a founder create the conditions for good political rhetoric, even when they do not know in advance what will be on the political agenda? As these questions suggest, is difficult to evaluate a given exercise of leadership without being familiar with the substantive issues at stake. In times of urgent crisis, for example, moderate and rationalistic rhetoric will be inappropriate, just as inflammatory rhetoric will be inappropriate during times of normalcy. But who gets to decide whether the times are normal or not, and therefore, whether the rhetoric in question is appropriate? How can we make it likely that leaders will be punished for inappropriate rhetoric and rewarded for rhetoric that advances the common good?

The American founders' answer to this question is well known. They believed they could create conditions within government that would continue to be hospitable for reasoned debate, and that would incentivize officeholders to speak publicly in ways that allowed other officials and the public at large to understand and engage with the relevant range of perspectives on complex matters of public policy. Less well understood is how to determine whether the system is succeeding on its own terms—whether the system is generating and incentivizing the kinds of leadership that show the regime as a whole to be functioning as the best version of itself. How do we know if the rhetoric our leaders are using is beneficial for the polity, without a background theory of what constitutes "good" rhetoric in our political system in the first place?[1] Though our constitutional

Demagogues in American Politics. Charles U. Zug, Oxford University Press. © Oxford University Press 2022.
DOI: 10.1093/oso/9780197651940.003.0004

order is designed to incentivize good rhetoric, there is no guarantee it will succeed; the Constitution is not "a machine that goes of itself."[2] Officeholders and the public they represent must understand both the ends that their political institutions were meant to realize, and what it means for those institutions to operate in a healthy manner, in order to hold the occupants of those institutions to account and, more broadly, to diagnose the relative health of the system of which those institutions are a part. The following chapters are an attempt to perform such a diagnosis in reference to rhetorical leadership in the American constitutional order.

Rhetorical Leadership and Ordered Politics

The American Constitution sets up a political framework in which exercises of governance are ordered and regulated through formal institutions. To gain and hold power within such a framework, officeholders must avail themselves of rhetorical forms that make success within the constraints of that framework more likely. Unlike in participatory democracies, the actual exercise of governance in the American system does not hinge on the ability of private individuals to develop a following in a popular assembly. To be sure, actors within the private sphere can exert pressure on public officials to act in their preferred ways, and officeholders can appeal to the public for their preferred policies and outcomes. But as James Madison famously observed, at the federal level the actual exercise of governance itself never directly involves the general public.[3] Elected officials in constitutionally established positions of authority must respond to various pressure points of influence (e.g., donors, lobbyists, primary elections, the media) and calculate the likely effects of their conduct on their chances for reelection before making authoritative and publicly binding decisions for themselves.

The basic rationale for choosing a representative system of this nature, instead of a participatory scheme designed in accordance with the classical model, is familiar enough, though a brief outline of its logic is perhaps useful in approaching the subject of demagoguery in the American context. When governance is exercised in an informal, contingent manner, basic political questions such as whether a law will get passed and administered or whether and how a legal case will be adjudicated are highly dependent on chance. How many popular orators will assert themselves into the contest? How will their oratory affect their audience? How will the audience react to multiple and divisive orators? "Where authority is based on a leader's supposed representation of the people's will," writes Ceaser, "competition for popular favor is bound to become the mode of soliciting office and with it the cultivation of whatever currents of opinion seem likely to provide a popular following."[4] As glimpsed in Xenophon's *Memorabilia* in Chapter 2, the ability of leaders to act in such a regime depends heavily on the disposition, favor, and enthusiasm of the popular assembly. By the same token, insofar as orators are incentivized to exploit these for their own advancement, negotiation and deliberation are disincentivized as modes of decision-making.

By contrast, a formal arrangement of offices and institutions, though by no means immune to various forms of public pressure, circumscribes nonetheless the range of contingencies and narrows the range of political outcomes: "The perspective of an officeholder with a limited sphere of responsibility and interest is one that resists demagogy because it does not presume the possibility of wielding final or sovereign authority."[5] By reducing the number and range of questions that must be answered at each stage of political action—for example, who should be allowed to speak and for how long, what counts as a majority, and who answers to whom—political forms impose order and focus on politics and political speech: "deliberative institutions focus debaters on particular questions and limit the audience they are addressing. Such settings impart a natural discipline to the speeches given within them, encouraging substance."[6] For this reason, many of the American founders held that the proper setting for routine policy formation and decision-making was "the institutions of government themselves, not the campaign trail. Legislatures and parliamentary assemblies had evolved over centuries to encourage substantive discussion of concrete policy choices and to reduce the danger of demagoguery."[7] All of these were selling points for the founders, who wanted a system that would incentivize substantive debate. Thus, "by giving authority an institutional basis in the Constitution, the Founders doubtless thought that there would be no further need for leadership"—at least, leadership of the kind that tended to dominate the classical republics.[8]

This in turn allows for more devotion to the substance of politics itself. Where officers do not have to fear violence against themselves precipitated by an adversary vying for popular acclaim, the more limited scope of their business will permit them to concentrate on the tasks their offices were designed to execute.[9] Fixed terms, for example, tell us who will be governing and for how long, which relieves officeholders of the fear of being suddenly replaced or worse. Though elected officeholders are ultimately answerable to their constituents during elections, there is nothing their constituents can formally do to constrain their official conduct between elections.[10] Further, federal judges have no popular constituency, and depend only on Congress' understanding of "good behavior" in order to retain their place in the federal judiciary. Hamilton sketches the basic rationale for fixed terms at the beginning of *Federalist* #71:

> It is a general principle of human nature that a man will be interested in whatever he possesses, in proportion to the firmness or precariousness

> of the tenure by which he holds it; will be less attached to what he holds by a momentary or uncertain title, than to what he enjoys by a durable or certain title; and, of course, will be willing to risk more for the sake of the one than for the sake of the other.

A more recent but nonetheless helpful articulation of this rationale was given by Justice John Paul Stevens in *U.S. Term Limits, Inc. v. Thornton,* a 1995 case involving the question of whether states have the right to add additional qualifications for membership in Congress. Writing for the majority, Stevens argued that "the power to add qualifications is not within the 'original powers' of the States" because "the Framers intended the Constitution"—not the state governments—"to be the exclusive source of qualifications for members of Congress."[11] Stevens continues:

> Each Member of Congress is "an officer of the union, deriving his powers and qualifications from the constitution, and neither created by, dependent upon, nor controllable by, the states." . . . Those officers owe their existence and functions to the united voice of the whole, not of a portion, of the people." . . . Representatives and Senators are as much officers of the entire Union as is the President.

Stevens points to several constitutional provisions that corroborate his argument, including Article 1, Section 6, which provides that the salary of congressmen is to be paid by the federal treasury and not by the individual states. This provision reflects "the view that representatives owe their allegiance to the people, not to the States."[12]

One might point to other provisions in the Constitution, such as equal state representation in the Senate (as well as the last clause of Article V insisting that no amendment be passed depriving the states of equal representation in the Senate) as evidence of the fundamentality of the states. This objection, while containing a modicum of truth, falters in several ways. There are many more nationalizing components to the Constitution than there are components favoring state power. For example, Article VII gives the power to ratify the Constitution not to state legislatures but to specially appointed ratifying committees appointed within the states.[13] The Constitution gives the federal government nationalizing authorities like the power to impose "full faith and credit" among the states as well as the power to judge whether a state has a "republican form of government." In addition to binding all public officials—federal and state—to support the federal Constitution, not their own state constitutions, Article VI declares the federal Constitution the "supreme law of the land."

National supremacy over the states is also reflected in the design of the Senate, the very institution frequently held to symbolize and guarantee states' rights. It is correct that, institutionally speaking, equal state representation in the Senate builds the interests of the states qua states into the legislative and governing process—this kind of discretionary power is perfectly compatible with a regime that invests ultimate decision-making authority in the national government. Indeed, a legislature that *truly* represented the states qua states would—as the Confederation Congress had done—give the states the authority to recall legislators as punishment for conduct that the state government regarded as harming the state's own interests. The decision to deny powers of these kinds to the states (and for that matter, to the people writ large), not just in the Senate but in all constitutional offices, reflects a rejection of the logic of the Articles of Confederation, a genuine "states' rights" constitution based on representative democracy.

Generally speaking, we might choose constitutional offices over a scheme of representative democracy such as the Article of Confederation because we would anticipate that the former would afford elected officials political space within which to think and debate from a national as opposed to a purely local perspective. By the same token, the foundation of relationships in smaller communities tends to be intimate and familial; the basis of political decision-making is therefore personal trust and other affective experiences rather than transparent negotiating and reasoning. "The small size and scope of [direct democracies and ancient republics] allowed for clear and quick divisions which leaders could exploit and manipulate for their own ends."[14] As Hamilton observed in responding to the idea that the Union ought to be divided into separate, autonomous republics:

> Such an infatuated policy, such a desperate expedient, might, by the multiplication of petty offices, answer the views of men who possess not qualifications to extend their influence beyond the narrow circles of personal intrigue, but it could never promote the greatness or happiness of the people of America.[15]

Small communities breed familiarity, which in turn breeds either unreflective solidarity based on shared prejudice or resentment based on envy and other sources of fraternal enmity. As a consequence, "in the ancient republics, where the whole body of the people assembled in person, a single orator, or an artful statesman, was generally seen to rule with as complete a sway as if a sceptre had been placed in his single hand."[16] Leaders in small, homogenous communities are incentivized to exploit the unarticulated feelings and sentiments of their fellow citizens because, as political experiences, familiarity and solidarity seem to dispense with the need for impartial, transparent articulations of justice and the common good. "If people are friends," wrote Aristotle, "they do not need justice."[17] The sinister implications of this view within the political realm are not hard to imagine. "Friends" understand who the community's enemies are; "friends" therefore do not need to go through an impartial legal process, present evidence of guilt, and convince a jury of one's peers when pursuing and punishing the enemies of the state. For their part, founders like Madison were keenly aware of how inadequate fraternal feelings and moral exhortations had demonstrated themselves to be in the face of an incensed majority in a small community:

> If the impulse and the opportunity be suffered to coincide, we well know that neither moral nor religious motives can be relied on as an adequate control. They are not found to be such on the injustice and violence of individuals, and lose their efficacy in proportion to the number combined together, that is, in proportion as their efficacy becomes needful.[18]

Stated more broadly, the familiar institutions of modern constitutional government are based on this very understanding—namely, that trust and exhortation are inadequate as political principles, that the personal feeling of uprightness experienced by a republican citizenry is by no means a guarantee of desirable political outcomes, and that reason-giving is therefore fundamental in a community of free and equal human beings.

This principle is reflected in the design of the American constitutional system. In a government of officials chosen by a diverse coalition consisting of many and often competing interests, a premium will be placed on rhetorical transparency and impartiality because mutually suspicious groups will be less inclined to take it on trust that their interests will be represented when the officials who represent them are making decisions. To extend Aristotle's analysis, we might say that within the realm of collective action, "justice"—that is, transparency and impartiality—is required as a substitute for the trust that friendship within an intimate community provides. Officials in a large, relatively impersonal constitutional democracy can be expected to depend less on familiarity, shared sentiment, and mutual prejudice as means for persuasion than leaders in a small republic might.

To illustrate the point, consider a hypothetical scenario. A representative from Seattle, Washington, is likely to be unimpressed with the popular following that a representative from West Virginia has in Charleston—unless that following can be translated into, and leveraged for the sake of, achieving some political goal that the member from Seattle wants to realize. But the medium of exchange that the two members will use to pursue their respective goals will be a reasoned account of the relative importance of those goals for the members who are pursuing them. Knowing that their constituents are unlikely to favor a climate bill that effectively ends the coal industry in the United States, the member from West Virginia might express their willingness to support a climate bill that carves out room for coal subsidies, basing their bargaining position on the rationale that the real economic needs of their constituents ought to outweigh the scientifically projected needs of the environment. For their part, the member from Seattle (who needs the West Virginia member's support if their bill is to pass) is also fully cognizant that the environmental lobby in their own district will react adversely to a climate bill that perpetuates the coal industry through subsidies.

In this scenario, the need for a bill together with the threat that such a bill will likely pose to the coal industry creates the pressure for a policy solution that will speak to the real needs of all parties involved and whose rationale can be accessed and validated by the entire community. Instead of taxing the coal industry into oblivion, *and* instead of agreeing to a coal subsidy that will almost certainly result in a primary challenge, the member from Seattle proposes a phased-out approach to coal production in West Virginia and other states coupled with subsidies for green-energy facilities whose construction and operation will employ former coal miners, thereby ameliorating the negative economic impact of the climate bill without perpetuating the very industry that the climate bill was originally designed to terminate. At no point in this transactional process do any of the players involved need to be motivated by upright intentions—the member from Seattle does not need to care about the welfare of coal miners, nor does the member from West Virginia need to be concerned about the welfare of planet Earth.

Generally speaking, we might conclude that in order to advance their mutual ambitions for legislative success, officials within an institutional incentive structure like this one are led to appeal to each other in terms that would be attractive to individuals from different backgrounds who cannot fall back on presumed commonalities, affections, and shared experiences. While as a person a member of Congress might not be particularly rational or deliberative, the conditions for their success—a record of high-quality and nationally popular legislation leading to reelection—will incentivize them to find common ground with other members whose cooperation is necessary for the realization of their own individual ambitions. Reasons that can be understood, corroborated, and validated by individuals who do not share a background, who do not necessarily trust each other, and who therefore need to make explicit and transparent the terms of their interactions and agreements therefore become the rhetorical currency on which discourse in the regime trades.

Demagoguery as the Constitution Understands It

National office is meant to extract rationality from individuals who might otherwise be narrow, prejudiced, and parochial.[19] What does this aspect of the Constitution mean for the rhetoric of officeholders? How does the Constitution, which displaces the moralistic classical understanding of demagoguery, want us to think about the kinds of rhetorical tactics that would have been classified as demagogic in earlier times?

The most important point is that the character and personal ethics of individual officers do not need to evolve or improve in the process of governing for the system to function properly. Rather, publicly beneficial conduct can be elicited from the outside through incentivization: "At no moment need the actor be motivated by his or her arguments, even though he or she feels compelled to respond to the arguments of others. As long as politics is induced to trade on the plane of reasons, no matter what the motivations, constitutional democracy succeeds."[20] Office "supplies the defect of better motives."[21] This distinction between moral character and official conduct is core to the Constitution's design. Thus, under the Constitution "only a minimal ethical floor of individual virtue was necessary for well-functioning government. Under this theory, ordinary self-interest can be tied to institutional place and transformed into public-regarding behavior, regardless of whether individual political motives are authentic or sincere."[22] Constitutional functionality thus does not presuppose a "constitutional conscience" among officeholders, as Signer maintains, if by conscience we mean the inner awareness that one's actions are just or unjust.[23] The Constitution neither requires officials to be convinced of their own uprightness nor requires the public to make judgments about the uprightness of leaders.

What *does* the Constitution require? In Chapter 5, I will describe in some detail the different kinds of rhetorical practices the Constitution wants different officeholders to abide by in executing their offices. For now, let me summarize the new, instrumental—as opposed to moralistic—understanding of demagoguery that the Constitution presupposes.

The most important feature of demagoguery for the founders was not that it rewards unjust officials, though this is certainly undesirable. Rather, it is that it leads groups of people to authorize measures, or to do things themselves, without weighing competing arguments for the merits of those measures. A variety of rhetorical appeals can accomplish this end. Some appeals promise an object or outcome that is desirable for a part of the community at the expense of the whole. Others paint an enemy, foreign or domestic or both, as the object of fear or hatred. What made this kind of rhetoric undesirable from the standpoint of the founders was not that it identified a goal as desirable or that it singled out a group of people as threats to the community. After all, some goals *are* desirable, and some groups *are* threats, and it is the job of a leader to make these clear in terms that all members of the community can weigh for themselves. What makes the kinds of rhetorical tactics the founders associated with demagoguery bad is the particular way in which they coerce groups of people into acting. Demagoguery's defining characteristic is that it leverages sources of human motivation without supplying reasons for why someone who is not already committed to pursuing a certain end ought to be. Characteristically, demagogues speak as though their audiences know already that the positions being taken and the measures being proposed are necessary and just, and they withhold reasons for *why* they should be understood as necessary and just.

Of course, the founders recognized that day-to-day political discourse would incorporate a variety of rhetorical appeals and that differences in the structure of offices would incentivize more or less demagoguery, with House members, for example, likely being more intemperate than senators. Accordingly, the rationales that officials articulate would vary in persuasiveness (rhetorical presentation) and inherent quality (argumentative rigor and empirical veracity). For the system to work well, officeholders and the public must be prepared to hold speakers to the rhetorical standards that thoughtful decision-making requires. Politics must trade on the plane of reason (that is, the quality of arguments offered) and not on speculation about the purportedly vicious or virtuous motives behind those reasons. Like Machiavelli, the founders were frustrated by "professions of good" that distracted from the serious business of politics, and they sought to reconstruct rhetoric on a Machiavellian foundation. They were committed to deliberative politics not simply for its own sake but because they thought that the common good was more likely to be realized in a regime whose discourse traded in contestable and, to some extent, verifiable arguments about the general welfare. Unlike virtue—or worse yet, claims about divine revelation—the general welfare is something tangible, comprising economic health, personal security, and the protection of individual rights: something about which, in principle, everyone knows something and can therefore contribute to by making and responding to ever more refined and nuanced defenses of public policy.[24] By the same token, a form of politics marked by speculative judgments about the character and motivations of leaders lends itself to unhelpful demagoguery.

Consent and the Common Good

Ultimately, thoughtful decision-making is held by the Constitution as the best way to secure the public's consent to publicly beneficial measures, and within this understanding we find room for demagoguery in the Constitution—even if the Constitution's founders never described the system in precisely those terms. Rather, as I will suggest here, we are led to the conclusion that demagogic rhetoric can be good within the constitutional order by thinking through the design choices that went into the Constitution itself. By taking the Constitution on its own terms, we are led to an understanding of what the Constitution permits, forbids, and requires that can differ significantly from what the founders and defenders of the Constitution wrote during its drafting and ratification.

The Constitution is instrumental in the sense that it aspires to bring about a just and beneficial state of affairs.[25] But because it is also cognizant of the contestable character of the common good, it does not empower one ruler or element within the regime to decide what the common good demands in terms of concrete governance.[26] It recognizes that the public must ultimately consent to a particular understanding of the common good, and that consent requires reflection and choice. A policy that is simply imposed on a people cannot be unqualifiedly good unless those people have some verifiable understanding of its merit.

What does the aspiration to consent-based governance demand in terms of the actual conduct of officeholders under the Constitution?[27] Consent presupposes or entails a voluntary choice; we can only truly be said to choose something voluntarily to the extent that we have understood the principles or merits of what we are choosing.[28] Consent requires a degree of knowledge of the terms of an agreement, and a person who did not know what an agreement entailed cannot be said to have truly consented to the agreement in the first place, even if (and crucially for our purposes) they were tempted into the agreement by a passion or a desire.[29] For this reason, governance based on popular consent requires public officials to be "accountable" to the people they govern. To be accountable means to owe an account—that is, a reasoned explanation—of one's actions; it means not being able to act with impunity or unlimited discretion, in the manner of an authoritarian ruler. Public officials owe an explanation of the actions that they as officers of the public trust have undertaken and plan to undertake on behalf of the public, so that the public can in turn make an informed judgment of their conduct and their worthiness to hold the public trust in the future.

Consent at the political level requires an articulation, by those who govern, of the purposes of and reasons for their actions. As Muirhead and Rosenblum observe in criticizing public officials who fail to contradict conspiracist claims, "They need to educate citizens about government and offer true explanations of public actions while refuting unwarranted ones."[30] Such explanations are not just a strategic option; they are a responsibility. It is for this reason that courts do not simply issue holdings but rather write opinions, available to the public, articulating the *reasons* for their holdings. It is why the Senate must give its "advice and consent" on presidential nominees rather than simply voting on them. It is why the president is required to "give to the Congress Information of the

State of the Union, and recommend to their Consideration such Measures as he shall judge necessary and expedient," and also why the president in vetoing a bill cannot simply refuse to sign it into law, but rather must "return it, with his Objections to that House in which it shall have originated, who shall enter the Objections at large on their Journal, and proceed to reconsider it." Articulations of the reasons for state action are necessary if, among other things, the public is to comprehend the terms of their agreement to be governed—that is, if they are to understand what it entails to be governed by these particular officials and what precisely they have agreed to in consenting to be governed by them.

Within this framework, demagoguery is rhetoric that seeks the acquiescence of others in what the orator wants by framing claims in terms that cannot be validated or scrutinized—terms that cannot be consented to. As Barber explains, the Constitution's commitment against this kind of acquiescence can be inferred from its structural features, such as Article V, which impose significant procedural requirements on momentous state action. The Constitution anticipates that these requirements will reward proponents for state action who are able to develop a rationale capable of persuading large as opposed to narrow majorities:

> The Constitution itself evinces in several ways an expectation that most of us will want to act contrary to our principles. Consider the amending provisions of Article V, provisions whose stringency makes sense if we realize that what is morally and intellectually best in us is typically weaker than our immediate demands, that nations have better and worse moments just as individuals do, and that the best moments, though rarer, are the most authoritative. Because we have an awareness of all these things we try to fortify the best in us with constitutions that restrain the worst in us.[31]

Constitutional officers have a responsibility to explain their actions in a way that creates the conditions in which other officers and citizens will make informed choices between alternative courses of state action, as opposed to indulging their immediate desires and demands. Of course, this is not to say that citizens *will* make an informed decision when faced with such rhetoric, or that they will internalize much or any of a given public utterance's meaning. The best we can do is to attempt to evaluate the quality of the rhetoric itself by looking at public utterances in light of the kind of speech that the best version of a constitutional officer would employ.

To the extent that rhetoric evinces demagoguery, insulating itself from contestation and external verification, it rejects the principle that all members of the community must be treated as capable of evaluating reasoned claims regarding why their assent deserves to be given to state action. Demagoguery is problematic not as an ethical matter but because it makes citizens more likely to authorize state actions "adverse to the permanent and aggregate interests of the community," actions to which, upon reflection, a rational person would be less likely to consent.[32] Demagoguery so defined induces citizens to "support" state actions that flatter their unreflective prejudices and desires, while at the same time preventing citizens from truly consenting to those actions. It is for this reason that, as we have seen in examining Shays' Rebellion, polities based on the classical understanding of demagoguery are so prone to instability, factional conflict, and civil war. Citizens in such regimes are more likely to be swayed by demagogues to support actions whose merits and consequences they do not fully, or even partially, understand.[33] For these reasons, the Constitution empowers a system of constitutional offices whose design would induce officials to explain their conduct in a way that provided other officeholders, and ultimately the voting public, with the opportunity to make informed choices based on the merits of alternative policies and policy visions. Such a system

> will be less apt to be tainted by the spirit of faction, and more out of the reach of those occasional ill humors, or temporary prejudices and propensities, which, in smaller societies, frequently contaminate the public deliberations, beget injustice and oppression towards a part of the community, and engender schemes, which, though they gratify a momentary inclination or desire, terminate in general distress, dissatisfaction, and disgust.[34]

Such a system would make it more likely that the public would be in a position to follow their *interests* (ends that a rational person would choose after deliberate reflection on their merits as well as the merits of their alternatives) instead of merely following their *inclinations* (ends that come to sight as attractive before their merits have been elaborated and weighed).

Instrumental Demagoguery: A Dilemma

The Constitution's design is based in part on the expectation that, when given the opportunity to choose between alternative articulated conceptions of the common good, governments and the publics they represent will tend to embrace the most rational of those conceptions. This hope accounts in part for the existence of deliberative institutions—forms of government designed to elicit better articulations of public policy between which the public and their governments can decide responsibly. Yet crucially, this expectation is not guaranteed to succeed; reason in politics is not self-executing. Unlike either deliberative democracy, which views public reason as irreducible to public goods, or interest group theory, which conceives of politics as bargaining over goods and rights, the Constitution appreciates that deliberation and the common good are desirable ends that sometimes conflict and that political judgment is needed to mediate between them.[35] Drawing on the insights of Machiavelli and modern political philosophy, Hamilton, for example, insisted there would be times when statesmen would have to produce political effects because reasoned explanations of proposed action would be insufficient to gain the public's consent to a necessary political decision. The public good might demand a subordination of deliberation because public reasoning sometimes fails to realize the goods for the sake of which it was enlisted in the Constitution, thereby justifying a non-deliberative solution to bridge the gap. In this view, demagoguery could serve as a tool when other means prove unsuccessful, though it can also supply a temptation to politicians who feel they can profit politically from using it as an end in itself. From the Constitution's perspective, demagoguery can subvert the constitutionally enjoined ends that a leader might legitimately enlist demagogic tactics to pursue—hence the dilemma.

On the one hand, deliberation alone cannot guarantee desirable outcomes, especially in emergency situations where decisive action is needed. On the other hand, this very fact can serve to justify and empower modes of politics that are damaging to the community; it incentivizes, for example, the manufacture of emergencies to achieve results that would not be achievable through normal political rhetoric.[36] Because the Constitution is committed both to the view that deliberation tends to be conducive to the general welfare *and to the general welfare itself*, no adequate constitutional theory of rhetoric can ignore these twin commitments. Because demagoguery is more likely to be used for harmful political ends than for beneficial ones, the Constitution imposes a steep hurdle in front of all uses of demagoguery—a hurdle that is not impossible to clear, however. This hurdle asks whether appeals to non-rational sources of public motivation were rendered necessary by recalcitrance—by the public, the government, or both—that could not have been surmounted otherwise and that was likely to harm the community. Or, the more likely alternative, was it rendered "necessary" from the demagogue's own standpoint because the demagogue failed to argue for their position in a sufficiently compelling way? Was a non-demagogic (or less demagogic) rhetorical alternative open to the orator in question, such that they might have effected the same outcome without resorting to sub-rational appeals?

Regarding demagogues and demagoguery, then, the Constitution asks not what the politician's motives were—did they circumvent deliberation out of moral depravity (for example, laziness and ambition)?—but whether their demagoguery can be justified with a view to the Constitution's own reluctant but decided recognition of the inherent weakness of deliberation itself. In most cases, it cannot, but this does not excuse us from seeking out and understanding those cases where it can. Indeed, the Constitution's multiple commitments create the pressure for the inquiry we are pursuing here.

Constitutional officeholders have a duty to conduct themselves in a way that vindicates the function of their office. But they also have a duty to explain publicly how their official conduct accords with the duties that their office entails, because the government and the public they represent need to be able to weigh the merits and reasons for official conduct—conduct that might be interpreted in different (i.e., more or less constitutional) ways. This principle can aid in classifying and evaluating political rhetoric and demagoguery. Recognizing and articulating the Constitution's commitment to deliberation *and* the general welfare, it is conceivable that an officeholder would deploy demagogic rhetoric tactically in conjunction with an argument about why the political situation they are facing has rendered demagoguery necessary. Defensible demagoguery must be integrated with an explication of the purpose and justification of the demagogic rhetoric in question; the orator must evince self-awareness of the purpose and rationale of their rhetoric. Rhetoric of this kind would, accordingly, consist in a diagnosis of the factors that the officeholder believes to be responsible for unjustified recalcitrance on the part of the audience that requires persuading—for example, a particular institution, the whole government, or the public at large. The plausibility of an argument of this kind would hinge ultimately on two questions: (1) whether there is sufficient reason to think that *not* using demagoguery would fail to move the audience, and (2) whether such a failure would result in some genuine harm to the polity.[37] Defensible use of demagoguery thus hinges on the tenability both of the diagnosis offered and of the orator's explication of their own rhetorical conduct. To be well used, demagogic rhetoric must be integrated into an account of how such rhetoric connects to, and is likely to ameliorate, the political dysfunction highlighted in that diagnosis.

5

Demagoguery in Office

> The Senate is broken . . . the structures we have built reward us for hurting one another. We need to reform those structures or we will never make progress.
>
> —Sen. Tom Udall, Farewell Address to the Senate

The conventional interpretation of the American political system—originally articulated in *The Federalist* and developed subsequently by scholars and commentators—contains an important theoretical puzzle. According to that interpretation, institutional design can, in important respects, serve as a substitute for public-spiritedness. In the classical understanding, public officials were expected to make choices about governance and statecraft in accordance with their understandings of justice and the common good. They were, of course, free to choose injustice over justice, denying what their consciences told them to be right; but the hope was that public-spiritedness—itself derived from civic education provided by the community—would make it more likely that they would choose justice. That leaders should choose to act for the right reason—that is, virtuously—was just as important (in this view) as their choosing the right course of action for the community. Leaders must be entrusted with the freedom to act virtuously; and should they act viciously, they ought to be punished for it.

The founders saw two defects in this model. The first, a philosophical one, is that it is difficult to hold a leader accountable for choosing injustice over justice, because it is difficult to determine whether they knew what they were choosing was unjust in the first place. This difficulty is a problem if the personal motivations of leaders are held to be just as important as how the political outcomes of their decisions affect the community. How can you be sure a leader did not genuinely believe what they were doing was just, especially if they themselves insist this to be the case? Further, how can you be sure that what *you* believe is just and unjust is truly so, and not your mere opinion? Punishing a leader for choosing what they thought justice demanded but which you regard as evil presents a moral

Demagogues in American Politics. Charles U. Zug, Oxford University Press. © Oxford University Press 2022.
DOI: 10.1093/oso/9780197651940.003.0005

difficulty if it cannot be determined whether the choice was truly just or evil. The model assumes that there exists a single right decision in every case, that that decision can be known objectively, and that leaders can be justly rewarded for choosing it or justly punished for choosing otherwise.

Practically, the model flounders because, as common sense testifies, the pull of self-interest frequently proves more powerful than the pull of the public interest. The founders—and Enlightenment thinkers, generally—believed that it was misguided to put human beings in positions of power and expect them to resist the myriad temptations that come with power. Becoming indignant at leaders who misuse their power instead of incentivizing them to use their power for the common good reflects a characteristically aristocratic preoccupation with elite character, and a disregard for the basic necessities of ordinary people whose welfare depends on the actions of elites. If, in contrast, the priority is justice for the community—justice understood as public policies that advance the welfare of *all* citizens, and not just a favored class or social element—then it makes more sense to create an incentive structure in which public officials do not have to make frequent difficult choices between the public interest and their self-interest—or at the very least, one in which those choices are less radical and dichotomous: "The government [the founders] constructed was . . . understood by them all to be unusual in the relatively small demands it placed on a political aristocracy and in the relatively great demands it placed on the people."[1] In this scenario, leaders will be less heroic but they will also be less inclined to betray the interests of those without political power, because they will see those interests as in some way aligned with their own. Most importantly, whether the government discharges its duties and responsibilities correctly will depend less on the self-restraint of political leaders and more on the judgment of the voting public, whose responsibility it is to decide whether those leaders are living up to their constitutional oaths and therefore deserve to hold office.

At the same time, there would appear to be a contradiction within this view. Does not a system of institutions designed to incentivize publicly desirable behaviors in leaders—rather than entrusting leaders to exercise heroic levels of nobility and self-control—in some way dispense with the need for public judgments of leaders' conduct? That is, if the system is supposed to incentivize the kind of conduct we want in government, why would we need to judge for ourselves whether that conduct is good? Should not the system, as opposed to the prospect of praise or blame by the public, provide the impetus for leaders to do their jobs well? As this characterization of the Constitution suggests, the idea that institutional design can simply replace the need for judgment on the part of public officials is highly simplistic. The argument I will articulate in the pages that follow is that this idea is in fact a crude version of what turns out to be a sophisticated *new* understanding of the role of public judgment in a democracy.

According to this understanding, the Constitution does not aspire to replace public judgment, but rather to recalibrate it in line with a new set of priorities. It is true that, by design, those holding office under the Constitution do not have to exercise the same degree of judgment as classical statesmen did, because they themselves are not the holders of sovereignty and the basis of their own prerogative. Rather, their prerogative is derived from a publicly authorized regime—the Constitution—that constitutes their authority.[2] Their roles are therefore circumscribed by the offices they inhabit and, more importantly, by the levers and veto points that the other offices that constitute the separation of powers system have at their disposal.[3] Within this system and at every stage of policymaking and administration, officials both propose and choose from a range of alternative courses of action for themselves and other leaders, some of which are better for the public and some of which are worse. Within this system, the Constitution cannot guarantee that officials will always choose the best of these options; officeholders can fail at their jobs even though the Constitution's design nudges them in the right direction. Finally, the Constitution does not leave it up to officeholders to decide whether their conduct has been satisfactory or not, as the constitution of an authoritarian state would do. Rather, in some cases (e.g., impeachment and removal) it puts the authority to make such judgments in the hands of other publicly elected officeholders, and in others (the selection of elected branches) in the hands of the voting public themselves.

Under the Constitution, officeholders are ultimately accountable to voters, and voters need a way to judge whether their own interests are being served and officeholders deserve their trust. What standards should the public look to in deciding whether governing officials have done their respective jobs well? Answering this question is the work of political diagnostics: furnishing members of a regime with the standards and modes of assessment needed to make informed judgments about the health and functionality of the regime of which they are a part. Political diagnostics are necessary because political regimes do not necessarily reproduce the kinds of understandings (in citizens and in public officials) that are necessary to determine whether institutions and the broader system are properly functioning. For example, it is a truism that American public officials must be held accountable for their actions by the people. But what does it mean to hold someone accountable if their job entails very specific responsibilities? How can you judge someone's performance unless you have an accurate mental picture of what they are supposed to be doing in the first place? For example, holding the coach of an athletic team accountable means something very different from judging the performance of a chef, not just because what "success" means in the two cases differs radically but because the character of each *activity* is different.

One possible response to this last point is that the rules written in the Constitution provide all the resources we need to make such judgments. While partially true, this answer is analytically impoverished. The "rules" that the Constitution furnishes—particular responsibilities, length of term, and so on—do not provide clear answers for how leaders should comport themselves in particular scenarios (e.g., what kind of speech should be given or court opinion should be written, how a deal should be negotiated, whether to deploy troops). Strictly—that is, "constitutionally"—speaking, a president could go their entire term without making a single public speech, and a Supreme Court justice could cast every vote without writing an opinion, since neither of these conventions is explicitly mandated in the text of the Constitution itself.[4] But would we ever say that a president or judge who acted this way was really doing their job under the Constitution, let alone *succeeding* at their job?

That the answer is clearly no indicates that we have something much more robust in mind when we discuss the conduct of constitutional officers and debate whether they did their jobs well or poorly. This is because the Constitution creates a political architecture within which political actors must navigate their respective ways and make decisions about what kind of role they will perform. As the layout of a museum or auditorium is designed to steer the flow of foot traffic and direct people's gazes in a particular direction, the design of the Constitution's political architecture too is meant to nudge officials into making certain kinds of choices—even though it cannot guarantee what kinds of choices they will make in particular situations in advance. Accordingly, the Constitution's design leads us to suspect that officeholders will behave in certain ways; but it does not *necessitate* that they will, because officeholders are relatively free to decide to act in ways contrary to the office, in the same way that museum attendees can choose to walk against the flow of the crowd.[5] For this reason, the Constitution requires the public and other public officials to exercise their own judgment about whether leaders are behaving correctly, and to express their judgments in constitutionally prescribed ways (e.g., elections, nominations and confirmations, impeachments). This is to say, the public has a role to play in deciding whether governing officials are executing their constitutional offices correctly, while at the same time, the structure of the Constitution is incentivizing those officials to act in the way *it* wants them to. The government the Constitution creates "is like a glass-enclosed clock. Its 'works' are visible to all and must be understood and accepted by all in order to function properly."[6] For the system to work well, governing officials and ultimately the public at large must understand how the Constitution steers behavior, so that they can know whether leaders are executing their offices correctly.

Rhetorical Standards

Rhetorical conduct is an important aspect of executing one's office correctly because rhetoric—the way in which speakers articulate their views and positions before an audience—affects the government's and the public's abilities to understand the reasons for and against governmental action. Rhetoric is therefore a kind of behavior that the Constitution is designed to shape and that the public must know how to judge. What are the considerations we should look to in evaluating rhetoric as deployed by different officeholders? Here I sketch some of the ways in which the different designs of the presidency, the Supreme Court, and Congress suggest to us what it means to speak correctly in those roles.

The Constitution's architecture punishes and rewards behavior through the selection process and through the execution of the office itself. Originally, the House was the only directly elected office; would-be senators had to please their state legislators and would-be presidents had to please electors in the Electoral College. The kinds of conduct it takes to satisfy a crowd at a rally can be expected to differ considerably from the kinds it takes to reassure a small group of state elites, and the Constitution anticipates that these external requirements will incentivize would-be candidates to fashion themselves in a way that increases their chances for success. Even today, in the wake of the Seventeenth Amendment and developments in the Electoral College, candidates for the Senate and the presidency must still clear certain characteristic thresholds to secure electoral victories. The Electoral College rewards candidates for tailoring their political platform to the demands of constituencies in swing states that they would not be forced to acknowledge in a national popular vote. Relatedly, senators have a statewide constituency, which translates into a larger number of competing interests than is likely to be found in a single congressional district, where aspiring House members are freer to indulge the narrower interests of a smaller constituency.

The workings of these differences in institutional design can be glimpsed in the characteristic behaviors they tend to spawn in officeholders—behaviors that serve both as sources of solidarity within the same institution (e.g., "senatorial pride") and as sources of derision between different institutions. Former president Barack Obama has described such derision astutely:

> Disdain between the houses of Congress is a time-honored tradition in Washington, one that even transcends party; senators generally consider House members to be impulsive, parochial, and ill-informed, while House members tend to view senators as longwinded, pompous, and ineffectual.[7]

Officeholders in these different positions see caricatured versions of each other because their own offices force them to have a different outlook on the same political phenomena. To senators, House members seem parochial and ill-informed because their relatively smaller districts and significantly shorter terms of office bind them more tightly to their constituents' concerns and prevent them from immersing themselves in policy in the way that a six-year term would. To House members, senators appear long-winded and pompous because of the Senate's privileged position vis-à-vis confirmations and treaties, a senator's more significant constituency (a whole state as opposed to a district within a state), and the longer term of office that each senator has.[8] These observations about the House and Senate apply to each constitutional office as well.

Judicial Demagoguery

The idea of judicial demagoguery will strike many as strange, since judging is not typically thought of as a role that entails public speaking or rhetoric. Indeed, at least within the Hamiltonian framework, judges are expected to rise above the tumult of ordinary politics, ruling on questions of law without having to concern themselves with coalition building, audience persuasion, and other tasks that require rhetorical expertise. Furthermore, as some recent events confirm—most notably Justice Ginsburg's vocal criticisms of Donald Trump and Justice Brett Kavanaugh's impassioned testimony before the Senate Judiciary Committee—the rules and norms that have developed around the American judiciary, especially the Supreme Court, unambiguously reflect the expectation that judges remain within relatively narrow rhetorical bounds.[9] As the *Post* wrote in an editorial censuring Justice Ginsburg for her aforementioned public remarks about the then presumptive Republican nominee:

> However valid her comments may have been . . . and however in keeping with her known political bent, they were still much, much better left unsaid by a member of the Supreme Court. There's a good reason the Code of Conduct for United States Judges flatly states that a "judge should not . . . publicly endorse or oppose a candidate for public office." Politicization, real or perceived, undermines public faith in the impartiality of the courts.[10]

And yet, counterintuitively, it is this very fact that makes the Court a particularly helpful site for observing and describing the phenomenon I have tried to sketch above. Precisely because the Court, unlike Congress and the presidency, has maintained such strict rhetorical norms into the twenty-first century, it makes sense to say that we are more attuned to the significance of rhetorical norm violations by judges than we are to violations by presidents and members of Congress, whose rhetorical responsibilities—while certainly not non-existent—tend to be harder to see. The persistence of rigid norms in the judiciary, together with a more broadly shared consensus about what judicial conduct requires, makes it easier both to recognize judicial demagoguery when it happens and to study its significance for the institution and the regime as a whole.

Regardless of how logically sound and rationally coherent judicial opinions actually are, judging is a role that idealizes the notions of reason and passionless argumentation. To this end, judges seek to distinguish themselves from other institution members by emphasizing the role of logic and impartiality in judicial decision-making, as if judging were a purely deductive activity. Here, the words John Roberts often repeated when he was a circuit court judge, "balls and strikes," are particularly revealing.

The roots of this idealization are traceable to the status that the notion of impartiality and impartial justice will reasonably occupy in any regime dedicated to the principles of liberty and equality. In such regimes, political outcomes are not supposed to be reached simply because a particular class, religious sect, or party preferred them. Rather, it is assumed that all members of the polity could in principle participate in the decision-making process and, by the same token, that citizens should be persuaded of the merits of public policy to the furthest extent possible.[11] Such a state of affairs would be impossible to achieve in practice, of course, but it remains the normative goal to be aspired to. And to the extent that this ideal remains authoritative, it makes sense to conclude that citizens will retain a degree of suspicion or distrust toward institutions that are more explicitly based on non-impartial modes of decision-making, such as bargaining and majoritarianism. As Hamilton explains in *Federalist* #78, norms in Congress and the presidency accommodate "will" and "force" but the judiciary is supposed to exercise "judgement only." This means that whereas the "political" branches are *more*, though by no means *simply*, committed to simple majoritarianism (i.e., an expression of majority will lacking in a deliberative justification), the courts are committed to the principle that judicial decisions should be made impartially, on the merits, irrespective of the personal and factional interests of the judges themselves.

Accordingly, the aspiration on which the judiciary is based is that judges should be institutionally shielded from the sorts of emotional and factional pressures that induce other political actors, especially members of Congress, to deviate from a strict adherence to principle; judges are therefore supposed to be able to make the decisions that, in principle, any member would make if given the opportunity to exercise their reason in an impartial way. This constitutional expectation is reflected in the fact that judges accompany their official decisions with opinions enumerating the reasons for those decisions, even though there exists no explicit mandate for opinions in the Constitution. Simply deciding without articulating a rationale would suggest a degree of willfulness unacceptable for an office that is held to the highest standards of deliberativeness.

So understood, the normative ideal of courts is in considerable tension with the idea of political rhetoric, whereas rhetoric is perfectly at home in Congress, where expressions of will are taken for granted. As we have discussed above, rhetoric is the art of presenting ideas and arguments in a way that makes them more persuasive than they would otherwise be. Rhetoric thus presupposes that logic and facts are not themselves necessarily attractive or compelling; they need additional help to become effective, and so how they are presented helps determine whether they gain the consent of an audience. Viewed this way, rhetoric is a concession to the part of our nature that does not simply respond to the merits of an argument. This means that in a regime based on the idea that governments derive their just powers from the rational consent of the governed, rhetoric is always potentially a source of coercion, insofar as it can be used to move audiences by means of their passions instead of through reasons that are universally accessible. Regardless of how close it could ever come to realizing this goal, constitutional democracy aspires to a state of affairs in which individuals have the resources to freely choose the best political option from a range of proposed alternatives. By the same token, choosing on account of a consideration other than the merits of a proposal implies illegitimate influence of some kind. Because they emphasize the principle of impartiality and the promise that justice can be achieved in particular cases through the application of universally accessible reason, without reference to factional interests or personal ambitions, courts and the judges who administer them embody this particular aspiration of constitutional democracy.

As we have suggested, the American Constitution is not best understood as embracing a conception of constitutionalism in which courts have the final or even the most authoritative role in constitutional decision-making. At the same time, courts are, by virtue of their institutional features, better positioned to take up certain political and constitutional questions than are the other branches; but this means that individual judges should actually be held to the standards that justify having a relatively autonomous judiciary in the first place. Evaluating judicial rhetoric will consist in abstracting the kinds of behaviors and attributes we would want to see in any judge and then looking at individual behavior in light of those standards.

What are these behaviors and attributes? Most importantly, judges—unlike the other officers of the Constitution—are not the advocates of an electoral majority; they cannot be held accountable by the voting public in regular elections. For this reason, judges cannot justify using popular rhetoric as a means to gauge public support for particular judicial actions and rulings, as the elected branches are obligated to do. Procedurally, then, judges are not positioned in a way that would allow them legitimately to claim to be ruling in a way that a certain portion of the public wants them to rule. Because they are electorally unaccountable, they must speak publicly in a way that acknowledges that no element of the polity is empowered to remove them from office on account of their rulings alone: a judge's authority is purely abstract and cannot be derived from a concrete public act, such as an election or reelection. By the same token, speaking in a way that presumes public support would—as I will suggest in my discussion of Chase—authorize Congress to consider impeachment and removal.

The written judicial opinion, though nowhere explicitly required in the Constitution, is nevertheless a constitutional norm that nicely captures the essence of judicial rhetorical responsibility and translates that responsibility into material form. As a form of communication, writing is more deliberative than speaking because it removes the reader from sources of influence that come from personal exposure to the individual who is writing—for example, charismatic appeal, personal appearance, and tone of voice. Though writing certainly has the potential to be non-deliberative, even demagogic, its abstract character forces the reader to confront the impersonal medium of a text instead of the personal form of a speaker's living presence. Insofar as judges must provide a public rationale for their rulings (so that other judges and political actors, as well as the public at large, can decide for themselves if the bases of those rulings are sound), they should do so in a way that deflects attention away from their own personal characteristics and focuses attention on the reasons that might plausibly convince someone of the soundness of the ruling in question.

Further, insofar as judges decide to speak publicly instead of confining themselves to their official opinions, they should refrain from using speeches as a means to drum up support for themselves and their preferred rulings. Unlike elected officials, whose authority hinges on their ability to persuade voters to return them to office, judges do not need to shape public opinion in order to decide as they wish; life tenure protects them from this requirement. But for this very reason, it also renders constitutionally unjustifiable any attempt by a judge to use public speech either to gauge public opinion or to sway it in their favor. Judges do not need public rhetoric to execute their offices, and so they should be discouraged from using it.

Congressional Demagoguery

Following the 2018 midterm elections, House Speaker Nancy Pelosi publicly scolded freshman Representative Alexandria Ocasio-Cortez, along with several other outspoken junior members, for indulging in rhetorical excesses while failing to put in the kind of legislative work necessary for a well-functioning Congress. "While there are people who have a large number of Twitter followers," argued the Speaker, "what's important is that we have large numbers of votes on the floor of the House."[12] For her part, Ocasio-Cortez defended the rhetorical tactics she had employed on social media, arguing that they were necessary for raising awareness of issues that would receive insufficient attention if Pelosi's conception of House leadership hierarchies and congressional norms were allowed to prevail.[13]

Rhetorical norms like those Speaker Pelosi presupposed in chastising her junior colleagues must be evaluated in light of Congress' commitments to the values of democracy and republicanism. Thus, whereas Representative Ocasio-Cortez held that a rhetorically aggressive approach was warranted by a democratic deficit in Congress and the political system generally, Speaker Pelosi maintained that a greater respect for House norms and hierarchies on the part of individual members was itself the best means to achieving legislation that would vindicate the polity's commitment to democracy.

How should we adjudicate these competing claims? A member of Congress is part of a lawmaking assembly, one of whose purposes is to bring to bear competing perspectives from around the country on matters of public policy affecting the whole. Members of Congress, and legislators in general, have a duty to communicate the needs of their constituents and other members of the polity in order to advance their interests. At the same time, legislators are not *simply* advocates of their voters. They are responsible for the welfare of everyone in their district and, as members of the national legislature, for the welfare of the whole constitutional order. Their ability to advocate for their own constituents therefore hinges on their ability to convince a congressional majority and the president that the common good of their district or state is connected to and advances the common good of the whole country: "Whether and how political decision makers respond to group claims will depend not simply on the political strength of those making the claim, but also on the persuasiveness of the case they make, connecting their partial interest to the well-being of the whole."[14]

What this rhetorical duty on individual legislators demands in terms of real-life political action is a blend of forceful advocacy, dissemination of information, and oversight. Getting Congress the "facts-on-the-ground" information it needs to legislate well—that is, the lived experiences of one's constituents—is a necessary, but not sufficient, condition for actually getting one's case heard by those in Congress who most need to hear it. For a variety of reasons, Congress can prove recalcitrant in the face of issues that, in the perspective of individual members, deserve urgent attention. Because each member of Congress is only one among many legislators, their office entails a responsibility to avail themselves of rhetorical means that more constitutionally exposed offices—those of judges and presidents—should avoid, or use only on occasion.

In addition, members of Congress are not solely legislators; the Constitution also assigns oversight roles to the legislature, and these roles require members to both supervise the activities of the other branches—especially the executive bureaucracy—and alert their colleagues, constituents, and the broader public regarding these activities, for better or for worse. As we will discuss in our case study of Joe McCarthy, Congress' oversight role provides committee members with significant opportunities for rhetorical display: members can use their institutional powers to investigate governmental officials and agencies with a view to defunding and even formally reprimanding them. Skillfully deployed demagoguery can enhance a member's power in this respect, especially because committee members in their oversight capacities can gain access to sensitive information that is available neither to other members of the government nor to the public. For this reason, members of Congress have numerous opportunities to use the rhetorical prominence that their oversight powers confer upon them for good ends as well as bad ones. A member who suspects maladministration or corruption can use their oversight position to direct attention toward the suspected malefactor in the form of investigations and hearings, leveraging the sensitive information they already possess to ferret out more information about the problem they are investigating. Demagoguery might be permissible under these circumstances should government officials or other members of Congress attempt to stymie the investigation or simply ignore it. Yet as the case of McCarthy shows, this same oversight authority also provides members of Congress with the opportunity to leverage their rhetorical position in ways that enhance their own notoriety while harming the government and members of the public.

Presidential Demagoguery

Of the three constitutional offices, the presidency is perhaps the most difficult to analyze with respect to rhetoric because so many contending theories have been advanced regarding how presidential rhetoric has changed and what standards should be used to evaluate it. It is difficult to form a stable picture of the ideal of presidential rhetoric because, as many have observed, the Constitution itself offers very little guidance in this regard, and because the standards for what kinds of rhetoric are appropriate for presidents have changed so dramatically. Many scholars regard the modern or post-FDR presidency as having established an entirely new set of criteria, with the result that pre-FDR presidents are largely irrelevant in an analysis of contemporary practice.[15] In this view, pre-modern presidents were excessively constrained by the separation of powers system; after FDR, older, more legalistic ways of evaluating presidential conduct simply ceased to be relevant.[16] Thus, beginning with Richard Neustadt and continuing with Samuel Kernell, who applied Neustadt's framework to presidential rhetoric, scholars have envisioned a presidency significantly liberated from constitutional constraints and free to both pursue and execute the kinds of public policies they want.[17] Others, in sharp contrast, have sought a return to earlier paradigms such as that of Washington and Lincoln, arguing that more popular conceptions of presidential leadership amount to fundamental perversions of the Constitution's ideal of the presidential office.[18]

There are merits to both of these views. Followers of the modern-presidency school rightly observe that the constraints that earlier conceptions imposed on presidential conduct rendered presidential leadership inadequate to the evolving governmental tasks of the modern world. On the other hand, critics of the modern presidency rightly point out the dilemmas of a conception of presidential leadership according to which "everything goes." Do we not implicitly concede the existence of standards, perhaps an ideal, when we speak of better and worse *presidents*—as opposed, say, to better and worse generals or CEOs? That the answer is clearly yes indicates the need for an evaluative framework that can tease out and apply the particular qualities and virtues we instinctively associate with presidential leadership.

Because both of these general approaches to presidential behavior and presidential rhetoric offer strong arguments, my aim is to elaborate a standard for presidential rhetoric that captures the strengths of each while remaining attentive to the ambivalences inherent to the presidential office, that is, to its contestable character. In a recent book, Stephen Knott has attempted to do the same thing, and so Knott's conception of the presidency naturally recommends itself as one after which I might model my own. Knott maintains that Donald Trump is the archetypal demagogue-president and, as such, should be interpreted as the antithesis of the presidential ideal, which was articulated by Hamilton in *The Federalist* and put into practice by George Washington.[19] Knott tries to demonstrate that the presidency has suffered from a gradual decline—from dignity and restraint into demagoguery—as a result of changes in presidential norms effected by several key presidents, beginning with Jefferson and Jackson and culminating in Wilson, FDR, and Kennedy. Whereas presidents who modeled themselves after Washington understood their authority to be derived solely from the constitutional office, demagogic presidents claimed to represent the people writ large and used this claim to justify departures from the original ideal.[20] Knott advocates a return to the Washingtonian model, which prizes rhetorical restraint, energetic leadership in foreign affairs, and a minimalistic conception of presidential leadership in domestic policy.[21]

In urging us to develop a model for evaluating presidential leadership based on constitutional design and historical practice, Knott is certainly pointing in the right direction. And yet, Knott's moralistic conception of demagoguery—which he shares with other authors discussed in this book—together with a rigid and unnuanced conception of the constitutional meaning of the presidency, leads him to misinterpret past presidents in light of his clear (and understandable) disdain for Trump.

Knott begins by acknowledging that the presidency is designed to be a powerful and energetic office, but he argues that it was designed to be so in a specific way. For Hamilton and Washington, according to Knott, presidents were supposed to play no role whatsoever in influencing public opinion; rather, they were supposed to resist changes in public sentiment in order to maintain stability in the government and to foster a deliberative ethos.[22] All of this changed with Jefferson and Jackson, who "displac[ed] the founders' constitution" by taking a more active role in trying to mold public opinion and advocating for a more majoritarian conception of presidential leadership.[23] The precedents set by these presidents were then invoked by progressives in the early twentieth century, who "disregard[ed] the Constitution" by "promis[ing] too much of the federal government, and of the presidency."[24]

There are several problems with this analysis. First, Knott alleges that Jefferson and Jackson were demagogues, but he never articulates what theory of demagoguery this allegation presupposes. Instead, he seems to presuppose a boilerplate moralistic conception akin to the one that in previous chapters we have argued to be inadequate.[25] Accordingly, what Knott means in accusing Jefferson and Jackson of demagoguery is not that they deployed certain identifiable demagogic rhetorical tactics in their capacities as presidents. Rather, it would appear that he suspects them of having been motivated by the wrong kinds of impulses, ones unbecoming of a leader with a "magnanimous soul."[26] He frequently mentions unseemly anecdotes about these men, alleging, for instance, that "Jackson's vindictiveness was all consuming, and when he was finally elected in 1828, a major prerequisite for an individual to be awarded a cabinet post was that one had to demonstrate an appropriate level of hatred for [Henry] Clay."[27] While ugly, this anecdote has nothing to do with Knott's purported subject of demagoguery; it is merely part of an effort to make Jackson seem morally unattractive.

As for instances of actual demagoguery, the evidence Knott supplies is taken from these presidents' private, unofficial writings (Knott quotes a private letter from Thomas Jefferson to Levi Lincoln, in which the latter promises to "sink federalism into an abyss"),[28] from statements made before or after they held the office,[29] and from fellow partisans and campaign officials other than the presidents themselves.[30] By the same token, Knott pays almost no attention to what these presidents publicly said *as presidents*. This is clearly a problem, since once in office, neither Jefferson and Jackson gave frequent public speeches—let alone *demagogic* speeches—even though Jackson in particular had been fond of public speaking and aggressive rhetoric before assuming office.[31] Rather, their behavior emphatically confirms a nineteenth-century norm against presidents using public speeches to agitate for their own policies—a fact Knott himself acknowledges when he observes that Jefferson characteristically refused to advocate for the Twelfth Amendment publicly.[32] Indeed, Knott writes, "Jefferson avoided the type of overt public appeals that would characterize twentieth-century American presidents."[33] Further, in his chapter on Trump, Knott concedes (accurately) that "by and large presidents prior to the twentieth century relied on surrogates to savage their opponents, although there were some exceptions to this norm. Pre-twentieth century, presidents generally confined personal attacks to private correspondence, a tradition which is sadly lost."[34] For his part, Knott appears to be unaware of the extent to which this admission undercuts his characterization of Jefferson and Jackson as demagogues. After all, the behavior for which he faults these presidents was overwhelmingly private and anonymous and lacked the public rhetorical character that warrants calling it "demagoguery." Yet Knott goes so far as to accuse Jackson of being a conspiracy theorist at the level of Trump, giving the impression that Jackson undertook a public rhetorical campaign against the man he believed to have been responsible for the attempt to assassinate him, U.S. Senator John Poindexter.[35] This impression is misleading. Jackson is *reported* to have made this accusation in the moments immediately after the attempt, while the would-be assassin—who had attempted to fire two pistols at the president from point-blank range—was lying, restrained, in front of him.[36] If true—the report was published in the *Baltimore Patriot*, then a Whig publication edited by the apparently anti-Jacksonian Isaac Munroe—Jackson's utterance looks more like a momentary outburst from a man who had nearly been killed than a purposeful public presidential message akin to Trump's incessant tweets and rally speeches promoting conspiracy theories.[37]

By the same token, the relatively few public speeches nineteenth-century presidents *did* give—Jefferson and Jackson included—tended to be unifying and ceremonial rather than popular and partisan.[38] The office both constrained and elevated their discourse.[39] Relatedly, their written public communications reflect a high degree of argumentative sophistication; consider especially Jefferson's First Inaugural and Jackson's Bank Veto Message. Knott, however, mentions none of this, and his characterization leaves one with the erroneous impression that Jefferson and Jackson regularly gave Trump-esque public harangues, when in fact each maintained a high degree of decorum and sought to honor the Constitution's commitment to deliberation. Neither president is properly understood as having "displaced the founders' constitution," at least in the way

Knott claims they did, and Knott is clearly reading his own underdeveloped notions about demagoguery back into the historical record so as to substantiate his argument that the roots of Trumpism can be traced to Jefferson and Jackson.

From this initial source of confusion in Knott's argument, several additional problems flow. Knott seems to think that presidents who try to shape and direct public opinion, and who do not simply oppose public opinion, are somehow violating the Constitution.[40] This argument is strange in itself. Why should it be a "principle" of the office that presidents should oppose the majority as expressed in an election, as Knott claims it is?[41] Certainly it is an option for presidents to do so, as Hamilton argues in his defense of executive independence from the other branches, and sometimes a duty when the president regards the majority's sentiments as dangerous for the common good or individual rights. But there is nothing in the logic of the office demanding that presidents *always* resist the majority—why should they if they think the majority is right? In addition, Knott himself emphasizes that the Constitution is designed to "refine and enlarge" the public's views.[42] Why not view Jefferson and Jackson—who, after their respective elections, developed deeper and more nuanced arguments to justify the positions for which they thought their own electoral majorities stood—as doing precisely this?[43] Why accuse them of demagoguery for trying to articulate a rationale for the positions and policies they thought they had been elected to hold and carry out? Knott himself seems to admit precisely this in describing Jefferson's understanding of his role as public opinion leader: "Jefferson's presidency was both gauging public opinion and at times shaping it and moderating it, using the presidency 'to direct the public's constitutional understanding and to unify public opinion.' "[44] This characterization sounds more or less the same as Madison's notion of enlarging and refining public opinion, which Knott aptly summarizes: "The task of a chief executive was to serve as a 'medium' by which the public's views were refined to ensure that the 'true interests' of the country were protected."[45] Accordingly, it is hard to see why Knott sees Jefferson and Jackson as manifesting demagoguery. Even though these presidents believed that they should be more attentive to majority opinion than previous presidents had been, it is hardly obvious that such a modification amounts to a full-on rejection of the "constitutional presidency." At most, it seems like a legitimate attempt to make the office as energetic as Article II implies it should be.

In each of these respects, Knott's analysis showcases the weaknesses of a moralistic conception of demagoguery. Knott wants to be able to draw clear distinctions between "good" and "bad" presidents, between Constitution-lovers and demagogues. This moralistic lens leads him to make strange suggestions. For instance, he groups Jefferson and Jackson together with progressives like Wilson and FDR because, he insists, all four rejected the constitution in favor of a demagogic concern with majoritarianism. Accordingly, he faults the "demagogues"

Jefferson and Jackson for introducing patronage into the federal government and for rejecting Washington's commitment to merit-based appointment.[46] In so doing, he ignores or disregards the fact that one of the core principles of progressivism was the idea of enlightened administration, which rejected the hackery and cronyism that marked the patronage system and tried to replace it with a competent professional bureaucracy. In trying to group the "demagogic" presidents together, Knott draws a Manichean picture of presidential history. The moralistic lens through which he views the presidency and American politics generally causes him to smooth over complications and to ignore the complexity of the subject, which is more contestable and less amenable to moralism than he is willing to admit.

My approach in this chapter is based largely on Tulis' *The Rhetorical Presidency*, which develops a powerful case for the rhetorically restrained "constitutional" presidency that preceded Theodore Roosevelt and Woodrow Wilson, while at the same time acknowledging the strengths of Wilson's critique of that older view. For Wilson, the office of the presidency as created by Article II promised more power and effectiveness than could be delivered by the norms that had grown up around the presidency—norms based on the original interpretation of the presidency by founders like Hamilton, Madison, and Washington. Such power and effectiveness had become dearly needed with the rise of industrialization, modern military technology, and a nationally integrated economy. Through constitutional interpretation as opposed to constitutional amendment, Wilson created a new set of authoritative standards for what kinds of presidential rhetoric were appropriate, standards that competed with yet never fully displaced the preceding ones. Whereas the old way constrained presidents from using direct rhetorical appeals to the public as a means for pressuring the other branches to take political action, the new way as articulated by Wilson permitted—indeed, encouraged—presidents to make such appeals a part of routine governance. Because the health of the constitutional order required a fully energized presidency, presidents would regularly go to the public to agitate for passage of the specific public policies they envisioned.

Though Tulis demonstrates the extent to which these alternative conceptions presuppose differing standards for evaluating presidential rhetoric, he also shows how the rhetorical presidency has so far failed simply to eclipse the constitutional presidency. Rather, the former has been layered on top of the latter, with the result that presidents since Wilson have been pulled and hauled between the two constitutional paradigms. Sometimes presidents fully exploit the advantages of being rhetorically liberated, while at other times they make use of the restraint and reserve that marked the old way. Accordingly, until President Trump, presidents have successfully toggled between these two modalities without fully embracing the rhetorical presidency—that is, without being fully rhetorical all the time.

Paradoxically, the presidency's ambivalence suggests its own kind of hybrid standard for evaluating presidential rhetoric. According to this standard, presidents are evaluated on the basis of their ability to toggle between these two rhetorical modes, and part of the evaluation includes whatever rationale the president supplies for the conduct they choose to adopt. The framework is more supple and permissive than either the old or new way by itself, because it leaves room for restraint as well as direct popular appeals and demagogic tactics so long as the latter are integrated into a broader publicly-articulated argument. In essence, the standard sought here is built around the standard elaborated in the rest of the book—namely, that presidents, along with the rest of the Constitution's highest officials, should be empowered to be rhetorical and to deploy demagogic tactics when they can give an adequate argument for why the Constitution's own structure and principles require such rhetorical measures.

6

Demagogues on the Supreme Court

In this and the following two chapters, I turn from a theoretical discussion of demagoguery in American politics to historical cases of demagogic leadership drawn from American political history. My goal is to illustrate the spectrum of constitutionally good and bad demagoguery through examples that fall at different points on that spectrum. Further, I use thick descriptions of these historical examples to tease out the different meanings that demagoguery takes on when it occurs in different institutional settings; each chapter is devoted to demagogues within one of the three branches of American national government. As I noted in Chapter 1, these cases are by no means exhaustive; I have chosen them because they are useful for demonstrating how my framework applies to the real world. Alternative cases could easily do the same kind of analytical work.

This section of the book begins with a discussion of judicial demagoguery before turning to demagogues in Congress and the presidency. I proceed in this particular order because, as I suggested in Chapter 5, today judicial norms regarding rhetoric and demagoguery are the strictest and therefore the easiest to recognize when they are broken. In contrast, Congress' norms are the most permissive, and so the contrast between these two branches helps to expose more vividly the modes of normative assessment I propose bringing to bear when we talk about demagoguery in American politics. This portion of the book culminates in the presidency because the office of chief executive combines norms that are at work in both Congress and the Court.

These case studies are by no means intended to accomplish a comprehensive analysis of the life, personality, and leadership style of each figure analyzed. Such an endeavor, while certainly worthwhile, is far beyond the scope of this project. Rather, I spotlight the rhetorical choices that these figures made during specific moments in their careers. For this reason, the assessment I provide in each case is not meant to be comprehensive of the figure's whole career; it is an evaluation of the specific choices they made in the context of a specific political debate. The same figure may well have made significantly better or worse decisions within

Demagogues in American Politics. Charles U. Zug, Oxford University Press. © Oxford University Press 2022.
DOI: 10.1093/oso/9780197651940.003.0006

the context of a different debate; and, if I am successful, the approach to demagoguery that I have proposed here could be used to analyze those decisions, as well.

Justice Samuel Chase and the Judiciary Act of 1802

Associate Justice Samuel Chase (1741–1811)—sometimes referred to as "Old Bacon Face"—was known by his contemporaries for both his aggressive personality and his skill as a jurist and politician, qualities Chase, a vehement Federalist, continued to display once appointed to the Court and which occasioned his impeachment trial before a Jeffersonian-dominated Congress in 1804–1805. Of Chase's disposition, district judge Richard Peters—who served with Chase on court panels when the latter rode circuit—once said that

> of all the others I like the least to be coupled with [Chase]. I never sat with him without pain, as he was forever getting into some intemperate and unnecessary squabble. [Chase] had the singular instinct for tumult which scents [it] at a distance from whence it is imperceptible to others['] eyes, and irresistibly impels a participation in it.[1]

Relatedly, President Washington hesitated before nominating him to the Supreme Court in 1796, likely because he was aware of Chase's reputation for imprudence and provocativeness.[2]

In retrospect, Washington appears to have been correct in his estimation. During the Adams and Jefferson administrations, Chase found multiple ways to push the boundaries of acceptable conduct for judges. After passage of the Alien and Sedition Acts, for example, he drew attention to himself by vigorously enforcing the laws, sometimes disrupting normal court proceedings in order to ensure the outcome he desired.[3] During Adams' reelection campaign in 1800, he openly campaigned for the president in his capacity as associate justice.[4] For our purposes, however, the most interesting of Chase's indiscretions was his decision to harangue a Baltimore grand jury with demagogic rhetoric in 1803, thereby revealing his own preferences and attempting to sway the jury in order to reach the outcome he wanted.

In 1801, a lame-duck Federalist Congress passed the so-called midnight judges law, which created sixteen circuit courts and, incidentally—Adams still held the presidency—filled them with Federalist judges. When the Republicans under Jefferson took office in March with majorities in each chamber, they set their sights on the 1801 act and, having repealed it, passed the scaled-down 1802 Judiciary Act, which got rid of the newly created judgeships (and with them, the newly appointed Federalist judges). This move on the part of the Republicans elicited the outrage of Chase, who had already established himself as a Federalist firebrand. In 1803, he delivered a lengthy and impassioned speech to the aforementioned Baltimore grand jury. What follows is the portion that most accounts of Chase's impeachment and trial quote from the *Annals of Congress*:

> You know, gentlemen, that our state and national institutions were framed to secure to every member of the society equal liberty and equal rights; but the late alteration of the federal judiciary, by the abolition of the office of the sixteen circuit court judges, and the recent change in our state constitution by the establishment of universal suffrage, and the further alteration that is contemplated in our state judiciary, (if adopted) will in my judgment take away all security for property and personal liberty. The independence of the national judiciary is already shaken to its foundation; and the virtue of the people alone can restore it. The independence of the judges of this state will be entirely destroyed, if the bill for abolishing the two supreme courts, should be ratified by the next general assembly. The change of the state constitution by allowing universal suffrage, will in my opinion certainly and rapidly destroy all protection to property, and all security to liberty; and our republican constitution will sink into a mobocracy, the worst of all possible governments.[5]

The demagogic thrust of the speech is clear: Chase is predicting that the repeal of the 1801 act will precipitate the complete overthrow of the American regime. At the same time, and as we will discuss in detail with reference to the rest of his speech below, Chase is integrating this message into a broader argument about the role of the judiciary in the constitutional order and its status vis-à-vis separation of powers. In his view, an independent judiciary is instrumental to the regime's ability to honor its own commitments to "equal liberty and equal rights." Regardless of who the judges happen to be, lower courts were necessary for the federal judiciary to administer its duties adequately because the Supreme Court alone was no longer adequate to the task. The abolition of the lower courts by the Republicans, though technically within Congress' powers, therefore touches on questions that reach to principles that are core to the Constitution. Leaving such a decision up to a regular electoral majority is momentous and, in addition to jeopardizing the rights of the present generation, sets a dangerous precedent for the future polity.

Despite Chase having couched his rhetoric within a deeper constitutional argument, the Republicans decided he had abused his office as judge in using rhetoric to attempt to sway a jury, which is supposed to be impartial and whose impartiality judges are supposed to strive to guarantee. To this end, in the impeachment that followed, the House crafted an article that explicitly addressed the question of Chase's judicial rhetoric and whether his speech amounted to an abuse of his judicial office. "Mutual respect between the Government of the United States . . . and the people . . . [is] highly conducive to the public harmony," begins the eighth article of impeachment,

> yet the said Samuel Chase, disregarding the duties and dignity of his judicial character, did, at a circuit court . . . pervert his official right and duty to address the grand jury then and there assembled, on the matters coming within the province of said jury, for the purpose of delivering to the said grand jury an intemperate and inflammatory political harangue, with intent to excite the fears and resentment of the said grand jury . . . a conduct highly censurable in any, but peculiarly indecent and unbecoming in a judge of the Supreme Court of the United States, and moreover, that the said Samuel Chase . . . under pretense of exercising his judicial right to address the said grand jury . . . did, in a manner highly unwarrantable, endeavor to excite the odium of the said grand jury, and of the good people of Maryland, against the Government of the United States, by delivering opinions which, even if the judicial authority were competent to their expression, on a suitable occasion, and in a proper manner, were at that time, and as delivered by him, highly indecent, extra judicial, and tending to prostrate the high judicial character with which he was invested, to the low purpose of an electioneering partisan.[6]

Here we see in stark relief an elegant and articulate description of demagoguery and the way its use by a constitutional officer can be interpreted as disrupting the substantive goals that the particular design of the institution in question, in this case the Supreme Court, exists to realize: the impartial administration of justice. In addition, we glimpse the core disagreement between Chase, who clearly thought his departure from judicial norms was warranted by the radical action of the congressional Republicans, and the Republicans, who made the case that Chase's deployment of demagoguery constituted a violation of the responsibilities that are particular to the role of Supreme Court justice (as opposed to members of Congress and the president).

Before evaluating Chase's rhetoric in light of his rationale, it will be helpful to consider some scholarly treatments of his impeachment and trial, particularly with a view to establishing how they have tended to diminish the importance of the eighth article. Indeed, scholarly treatments of Chase have focused on the question of whether the justice's impeachment and trial were legitimate uses of those constitutional powers by Congress. As a consequence, these treatments have tended to sidestep the more substantive question of how best to critically evaluate the behavior for which Chase was actually indicted. Raoul Berger, for example, holds that Chase should have been removed because contemporary norms proscribed the kinds of rhetorical outbursts he made as a judge.[7] Richard Ellis and William Rehnquist both contest this interpretation, focusing on the political motivations of the Jeffersonians and arguing that Chase's acquittal established the beneficial precedent that judges should not be impeached and removed for political reasons.[8] Ellis also disputes Berger's argument based on contemporary norms for judicial behavior, arguing that at the time of the Chase trial "there existed no clear-cut definition of proper judicial behavior, especially in political trials." Further, "the role of the judiciary in cases involving political and partisan questions was by no means a settled matter in those times. It cannot be said, therefore, that Chase had clearly violated established judicial procedures."[9]

But does the absence of an agreed-upon answer mean that an answer should not be pursued? Moreover, the fact alone that there was no consensus during the early republic regarding how judges should behave in their official capacities—that is, about the meaning of the "good behavior" clause—in no way means that a better answer to that question could not emerge and that new norms of judicial conduct could not be constitutionally constructed around that answer.[10] More generally, the absence of established constitutional norms governing a certain constitutional provision, such as judicial behavior, can serve as an invitation to think more critically about the substantive goals that the provision in question exists to realize and, accordingly, the kinds of norms that are most likely to facilitate those goals.

As a consequence, even though both of these views are plausible on their own terms, they nevertheless avoid confronting the more difficult yet more pressing question of what rhetorical responsibilities judges have in the first place. More deeply, both view the broader question of impeachment through the same analytical prism. It might well be true, as Berger contends, that contemporary norms forbade rhetoric like Chase's, but do these norms show the American judiciary in the most intelligent light? By the same token, the Jeffersonians may have overplayed their hand politically, as Ellis maintains. But this fact does not dispense with the legitimate questions the Jeffersonians raised about the proper way for judges to engage in public speech. Even if rhetoric like Chase's *was* insufficient grounds for impeachment—and this is by no means a settled issue—this alone does not remove the need for a critical evaluation of his rhetoric in light of the responsibilities that are implicit in the Constitution's conception of judging. We still need an intelligent way of organizing and refining the intuitions we all have about how judges should speak in their official capacities, intuitions that are more obviously shared today than are intuitions about how presidents and members of Congress should speak. More simply put, what does the best version of judging as envisioned by Article III demand in terms of public speech on the part of judges? The thought paradigm shared by these scholars gives us an analytically thin answer when a more capacious one is needed.

For his part, Chase himself appears to have contributed to the construction of this very thought paradigm in the course of his impeachment trial. As Keith Whittington helpfully outlines in his discussion of the Chase trial as a case of "constitutional construction," Chase based his defense on the familiar argument that only statutory crimes are a sufficient basis for impeachment and removal of judges.[11] By the same token, indiscretions and abuses of office, let alone rhetorical abuses, are too nebulous and subject to political partiality to count as the kind of charge that the Constitution's impeachment and removal power could be envisioning. As Whittington summarizes Chase's argument: "Without the fixed standard of criminal law to guide and constrain impeachments [of judges], personnel of the judicial branch would fluctuate with every party victory."[12] Fully thought through, Chase's argument displaces the question of what kind of judicial conduct (including rhetoric) the Constitution envisions, and replaces it with a set of minimal standards that apply equally to *all* constitutional officers (and, for that matter, private citizens)—namely, that only statutory crimes are punishable. It presupposes that even if there were responsibilities unique to the role of judge, responsibilities not shared by other officeholders, those responsibilities would not be a legitimate consideration in an impeachment trial.

Chase likely took this particular line of defense because it promised to be the most successful. Indeed, Chase was well positioned to frame the Republican case as illustrative of the very phenomenon he had been decrying in his own demagogic outbursts: their willingness to use legal and constitutional mechanisms to litigate purely political grievances (e.g., the appointment and entrenchment of Federalist judges), which ought to have been adjudicated through the electoral process or eschewed entirely. And after all, Chase did win, which suggests that his legalistic interpretation resonated with at least some of his audience's constitutional intuitions. Nevertheless, Chase came by far the closest to removal on the charge that he abused his office by haranguing the Baltimore jury: 19–15 in favor of guilty.[13] This fact suggests that his jurors and the public who influenced them felt that the strongest case that could be made against Chase—even stronger than his badgering of defense lawyers—was the charge of rhetorical irresponsibility. Indeed, the House managers emphasized precisely this point in trying to develop a rationale for judicial impeachment that would displace Chase's legalistic defense. Whittington summarizes this rationale as follows:

> What Chase's defenders characterized as minor issues of demeanor, the managers were able to represent as evidence of a "breach of trust," a "flagrant breach of duty," and "gross impropriety of conduct in the discharge of his official duties." Moreover, as part of his duty as a judge, Chase should have been as aware of his responsibilities on the bench as he was of criminal law. Far from being the retroactive application of a new political doctrine, the standard of good behavior was "the law of truth and justice. It is confined to no soil and to no climate. It is written in the heart of man in indelible character, by the hand of his Creator, and is known and felt by every human being." The duties and trust contained in high political office could not be reduced to detailed written law. Such duties and trust certainly were greater than the minimal conditions of criminal law but were nonetheless known and obvious to anyone likely to hold office.[14]

One might maintain reservations about the House manager's allusions to natural law and natural theology without rejecting their core contention regarding the duties and responsibilities inherent to constitutional offices like the Supreme Court.

For his part, Chase took the safer but less constitutionally rigorous path of arguing that such rhetoric does not amount to an impeachable offense, thereby sidestepping the substantive question of whether such rhetoric is appropriate in a judiciary. But does it really make sense to say that it would be a desirable state of affairs if all judges were at perfect liberty to deliver rhetorical tirades to juries like Chase's? Would justice really be better served, and would the judiciary better achieve its institutional ends, if judges tried to sway juries by means of demagogic appeals as a matter of course? Because the answer to both questions is clearly no, Chase's refusal to acknowledge and defend his rhetoric as unusual and in need of defense manifests a degree of bad demagoguery.

At the same time, and as noted above, it is important to distinguish Chase's defense of himself, which advances a thin and ultimately implausible conception of judicial rhetorical responsibility, from the rationale he developed in the speech for which he was impeached in the first place, his charge to the grand jury. Chase appears to have chosen the legalistic approach in his trial because it made strategic sense; trying to make a constitutionally capacious argument would have been more compelling from a theoretical standpoint; but it likely would have exposed Chase to more criticism from the Republicans, because it would have meant conceding their basic premise—that such conduct was unacceptable as a matter of judicial norms—even while defending his charge to the grand jury as an exception. Indeed, Chase would have had to convince enough of the Republicans that their own conduct, repealing the 1801 Judiciary Act, was constitutionally reprehensible enough to warrant his own demagoguery—a hard sell indeed.

What is the most responsible yet persuasive argument Chase might have made to the jury, in light of which we might judge his rhetoric and rationale as a whole? Consider the rationale he indicated in his charge to the grand jury, which, as we noted above, differs considerably from his trial defense. Chase began his speech by acknowledging that his audience would most likely regard his speech as extraordinary for a judge: "I will take the liberty to make a few observations, which I hope you will receive as flowing only from my regard to the welfare and prosperity of our common country."[15] In other words, Chase was well aware that what he was about to say would be regarded as originating in a spirit of partisanship unfitting for a judge. Chase went on to contend that "it is a very easy task to deceive or mislead the great body of the people by propagating plausible, but false doctrines, for the bulk of mankind are governed by their passions and not by reasons."[16] Indeed, "falsehood can be more readily disseminated than truth."[17] Given the limits of reason and the strength of passion, even judges who should normally confine themselves as far as possible to reasoned speech must, in extraordinary circumstances, "particularly the present," counter such "false doctrines" by means of rhetoric that has the power to steer the public's passions in a countervailing direction.[18]

Next, Chase proceeded to address the fundamental question of the American regime: in what form of government are "the purposes of civil society best answered"? In answering, Chase articulated the argument—familiar to the founders of the Constitution—that popular governments, or republics, no less than monarchies can tyrannize over the rights of individuals.[19] The constitutional ideal is a state of affairs in which "the same laws govern the whole society without any distinction," a state of affairs that Chase claims—somewhat improbably, given his own role in enforcing the Alien and Sedition Acts—to have been realized under the Federalist regime.[20] In contrast, Chase contends that "the abolition of the office of the sixteen circuit judges," together with the alteration of the Maryland state supreme court and the institution of universal suffrage in that state, will render the government "uncertain, partial, [and] arbitrary."[21] The basis for his argument is that, contrary to more radical conceptions of majoritarianism espoused by the heirs of the Anti-Federalists, the realization of freedom in civil society requires institutions to protect the rights of individuals from dramatic shifts in public opinion and sentiment—in short, that responsiveness to majority will is only one dimension of popular government, and not necessarily the most fundamental one.[22] Whereas critics of the Constitution tended to fault the new regime for the distance it placed between constituents and rulers, Chase, like Madison in *Federalist* #10 and, more specifically, Hamilton in his argument for an autonomous judiciary in *Federalist* #78, denies that merely devolving authority to local majorities is the best way to protect the rights of individuals. More deeply, Chase goes on to repudiate the view, also espoused by some significant Anti-Federalists, that governments should exercise only as much authority as is needed to protect pre-political, natural rights:

> The institution of government is really no sacrifice made, as some writers contend, to natural liberty, [since] previous to the formation of some species of government, a state of liberty could not exist. It seems to me that personal *liberty* and *rights* can only be acquired by becoming a member of a community, which gives the protection of the whole to every individual.[23]

Given these commitments, the aspiration of a society should be that every citizen, regardless of the changing sentiments of majorities, should enjoy "equal protection from the laws"—that is, impartial administration of justice. To this end, Chase advocates a separation-of-powers system in which the courts are afforded a significant degree of independence to contest and refine the views expressed in the political branches; and he doubts that "justice [will be] impartially administered by judges dependent on the Legislature for their continuance in office, and for their support."[24]

Given this argument, the reasons for Chase's opposition to the repeal of the Judiciary Act become clearer. The Constitution's commitment to the impartial administration of justice with respect to individual rights means that courts, which are better suited to protecting those rights, should be protected from the whims of shifting majorities as reflected in the legislature. Congress' repeal of the lower courts constitutes bad precedent because it seems to establish that the federal court system, which derives its authority from the Supreme Court created by Article III, is merely a creature of the most recent electoral majority.

Needless to say, the sophistication with which Chase developed this argument even as he deployed fear-inspiring rhetoric at the Baltimore grand jury ("our republican constitution will sink into a mobocracy, the worst of all possible governments") is considerable.[25] At the same time, Chase might have gone further in staving off an obvious criticism, one that featured prominently in his impeachment and trial: that he was deploying such rhetoric simply because he was a Federalist partisan attempting to entrench the Federalist regime by defending the appointment of the midnight judges.[26] Chase might have elucidated the meaning of his role as judge and, in so doing, acknowledged what it was that made his rhetorical outbursts from the bench controversial, even shocking. With this acknowledgment in view, he might have explained why the gravity of the event he had been denouncing—the repeal of the lower courts—could plausibly be understood as justifying his unconventional rhetoric. After all, as a Supreme

Court justice, he was uniquely positioned vis-à-vis that event. While Congress does have the power to create new courts, as specified in Article III, those courts are also ultimately answerable, in their capacity as courts, not to Congress but to the Supreme Court. The possibility that Congress was going to abolish an entire court system simply because it disagreed with the political dispositions of the judges currently in that system could be quite plausibly interpreted as a serious abuse of constitutional authority on the part of Congress. And who is better suited to draw attention to the issue than a member of the institution most directly affected by the abuse in question?

Chase went some distance in advancing a structural argument like this in his actual speech to the Baltimore grand jury. As we have seen, Chase focused on the role that courts play in helping uphold the principles of the American regime as he understood them, and he justified his attack on the Jeffersonians on the contention that repealing the Judiciary Act of 1801, while politically expedient for Jefferson (who saw the Federalist-dominated judiciary as a threat to his coalition's power), was nevertheless an assault on an institution that the regime needed in order to honor its own commitments to impartial justice and political freedom. The problem is that while Chase did elaborate a contestable argument criticizing the repeal of the Judiciary Act, he never took the next step of actually justifying his own rhetoric with reference to the institution he belonged to and that institution's place in the broader polity. He seems not to have been aware why his charge to the jury might have seemed problematic and why it needed a rationale to justify it—or if he was aware of this, he pretended not to *need* to be aware of it in his trial, where he argued that judges have no particular rhetorical responsibilities and that only statutory crimes are impeachable. By refusing to grapple with the constitutional merits of his decision to make that speech, Chase lightened his own burden during his trial but also diminished himself as a statesman. Like the popular yet unsatisfying assertions of free-speech libertarians, who invoke freedom of expression to avoid having to justify the positions they take, Chase's trial defense seemed to imply that even he was unwilling to defend his behavior, but that a defense was not needed because the Senate could not remove a judge for anything less concrete than a statutory crime.[27] Living up to the deliberative ideal of the Constitution would have required elaborating a rationale for why Chase's rhetoric, which would have been unacceptable during normal times, had nevertheless been rendered at least plausibly legitimate by the threat the Republicans posed to the judiciary. Chase was by no means a bad demagogue, and in some ways he exemplified judicial statesmanship.[28] Nevertheless, his demagoguery might have been more rigorously integrated into an accessible and comprehensive critique of the view he sought to oppose.

Justice Antonin Scalia and the Corruption of the Judiciary

Samuel Chase used demagoguery in response to what he evidently perceived as a threat to the basic integrity of the American constitutional regime: the autonomy of the judiciary within the separation-of-powers system. Regardless of his personal reasons for arguing publicly in this way—it is more than reasonable to infer that he was motivated by partisanship and personal ambition—his arguments reflect a thoughtful analysis of the American system that should have been taken on its own terms by anyone who did not have a direct stake in the outcome.

Like Chase, Antonin Scalia appeared to believe that he, too, was witnessing a monumental threat to the American judiciary—albeit one that was much harder to see. Whereas Chase had confronted a sitting Congress that was prepared to dismantle the existing federal court system for political reasons, Scalia believed that the American legal system had been infiltrated by a subversive left-wing culture that was corrupting the judiciary from within: a culture that favored social practices (such as homosexuality) that had hitherto been marginalized in American society. Further, Scalia held that lawyers, politicians, and the broader public were incapable of recognizing this corruption because they too had been shaped in their thinking by it. As a consequence, for Scalia, the Court's role as champion of these social practices and its authority to overturn legislation that regulated or forbade them had come to be regarded as legitimate, when in fact, according to him, they were not.

Accordingly, the nature of the problem that each justice offered a diagnosis of differed considerably. Chase presented himself as confronting a dilemma evident in the text of the Constitution itself. On the one hand, the Supreme Court is the head of the entire judicial branch and has an institutional interest in the ability of the broader legal system, consisting in both itself and all "inferior courts," to live up to their constitutional responsibilities, whatever those might be. On the other hand, it is Congress that is technically empowered to create (and get rid of) lower courts. Does this mean that literally *anything* Congress decides to do with the lower courts is constitutional? A purely textual reading of the provision in question would lead to the conclusion that Congress could, at any minute today, abolish the entire contemporary federal and the circuit courts, forcing the Supreme Court to either take on all the cases these courts had previously administered or let those cases go unheard. Alternatively, Congress could create two (or five, or ten) new court systems, staffed entirely by partisans appointed by the present Congress. In what sense would either of these acts be genuinely constitutional as opposed to merely textually constitutional?

As the difficulty of answering these questions suggests, the constitutional provisions with which Chase was preoccupied create a site for contestation between Congress and the Court, contestation born of the Constitution's conflicting commitments both to majority rule and to rights and the rule of law. When placed in a precarious position, Chase became a partisan for his own institution in the way we would expect and want him to be within the separation-of-powers system.[29] This fact alone does not mean that his argument constituted the final word on the question at stake; quite the contrary, it meant that his personal as well as his political interest caused him to make an argument in defense of the judiciary as such—an argument that is relevant to the broader community charged with deciding constitutional questions like this one. In contrast, and as I will argue here, Scalia took issue with a development whose relevance to the Constitution is far less clear than the question of Congress' proper authority over the judicial branch.

Scalia's well-known rhetorical provocations did not begin with his tenure on the Court. Indeed, he was notorious for his rhetorical aggression as a conservative before his appointment to the Federal judiciary.[30] But his rhetorical proclivities took on new significance when the Senate confirmed his nomination to the Supreme Court in 1986. Conservatives as well as liberals noted his willingness to use the Court's official mode of communication—opinions accompanying decisions—to deploy rhetoric singular for its intensity and vitriol. Conservatives, long accustomed to liberal hegemony on the Court, embraced Scalia's rebellious flaunting of judicial folkways. For conservatives, Scalia was a godsend because he was willing to use aggressive rhetoric as part of a broader strategy, inspired by Reaganism and "movement conservatism," to push back the advance of liberal jurisprudence that the Warren and Burger Courts had either embraced or countenanced. As Brisbin helpfully puts it:

> Today American conservatives are conducting a political revival meeting. Through their performance, they want to convince the public of the sins of post–New Deal American liberal politics and revive the value of what they allege to be the true American political creed. . . . Justice Antonin Scalia . . . [was] a leading preacher in the conservative revival.[31]

In this view, liberalism had effected a fundamental corruption of the American constitutional order, and this radical corruption justified and necessitated a justice willing to use unconventional means—including provocative rhetoric—to raise the public's awareness.

Liberals, in contrast, frequently questioned the mocking, often insulting style Scalia chose to adopt in his opinions. Laurence Tribe, for example, wrote in a comment on Scalia's *Windsor* dissent that the justice had "use[d] the occasion [of the decision] to insult the Court's majority, and Justice Kennedy in particular, an essentially *ad hominem* (and *ad feminem*) terms."[32] Accordingly, Tribe wrote his commentary "to highlight the extraordinary character of [Scalia's] particularly vitriolic and internally inconsistent dissent." Both reactions clearly differ in the interpretations they advance of Scalia while at the same time pointing to a deeper source of agreement. For all observers—advocates and critics alike—Scalia purposely and consistently wrote in ways that justices normally avoid.

For our purposes, the most interesting dimension of Scalia's role on the Court is the paradoxical relationship between the conception of judging he advocated and the way in which he advanced that conception rhetorically. On the one hand, Scalia is well known for defending an ivory-tower model of judicial behavior, according to which justices ought to maintain an emphatically professionalized, machine-like ethos: "Judges are selected precisely for their skill as lawyers; whether they reflect the policy views of a particular constituency is not (or should not be) relevant."[33] According to Scalia, judicial culture should remain untainted by political and social concerns; it should be pure and impersonal, focusing to the furthest extent possible on the written word of the law and eschewing moral and public-policy considerations. In his *Obergefell* dissent, for example, Scalia claimed to be writing "to call attention to this Court's threat to American democracy."[34] The Court's threat is vividly on display in *Obergefell*, a "judicial Putsch" and "a naked judicial claim to legislative—indeed, super-legislative—power; a claim fundamentally at odds with our system of government."[35]

On other hand, Scalia is remembered for advocating this cold, impersonal conception of the Court through rhetoric that was both highly personal and overheated. As Brisbin aptly puts it, "Despite his claim that he wants the Court to do 'lawyer's work' and stay out of policy controversies, the frankness of Scalia's language . . . appears more like the rhetoric of the militant political activist. Indeed, Scalia's opinions often ring with phrases like those spoken by the politicians and pundits of the . . . conservative movement."[36] Especially in his dissents, Scalia openly mocked his fellow justices and ridiculed the Court as an institution. He once called the Supreme Court a "junior varsity Congress" and, in his *Casey* dissent, asserted that his colleagues on the Court "rattle off a collection of adjectives that simply decorate a value judgement and conceal a political choice."[37] The *Obergefell* majority opinion, authored by Justice Kennedy, "is couched in a style that is as pretentious as its content is egotistic."[38] Scalia was at pains to deflate the inflated tone he perceived in the majority with proportionally barbed mockery:

> Rights, we are told, can "rise . . . from a better informed understanding of how constitutional imperatives define a liberty that remains urgent in our own era." (Huh? How can a better informed understanding of how constitutional imperatives [whatever that means] define [whatever that means] an urgent liberty [never mind], give birth to a right?)[39]

Scalia was also at pains to emphasize his conviction that no sober person could possibly be persuaded by the merits of a decision like *Obergefell*, in which "the Supreme Court of the United States has descended from the disciplined legal reasoning of John Marshall and Joseph Story to the mystical aphorisms of the fortune cookie."[40]

There is an obvious rationale for Scalia's conduct, one we alluded to above. For Scalia, like other movement conservatives, the Court had become irreparably corrupted by moralistic activist judges bent on subverting the American regime. Indeed, he believed, the Court had become captured by a conspiracy bent on overthrowing that regime. According to Scalia, the majority in *Lawrence v. Texas*

> is the product of a Court, which is the product of a law-profession culture, that has largely signed on to the so-called homosexual agenda, by which I mean the agenda promoted by some homosexual activists directed at eliminating the moral opprobrium that has traditionally attached to homosexual conduct . . . [T]he American Association of Law Schools (to which any reputable law school must seek to belong) excludes from membership any school that refuses to ban from its job-interview facilities a law firm (no matter how small) that does not wish to hire as a prospective partner a person who openly engages in homosexual conduct.[41]

Statements like this echo Scalia's earlier premonition in *Casey*, declaring that "the Imperial Judiciary lives" and that the Court's "unelected, life tenured judges" now conceive of themselves as "leading a Volk."[42] Given such entrenched corruption, emergency measures were—in Scalia's view—necessary to restore the Court to its proper place in the political order; to use Locke's well-known formulation, Scalia had to break the "law" (judicial norms) in order to uphold the "law" (the proper role of the judiciary in the American polity).[43] In his own estimation, Scalia was fighting fire with fire; in order to restore a Court and a broader judicial culture pure of moralistic influence, he had to moralistically raise public awareness of just how far the Court had deviated from its proper role. Scalia's judicial rhetoric is a classic case of demagoguery, and the question we will pursue here is how plausibly Scalia developed a rationale that would render his demagoguery legitimate. Was there really a fire, and if so, did Scalia's counter-blaze actually help put it out? More importantly, did he provide the public with an adequate argument that there was a fire that needed to be put out in the first place?

In many ways, of all the cases we will examine in this book, Scalia was the most well positioned to develop a coherent and exhaustive public rationale for his universally acknowledged norm-breaking rhetoric. The author of several books on judging and legal philosophy, Scalia had opportunities and proclivities that most of our other cases did not. Now, as we have suggested, Scalia's rhetoric presupposes that no legitimate disagreement over Scalia's own approach to constitutional interpretation is possible. Because, as Scalia maintained, reasonable disagreement over the merits could not possibly have resulted in majority decisions such as those in *Lawrence*, *Windsor*, and *Obergefell*, the only reasonable explanation of these decisions is that the Court was seeking power out of corrupt motives. To repeat, invoking the attempted overthrow of the Weimar Republic by Hitler and his Nazi followers, Scalia called *Obergefell* a "putsch," and in *Casey* claimed the majority was trying to lead a "Volk." Is Scalia correct? Must we have recourse to conspiracy theories to explain the Court's conduct in cases such as these? Did the Warren and Burger Courts so obviously transgress the sacred boundaries between the judiciary and the political branches that a reaction like Scalia's, which implies that "everyone knows what's right," was justified? Or did the Court in its turn have a defensible rationale that should have muted Scalia's vehemence, precisely because it presented a legitimate alternative to Scalia's own philosophy?

A helpful place to turn in answering these questions is Scalia's essay on legal philosophy, *A Matter of Interpretation*, and the critique of that essay by Ronald Dworkin. Scalia made a point of stating that his essay, which treats "the science of construing legal texts," was intended by him to reach not just judges and lawyers but "all thoughtful Americans."[44] In other words, Scalia intended for his writing to have an impact on the broader public—presumably because not only could he not have articulated as comprehensive a statement of his own legal philosophy within the confines of a legal opinion, but offering such a statement would have been inappropriate in that rhetorical context. His essay, by contrast, promises to offer a fuller picture to those who might otherwise be unconvinced by the legal philosophy of which Scalia was able to give only an incomplete picture in his combined opinions.

A Matter of Interpretation develops a critique of two alternative theories of legal interpretation and proposes a third theory that Scalia regards as superior in terms of the American regime's fundamental principles and the role of the Supreme Court. On the one hand, Scalia rejects legal interpretations that seek the original intentions of the text's authors, because he regards such interpretive efforts as too conjectural and because they invite and permit discretion on the part of judges that does not comport with the basic values of constitutional government. On the other hand, Scalia rejects interpretive efforts to update legal texts in light of new knowledge in accord with notions about living constitutionalism and judicial pragmatism—that is, the idea that judges should try to rectify injustices to which the political branches have failed to attend. Here too his rejection is based on the view that judges should refrain from policymaking and focus exclusively on understanding and implementing the legal text's meaning.[45] In place of these alternatives, Scalia seeks to advance a version of textualism that discovers the meaning of legal texts as they would have been understood by those who originally wrote those texts. Scalia believes that this interpretive method is the only way to keep judges within their judicial roles and away from questions that only the elected branches can legitimately answer.

Dworkin's reply to Scalia accomplishes two main goals. First, it shows that Scalia's rejection of authorial intentions is based on a mistaken conflation of different kinds of intentions. Authors intend to bring about a certain state of affairs by means of their writings; they can intend for their writings to have certain consequences and not others. Dworkin calls reading a text with a view to uncovering these anticipated consequences "expectations originalism." In contrast, authors intend to express certain principles or concepts through the words and sentences they write down, irrespective of the particular consequences they may have imagined resulting from those words and sentences.[46] Dworkin calls this "semantic originalism." As Dworkin goes on to demonstrate, these kinds of intentions are not the same, and to be guided by them in legal interpretation requires an entirely different process. To use Dworkin's own hypothetical, a boss who instructs an employee to "hire the best candidate" might have a certain consequence or state of affairs in mind—perhaps they want their son to be hired—but as long as their instruction is limited to "hire the best candidate" and does not include the clarification "I understand my son to be the best candidate,'" the boss has only instructed the employee to hire the candidate who is *in fact* best.[47] The boss has instructed their employee to exercise their own best judgment about which candidate comes closest to the standard they, the boss, laid down.

As Dworkin proceeds to show, though Scalia's judicial philosophy appears to reject the idea that authorial intentions should be sought, it ends up conflating the two abovementioned heuristics. Which heuristic comes closest to what Scalia envisions? More importantly, which best captures what Supreme Court justices ought to do? Should judges seek the intended consequences that the legislator(s) had in mind and try to realize those consequences through their rulings, or should they rule in accordance with their own best understanding of what the principle expressed by the legislator(s) demands in terms of a concrete ruling?

Dworkin illustrates these alternatives with reference to Scalia's own comments regarding Eighth and Fourteenth Amendment jurisprudence. "If Scalia were faithful to his textualism," contends Dworkin, "he would be a semantic originalist."[48] Instead, however, Scalia vacillates between the two philosophies because he has not grasped their differences. Regarding the Eighth Amendment, for example, Scalia holds that judges should enforce the view of capital punishment that those who adopted the amendment would have held—namely, that state executions are not forbidden as "cruel and unusual." By the same token, judges should *not* seek what a semantic originalist would seek—namely, "whatever punishments are *in fact* cruel and unusual."[49] Similarly, Scalia claims that "equal protection" did not subsequently require equal access to the ballot, because the authors of that clause did not intend to create a state of affairs in which all citizens had equal access to the ballot. But, as Dworkin points out, just because the clause's drafters did not expect such a result does not mean that the best understanding of "equal protection" has not always required equal access. Rather, the original understanding would seem to be a defective version of the principle in question.[50] By insisting that the text should be interpreted to mean what those who wrote it would have said should result from it, Scalia "reads into [the clause's language] limitations that the language not only does not suggest but cannot bear."[51]

From the sophisticated objections Dworkin raises here, it should be clear at the very least that Scalia's own interpretive approach is not manifestly the most coherent and therefore the most legitimate alternative. On the contrary, there appears to be plenty of room for legitimate debate. This fact alone would seem to require Scalia to temporize his dismissiveness and hostility toward judicial outcomes reached through interpretive approaches that differ from his own—it is simply not as clear as he makes it out to be that his preferred method is the only one acceptable for American judges. And yet, as I will suggest, not only does Dworkin's critique significantly complicate the picture Scalia originally tried to draw, thereby muting Scalia's demagoguery, but in his response to Dworkin, Scalia repeats his own initial set of arguments without demonstrating their superiority to Dworkin's, thereby giving us even more reason to adopt a skeptical disposition toward his demagogic style.

To extrapolate from the discussion above, Dworkin's core challenge to Scalia would seem to be as follows. In a constitutional democracy, which places limits on what a democratic majority can do and which seeks to achieve a rationale for state action that can obtain the *true* consent of its citizens—true consent requiring reasons for the merits of a decision—why would judges be obligated to defer to a particular majority's understanding of what an abstract principle demanded, when a demonstrably superior understanding was available to them? Why should the commitments of a particular group trump the more coherent understanding of another? Dworkin's model is an open-ended one, in which succeeding generations put forth their own best understanding of what the same principles require. What is Scalia's?

In his response, Scalia contends that the alternative Dworkin draws amounts to a false dichotomy. He says that his own method, rather than seeking the particular concrete state of affairs envisioned by the text's authors, aims to abstract—with particular reference to the Eighth Amendment—"the existing society's assessment of what is cruel."[52] Again, this goal differs from Dworkin's, which seeks the best understanding of what is in fact cruel, irrespective of what the society that legislated the policy in question thought was best.

Though Scalia insists on distinguishing the former two approaches, it is unclear what that distinction actually amounts to. After all, Scalia maintains that the fundamental goal of the judge is not to find the interpretation that makes the most sense of the principle in question, but to enforce the interpretation or "assessment" that those who wrote the language containing that principle thought was best, *even if that assessment is based on reasons that are demonstrably inferior to the reasons for an alternative assessment*. Why is this clearly the best conception of the judge's role, as Scalia evidently believes it to be? Scalia alludes to several reasons. In elaborating the argument above, he expresses disdain for the idea that judges acting like "philosophers" should be allowed to "play with" moral values set down by previous generations. Where Dworkin sees opportunity for dialectical refinement and clarification of the Constitution's directive principles, Scalia sees mischief and chaos—there is no room for improvement, only deterioration. Indeed, one might be tempted to say that Scalia prefers stubborn adherence to arbitrariness because it at least promises stability, and that he is ultimately a moral relativist. Yet at the same time, he proceeds in the next breath to dismiss Dworkin's approach because it offers "no protection against the moral perceptions of a future, more brutal, generation."[53] And in respect to the Eighth Amendment, he concludes:

> The Americans of 1791 [who ratified the Bill of Rights] thought that what was cruel was cruel, regardless of what a more brutal future generation might think about it. They were embedding in the Bill of Rights *their* moral values, for otherwise all its general and abstract guarantees could be brought to nought.[54]

Notice, even in *this* context, Scalia's demagogic emphasis on the possibility that a "future generation" will obliterate the protections of the Bill of Rights and replace it with a more brutal system. In so doing, he ignores two basic questions that were core to Dworkin's critique.

First, he ignores the possibility—which was also the historical reality—that the moral perceptions of the generation who legislated the text in question were themselves brutal. Indeed, how could a member of a polity that countenanced slavery, genocide, and state-enforced segregation speak as though progress is impossible and things can only get worse? To be sure, there is no guarantee that future judges will offer and enforce improved understandings of the Constitution's principles, in the same way that the separation-of-powers system that the Constitution as a whole creates cannot guarantee that deliberation between its institutions will expose public officials and citizens to arguments that would not have otherwise been articulated. Both institutions are based on the aspiration that, in the aggregate, better outcomes will emerge if the mild voice of reason is given a chance to be heard.[55]

This brings us to the second question: why would a member of a regime based on the principle of rational consent defer to a previous majority's inferior conception of a fundamental principle—for example, that "equal protection" tolerates "separate but equal"? Why would a judge, whose institution is designed to foster independent judgment in its members, privilege a less defensible conception of a previous majority over their own more defensible conception?[56] What, in short, gives a previous majority the authority to dictate, without question, a subsequent judge's interpretation of the Constitution's core principles?

Though Scalia alludes to several possible answers to these questions, he fails to develop any one of them, let alone the principles on which they are based. In addition to alleging that "philosophers" should not be allowed to "play with" constitutional concepts, he attributes to Dworkin the view that "the passage of time" can "reasonably be thought to alter the content of [rights articulated by a given constitutional majority]."[57] Relatedly, he opposes his theory of interpretation to some unnamed "thoroughgoing constitutional evolutionists."[58] Though it is unclear whether Scalia means to include Dworkin in this last group, he appears to be contesting a theory of interpretation that bears only a crude resemblance to Dworkin's. To be clear, neither Dworkin nor those judges who profess a legal philosophy akin to his espouse the view that time guarantees, or even makes more likely, more reasonable judicial conceptions of fundamental concepts.[59] They do not espouse a theory that could reasonably be called "evolutionist," which implies that in the course of legal development the better elements of each decision will be preserved (by a principle akin to natural selection) and inferior ones will be abandoned. To be sure, an aspirational theory hopes that the passage of time will conduce to better outcomes insofar as subsequent judges will have a larger number of arguments and alternative interpretations to confront, appropriate, and think through before making their own decisions. But—and this is crucial—there is certainly no guarantee that subsequent judges exercising their own independent judgment will make decisions superior to those made by judges who preceded them. To use the language of social science, time is not the independent variable; reason is.

For his part, Scalia appears not to see or appreciate this distinction. The question confronting us, then, concerns the distorting lens through which he is viewing the arguments in question, a lens that causes him to persist in the same errors that Dworkin initially identified. Dworkin himself indicates one plausible explanation:

> [Scalia] says the moral reading [defended by Dworkin] gives the people not too little but too much power, because it politicizes the appointment of Supreme Court justices and makes it more likely that justices will be appointed who reflect the changing moods of the majority. He fears that the constitutional rights of individuals will suffer.[60]

This interpretation squares with that of Brisbin: "In [Scalia's] vision, courts and laws are instruments that buttress order; courts apply law to annihilate the disorder and the anxiety associated with a selected set of conflicts."[61] This interpretation also squares with Scalia's own defense of judging as the enforcement of past majority decisions on the grounds that future decisions could be worse. At core, Scalia appears to be arguing that the prospect of instability flowing from a Court exercising independent judgment about constitutional principles necessitates the enforcement by the Court of arbitrary interpretations of those principles—"arbitrary" because, in Scalia's view, the Court is not supposed to evaluate the rationale behind those interpretations, which might entail seeking an interpretation based on a superior rationale (as Dworkin would recommend doing). Rather, it is supposed to uncover and enforce the original interpretation, not because it is better, but because it is original and change is dangerous.

There is some merit to Scalia's philosophy, which echoes arguments by Aristotle and Madison.[62] The question we have been pursuing, however, is whether there is so little merit to alternative philosophies, such as Dworkin's, as to justify Scalia's judicial demagoguery. I have suggested that this is far from the case, and that in the final analysis it is Dworkin's theory that is most attentive to the *range* of commitments—including deliberation and majoritarianism—that are embodied in the American constitutional order. In his dissents, Scalia presents his vision as if it were clearly the only legitimate one for a Supreme Court justice to maintain. At the very least, Dworkin shows that Scalia's vision contains serious sources of incoherence that render an attitude of openness toward other visions, like Dworkin's, legitimate. Accordingly, Scalia's rationale does save him from exhibiting the most extreme kind of demagoguery, for a more extreme version would have failed to articulate his philosophy to the extent that Scalia did. Nevertheless, Scalia's myopic concern with stability, which causes him to dismiss or ignore other constitutional commitments, taken together with his callous deployment of demagogic tactics in official Court communications, puts him closer to bad than to good demagoguery.

7

Demagogues in Congress

In turning from the Court to Congress, we cross the threshold into a different rhetorical world. Unlike members of the judiciary, and presidents for that matter, members of Congress have always understood themselves as rhetorical advocates, whether of themselves, their constituents, or the common good as they understand it. Of the three branches, members of the House and the Senate inhabit the most complex and multidimensional rhetorical habitat. As legislators, they are permitted—indeed, required—to become partisan advocates, eschewing pretensions of impartiality and open-mindedness in favor of commitment and zeal. At the same time, they are also negotiators tasked with assembling and functioning as a productive member of legislative coalitions, a task that can require a more deliberative and open-ended rhetorical approach. As discussed above, they are also national officeholders; they do not merely represent their own constituents but rather take an oath to uphold the Constitution of the whole country. But unlike presidents, who are tasked with the administrative responsibility of executing the laws of the United States—a role that requires both discretion and impartiality—members of Congress are tasked with the responsibility of actively creating legislation. They are tasked with acting impartially, like a judge or a jury, in cases of impeachment and removal, when both chambers take new constitutional oaths. Each of these roles creates the pressure for, and legitimates, a different rhetorical posture.

The figures we will encounter in this chapter confronted political challenges from the standpoint of legislators, and leveraged the various sources of power and influence that come with being a member of Congress. Some preferred open floor debate and public speeches outside of Congress, whereas others, like Joseph McCarthy, found the Senate committee to be the most useful platform from which to advance a cause. By contrast, Huey Long discovered that being *removed* from committee by his fellow Democrats could itself become a source of demagogic energy. We will consider each of their unique leadership styles in light of the arguments they developed to justify the rhetorical measures

Demagogues in American Politics. Charles U. Zug, Oxford University Press. © Oxford University Press 2022.
DOI: 10.1093/oso/9780197651940.003.0007

they decided were appropriate and necessary given the particular challenges they faced.

Rep. Adam Clayton Powell Jr. and Civil Rights

Adam Clayton Powell Jr. was the minister of the Abyssinian Baptist Church in Harlem, New York, and the first Black member of New York's City Council, elected in 1941. In 1944, he was New York's first Black member elected to the U.S. House of Representatives. Powell quickly developed a reputation as a compelling and aggressive rhetorical advocate for the Black community, a reputation that earned him at least as many allies as adversaries. Alluding to his public opposition to New York's mayor Fiorello La Guardia, a critic of Powell asserted in 1943 that "Powell is a notorious demagogue. . . . Only an ingrate and a professional troublemaker would attempt to turn New York's Negroes against Mayor La Guardia after all the Mayor has done for our people."[1] Similar impressions were echoed over the course of Powell's career. In 1965, William F. Buckley Jr. stated plainly that "Adam Clayton Powell, Jr. is a demagogue," and a year later the renowned political scientist James Q. Wilson quipped that "no one understands Powell better than Powell—his capacity for self-detachment is great, as is often the case with rogues and demagogues."[2] A 1971 book review in the *New York Times* averred that Powell had "clung to the demagogic style throughout his career—shrewdly amending and recasting it through different phases in the growth of racial consciousness among urban Negroes."[3] Similarly, in 1972, Thomas A. Johnson—also writing for the *Times,* though this time in a front-page obituary—characterized Powell as "a political demagogue, a Congressional rebel," "a wheelerdealer, a rabble-rouser," and "a grandstander."[4] More recently, a review of the 1989 Academy Award–nominated documentary *Adam Clayton Powell* claimed that Powell's "many accomplishments have been forgotten in the wake of the self-indulgence, arrogance, and demagoguery that dominated [his] later years."[5]

According to these characterizations, Powell was a political opportunist who manipulated a charismatic attachment with his constituents cultivated through impassioned rhetoric for the sake of personal advancement. To be sure, Powell's personal life was studded with indiscretions that sometimes verged on enormities. And he did frequently use his powers as an orator to obfuscate these matters.[6] Nevertheless, a consistent theme of this book has been that overemphasizing the personal motivations that we suspect to be driving rhetoric we find provocative and divisive can distract us from the potentially legitimate political strategy of which that rhetoric is a part and, further, the set of political understandings on which that strategy is based. Accordingly, focusing on

Powell's personal life and the dubious ethics that are alleged to have animated it undermines an earnest attempt to appreciate the normative merits his rhetorical leadership may have had.

Though his rhetorical style has been much discussed, its role in Powell's statesmanship has largely been ignored. This is because Powell's political achievements are generally regarded as having been accomplished *despite* his rhetoric. Scholars generally view the first fifteen years of his career—a time Charles V. Hamilton, author of Powell's comprehensive political biography, dubs his "congressional irritant" phase—as characterized by high rhetorical performance at the expense of low legislative performance.[7] In this reading, Powell did not become politically effective until assuming chairmanship of the House Committee on Education and Labor; most of the major political achievements political scientist John Davis lists, for example, are from this period.[8] Thus, Hamilton contends that "concrete results . . . were not [Powell's] to achieve," and that Powell was known for his many speeches but not for effecting real political change.[9] Accordingly, Powell was singled out critically by an electoral opponent on the grounds that, in Congress, "you get nowhere with rabble-rousing," and Hamilton points to several instances in which Powell's rhetorical aggressiveness appears to have actively undermined positive political change.[10] Daniels goes so far as to say that Powell's political career during this period was based on "verbal posturing" because he lacked tangible accomplishments, either in Congress or among his constituents, on which to base his claim to govern.[11] So understood, Powell was less than useful to legislators who were actually concerned with legislating. As Hamilton summarizes it, "To the legislative infighters, the ones who had to count the votes, make deals, sway doubters, and craft compromises, in the immediate postwar years into the 1950s, Powell was not particularly useful. Indeed, that was hardly his role."[12]

This is not to say that scholars necessarily blame Powell for his outspoken style. To the contrary, most view his rhetoric as having some plausibly defensible role. As Orr puts it, Powell's emphasis on his rhetorical "militancy by labeling himself as the first 'bad nigger' in Congress had its shock value."[13] Daniels suggests that the role of his rhetoric was one of "voter catharsis and vicarious revenge."[14] Hamilton frequently reiterates the "symbolic" importance of Powell's rhetoric.[15] Pollock contends that the main point of Powell's speeches was to shock audiences into awareness of issues they had not previously been aware of and perhaps to frighten them as well.[16] Daniels even goes so far as to suggest that Powell's rhetoric was one of his "most critical weapons," though he refrains from articulating what sorts of positive political consequences he thinks Powell used this weapon to bring about.[17]

The other side of the coin is that scholars have tended to view Powell's rhetorical style as of a piece with what many agree were his personal ethical shortcomings. In this view, Powell's ethics undermined his political effectiveness by lending credibility to the charges of his adversaries that he employed demagogic rhetoric in order to satisfy the desires toward which his self-interest impelled him. Thus, Orr observes that "Powell's handling of the Ester [*sic*] James affair and his subsequent actions combined with his history of being outspoken in Congress about civil rights had gained him many detractors in Congress."[18] Daniels argues that "Powell's self-aggrandizing ambitions were realized at the expense of both his desired image and his effectiveness as a political advocate for his constituency."[19] Hamilton states generally that Powell's allies supported him in spite of his moral character.[20] Davis draws attention to Powell's "womanizing," "tax problems," and "kickbacks," and observes that Powell had a reputation for "political unreliability" and a "willingness to attack, embarrass, and double-cross political colleagues."[21] Thus, Pollock correctly concludes that whatever real merits there might have been to Powell's political style have been obscured by "the furor surrounding the man."[22]

Laboring beneath these assumptions, scholars charitably disposed to Powell are nevertheless induced to focus exclusively on his "non-rhetorical" achievements, such as the specific legislation he passed. And yet, in seizing on what they feel to be the importance of his rhetoric—for example, its role as "catharsis" or "vicarious revenge"—scholars indicate that they have intuited some less obvious, but nonetheless genuine, political good or end for which Powell's rhetorical approach was, in their estimation, responsible. Daniels shows that he is on to this line of inquiry when he observes that studying Powell's rhetoric teaches that

> merely gaining political office is not tantamount to grasping and wielding political clout. If the current black penetration into the political system is to approach its potential, black politicians must devise and implement sophisticated and effective stratagems for acquiring and institutionalizing political power after the election.[23]

Indeed, my argument here is that Powell's rhetorical strategy is a prime example of such "sophisticated and effective stratagems." While the more tangible political achievements Powell realized during his role as Education and Labor chair might be easier to point to, this does not make the transformation in attitudes and norms he sought to effect by means of a carefully orchestrated rhetorical campaign less "real." Rather, it means we need a more nuanced tool set for apprehending and identifying the political and constitutional merits of the sort of rhetorical campaign Powell was waging. In such a campaign, purposely divisive and impassioned rhetoric—that is, demagoguery—is deployed tactically in conjunction with an understanding of political health and decay formulated at a high level of theorization. Accordingly, this chapter will begin by elucidating Powell's diagnosis of civil rights politics as symptomatic of political dysfunction and decay in the American regime. With this diagnosis in view, we will then interpret and evaluate Powell's use of demagogic rhetoric as a means for remedying the injustices for which these sources of dysfunction and decay were, in his understanding, responsible.

Powell's denouement in this role as "Mr. Civil Rights" was the famed episode of the so-called Powell Amendment (1955–1956). This amendment would have made payment of federal funds to school districts contingent on desegregation in those districts. The rhetoric surrounding this episode is indeed paradigmatic of Powell's broader rhetorical strategy during this period of his congressional career. And though we will turn to it shortly, it is worth noting that Powell had begun to develop this strategy from the outset of his career, as witnessed by a brief but revealing House debate in 1947 over a bill establishing a permanent military nurse corps. A look at this episode will help contextualize and reveal the issues that were at stake in the debate over the Powell Amendment, which took place eight years later. It will also highlight the character of the rhetorical norms in Congress Powell encountered and sought to transform in advocating for racial equality.

During the Second World War, Congress created a nurse corps in the Army and Navy that included a provision forbidding racial discrimination.[24] The law expired after two years, however, and so in March 1947 the House began debating new legislation, HR 1943, that would make the nurse corps permanent.[25] Support for the bill as it was initially crafted was overwhelming and bipartisan.[26] And yet, unlike the temporary law it was meant to replace, HR 1943 included no non-discrimination amendment. Accordingly, on March 13, 1947, when the House resumed debating the bill, Adam Clayton Powell urged the adoption of an amendment that would forbid "discrimination on account of creed, race, color, or national origin" in the hiring of Army and Navy nurses.[27] In the course of his initial speech, which lauded all other features of the bill, Powell observed that until passage of the 1945 law that preceded HR 1943, "the Navy had not appointed a single negro nurse." "But," he continued, "after it was passed by us unanimously, the Navy did appoint negro women to the nursing corps of the Navy."[28] From this fact among others, Powell drew the conclusion that the inclusion of women of color in this institution could not be taken for granted and that a provision in the law was necessary in order to guarantee equal hiring standards.

The reaction to Powell's recommendation by the bill's sponsors was swift and definitive. Representative Frances Bolton of Ohio said that she regarded it as "most unfortunate that this matter [a provision for non-discrimination] is brought up to us at this point." "The need is not there," she asserted, because "both the Army and Navy use Negro nurses as part of their corps. We have reached the point where Negro nurses have proven themselves, from here out their acceptance or rejection will depend on ability and qualification."[29] Bolton's was the familiar argument that once *some* progress in racial equality has been made it can be assumed that those in power will continue to do what is right by enforcing it. Accordingly, her view was that civil rights did not have to be explicitly provided for in legislation because they were in some important sense self-executing: once enforced, they could never be undone. Bolton exhibited the Hartzian faith that merit would replace race as the fundamental consideration and that the promise of liberty and equality would be progressively fulfilled.[30]

Setting aside for the moment the dubious basis of these hopes and assumptions, it is remarkable—and revealing as to the nature of House norms at the time—that Bolton felt no obligation even to acknowledge the fact that Powell had pointed out concerning the hiring (or non-hiring) of Black nurses prior to 1945. Indeed, Powell himself had to press the issue by requesting Representative Bolton to yield and then repeating his original observation, to which Bolton lamely responded: "I believe [no Black nurses were hired prior to 1945] because [the Navy] had no negroes at all."[31] Powell immediately corrected this response: "No; that is not the reason. . . . I am sorry to disagree with the gentlewoman, because at that time there were 28 [Black] commissioned officers . . . and I happened to be present at the time they were commissioned."[32]

Though Bolton went on to admit her ignorance of the matter, thereby conceding the limited point to Representative Powell, she did not then admit her originally erroneous supposition to be a sufficient basis for modifying her position vis-à-vis non-discrimination. Instead, she remained committed in her opposition but defended her position on a different ground entirely. Implored Bolton: "Does it not seem to the gentleman that when a matter such as this has been clarified, it would be unfortunate to dig up some of the past and insist upon bringing it into the present and extending it into the future?"[33] Bolton's not-so-subtle hint was that by insisting on explicit provision of non-discrimination, Representative Powell was drawing attention to a part of America's political legacy from which she, her white colleagues, and much of the white public would prefer to avert their gazes. The message of the hint was then amplified in an exchange between Bolton and Representative Robert Thomason of Texas.

MR. THOMASON. Is it true there is no discrimination now?

MRS. BOLTON. That is absolutely the case.

MR. THOMASON. The present system is working well so there is no necessity for any such amendment.

MRS. BOLTON. That is correct.

MR. THOMASON. *It would just help to stir the problem up.* Nobody is being discriminated against under existing law and this just takes care of a voluntary situation.[34]

Powell's retort, which cut to the heart of the matter—"If [digging up some of the past] would guarantee the future, I do not think it is unfortunate"—brings the principles being contested here into stark relief.[35] Representative Bolton and her white liberal colleagues were well-meaning indeed. They were not segregationists and it perhaps even made them happy to see racial equality advancing in the government and society.[36] As Powell remarked in raising his initial objection to Representative Bolton, "I know her attitude [regarding civil rights] and have known it for a long time before I came to Congress"—a remark that acknowledged Bolton's profession of good intentions: "I believe [Representative Powell] can have no doubt as to my stand, so clearly shown in my record."[37]

For Powell, however—as for Machiavelli—a profession of good intentions is irrelevant in the face of tangible harm.[38] From their hegemonic perspective in the regime, American whites can rest easy with "the present system working well" because they have nothing personally at stake in the system's continuing to work well—they will enjoy their liberties regardless.[39] But Blacks face the same issue from a fundamentally different perspective. For them, failing to obtain explicit assurance of non-discrimination is tantamount to agreeing to enjoy their civil rights at the sufferance of a ruler who could capriciously change his or her mind—a ruler whose past treatment of Black people (e.g., diaspora, slavery, and Jim Crow) fails to inspire confidence. For Powell, Black people are naturally better positioned to reflect on the American regime's fundamental commitments because, unlike white people, they cannot take the enjoyment of those commitments for granted.[40]

Thus, in response to the same objection to his amendment being posed later in the debate—when Representative Paul Shafer asked, "Is there discrimination now in the service?"—Powell explained with admirable patience: "Of course, they are in the service now, it is true. But what guarantee have we that this policy will obtain in the years to come unless we write it in the law?"[41] He then elaborated this point several minutes later:

> I would like to ask the gentlewoman [Margaret Chase Smith of Maine] what guaranties she has that what is beginning now without law will take place 10, 15, or 20 years from now? [Racial integration] did not begin in the service until 2 years ago when we passed an amendment offered by the gentleman from Ohio [Clarence Brown]. Twenty six years ago our Navy had negro commissioned officers, then changed its policy. When World War II came on we were caught and did not have

> them. During the war period we had to train them back all over again, change the policy back again. My amendment would merely guarantee this policy.

Powell's white colleagues could rest assured with a conception of racial equality in which progress was inevitable and permanent because they themselves were detached from the actual struggle over securing those rights; they did not need those rights protected for their own benefit and so they had nothing personally at stake in their realization. This view induced them to believe that progress in equality was inevitable and that an egalitarian current state of affairs could not be undone. Their confidence in inevitable progress was derived from the awareness on their part that even if Black people lost their freedoms, white people would be secure in theirs.

The debate over federal school aid unfolded for more than a year during 1955–1956 and witnessed some of Powell's most impressive congressional rhetoric. Specifically, it induced Powell to both deepen and broaden the insights he had begun to articulate in debates such as the one over HR 1943. The so-called Kelley Bill was an Eisenhower-sponsored plan to provide much-needed federal funds to public schools nationwide, a policy area traditionally reserved to states and local governments. Debate over the bill took place against the backdrop of the *Brown* decision of 1954 desegregating public schools, and the amendment Powell introduced made receipt of federal funds conditional on desegregation.[42] Powell's amendment was a moderate version of what could have been a more radically progressive rider. Instead of making dispersal of aid contingent on the entire state desegregating, it withheld funds only from school districts that failed to comply with the Supreme Court's ruling. In addition, the amendment proposed holding appropriated but not-yet-dispersed funds in escrow for a maximum of four years, during which time they would be released if non-compliant districts acquiesced.

Powell's amendment met with much of the same kind of resistance discussed above. In a well-prepared speech on the House floor on January 24, 1956, Powell provided evidence that executive branch agencies had been failing to enforce the *Brown* decision and that they were likely to continue doing so in the absence of positive legislation mandating enforcement and compliance.[43] Powell then proceeded to connect this observation to a constitutional argument about the role of the legislature and congressional abdication. In Powell's view, Congress would be abdicating its constitutional responsibility were it to fail or refuse to enact legislation making the promise of equal protection as the Court had articulated it explicit and real for those who were being denied equal protection in practice.[44] This argument was meant to rebut the contention, similar to the one elaborated by Representatives Bolton and Thomason in the HR 1943 debate, that civil rights did not need to be explicitly recognized and protected in order to be made real, that formal guarantees were sufficient. Indeed, in a lengthy speech opposing the Powell amendment on February 6, 1956, Representative Lee Metcalf of Montana insisted that it was the Court's role to enforce its own decision: "The Supreme Court has made it clear that the courts will enforce the constitutional requirement for non-segregation without the necessity of further legislation. This provision is a self-executing one soundly based on constitutional doctrine and cannot be circumvented by inaction on the part of Congress."[45] For Metcalf, it was enough that the formal hurdle of "separate but equal" had been cleared by the Court; the concrete hurdle of enduring segregation did not have to be cleared in order for the promise of equal protection to be fulfilled. Accordingly, Metcalf based *his* understanding of equal protection and civil rights on a broader argument about the nature and function of the American political system. The "doctrine" to which he referred was his conception of separation of powers, a principle that he interpreted to put no obligation on Congress to positively legislate the Court's constitutional interpretations. It is worth quoting Metcalf in full:

> There is a principle here that is fundamental to constitutional doctrine, that goes back to the separation of powers. I shall never concede that the enforcement of the great provisions of the Constitution, the liberties guaranteed by the Bill of Rights, and the 14th amendment are not effective until there is a specific legislative enactment by the Congress. The legislative branch of the government cannot by refusal or failure to act, deprive citizens of rights and privileges guaranteed by the Constitution. It is the duty of the executive branch to enforce these provisions of the Constitution in every law. These self-executing provisions of the Constitution are implicit in every law enacted in Congress and it is unnecessary to specifically mention them in legislation affecting the subjects in which these constitutional principles are involved.[46]

From this perspective, which is that of the hegemon—the element in the regime that enjoys its liberties at the sufferance of no one else—there is no urgently felt need to see that the abstract promises of the Constitution concerning rights be fulfilled through state action. Thus, Metcalf urged patience with states and localities that were only slowly and reluctantly complying with the Court's decision:

> As I read the amendment it will force the states to accelerate the process of desegregation.... The States that are making an effort to desegregate need the patient cooperation and the understanding of the rest of the

> nation. At its best the Powell amendment would do nothing more than the Supreme Court decision [in *Brown*] is now doing.[47]

Patience was required, according to Metcalf, because there was no positive duty for these states to desegregate. Rather, they were desegregating at their own sufferance and demonstrating considerable largesse and magnanimity in so doing.

Powell wasted no time in refuting this view of civil rights politics. The initial point he developed was that such a view reflects the hypocritical complacency of a person who has never felt their most basic liberties to hinge on the whims of an unpredictable despot. Yet this is precisely the condition in which all Black Americans find themselves. Thus, in his January 6, 1956, speech he observed with warranted asperity that

> one of the most ridiculous arguments made by many of my colleagues is that my amendments will hurt the Negro people. When I ask how do they know, they tell me, "Well, we know the Negro." . . . These men who say they know the Negro do not even know the white man. During the very week that the State of Virginia by a vote of 2 to 1 thrust education back into the Dark Ages and voted to scrap public education, the School Board of Arlington, Va., voted that they would integrate.

Black people are positioned to see the actions of white people more clearly than are white people themselves precisely because their very fate hinges on how white people decide to act. With respect to legislation, this presents a challenge because what white members of Congress will perceive as normal going-along-to-get-along—for example, not raising the issue of Black people being denied their rights—Black members will rightly feel to be the most urgent matter at hand. The same political phenomena thus take on opposite meanings. Powell elucidated that whereas white members of Congress view inclusion of explicit desegregation mandates as unwelcome reminders of the unreality of freedom for non-whites, Black members see failure to include such mandates as positive endorsement of the status quo under Jim Crow: "What would happen if the federal aid to education bill became the law of the land without my amendment? The decision of the Supreme Court of the United States [in *Brown*] would be ignored by Congress. Segregation, Jim Crow, and segregation would be more richly endowed than ever before."[48] More broadly, white members experience discussion of race as a disruptive distraction, whereas Black members see it quite correctly as an essential component of deliberation, insofar as legislating must be cognitively open to the "facts on the ground" in order to reflect a genuinely deliberative decision.[49] Their hegemonic position in the regime in fact blinds white people to the very considerations they would need to face squarely in order to realize the Constitution's promise to guarantee liberty for all citizens.

The second point Powell elaborated was in fact an extension of a constitutional argument he had previously made countering the kind of legalistic separation-of-powers argument advanced by Metcalf.[50] According to the "doctrine" cited by the latter, not only was Congress under no obligation to legislate the Court's interpretation of equal protection in *Brown*; it was actually forbidden to do so because the responsibility of enforcing the judgment of that case was the Court's and the executive's. On February 2, 1955, Powell advanced a radically different conception of separation of powers based on his contention that merely *implicit* support for civil rights by Congress would continue to function as a positive endorsement of the current state of affairs: segregation and Jim Crow. Like Abraham Lincoln, Powell held that each branch—including Congress—has a role in evolving and elucidating constitutional meaning: "Our President and our Supreme Court cannot do all this by themselves and, furthermore, we should not expect it."[51] Indeed,

> the executive and the judicial branches of our Government have passed us [Congress] by so completely and are so far ahead that the peoples of our Nation do not even look to the United States Congress any longer for any dynamic leadership in the field of making democracy real.[52]

Protecting constitutional rights is not—Metcalf's argument to the contrary—simply a matter for the courts who articulate them and the executive who enforces those articulations. Indeed, this is a mistaken understanding of American constitutionalism symptomatic of a deferential view of Congress' role in the political system. Rather, Congress has a positive duty to take part in constructing the Constitution, and refusing to take part in the debate over civil rights on separation-of-powers grounds is not just a mistake in political judgment; it is symptomatic of a decay in congressional culture and a loss of the institutional pride and solidarity necessary for healthy constitutional politics: "This legislative branch—this Congress—must immediately change its childish, immature, compromising, 19th century attitude, and not just become a part of the 20th century but a leader."[53] Congressional decay is manifested not simply in the fact that Congress has failed to vote on the measures Powell has proposed, but in the fact that it has limply refused to even take part in the debate around the issues those proposals concern on the grounds that it is simply not Congress' responsibility. As Powell put it:

> For 10 years, my colleagues and I have introduced civil rights amendment after amendment, civil rights bill after bill, pleading, praying that

> you good ladies and gentlemen would give to this body the glory of dynamic leadership that it should have. But you failed and history has recorded it.[54]

The thrust of Powell's argument here is not that justice requires civil rights legislation—he clearly believes it does—but rather that his colleagues should feel pride and ambition as members of Congress and that these passions should induce them to restore the House to its rightful place in the constitutional order: "I am proud to be a Member of the Congress of the United States. I am proud to be a member of the legislative branch of the United States Government and I know you are too. But I beseech you to transform this emotion of pride into the deed of leadership."[55] Powell's aim was to attach his diagnosis of why white members of Congress fail to understand the need to legislate civil rights to an appeal to the institutional pride of his fellow members.

As debates like the two we have been interpreting indicate, what would otherwise look like genuine, robust legislative deliberation in fact papered over a fundamental cognitive disconnect between white and Black people over what it means to secure basic rights and vindicate the Constitution's deepest commitments. Powell fully recognized that, unlike authentic segregationists, most members of Congress who opposed explicit provisions for non-discrimination did so not out of thoroughgoing racial animus, but out of a good-faith commitment to their own best understanding of what civil rights required. And yet, that understanding subverted the Constitution's own commitment to equality and justice.

The constitutional tragedy in this situation, of which Powell was a uniquely well-situated spectator, would seem to have been as follows. From the hegemonic standpoint, debates like that over HR 1943 and the federal school aid bill *seem* to witness Congress functioning well—with members arguing in good faith, with a wide range of positions being given voice, and with decisions being reached in accordance with majoritarian principles. For all intents and purposes, then, Congress would appear to be doing its job well, and so there was no clear way to indict the institution for dysfunction if those who would be judging the indictment were themselves white people. And yet, if allowed to proceed in this mode, civil rights for Black people would never receive the protections they needed in order to be made real. This fundamental disconnect—between deliberativeness, on the one hand, and vindication of the Constitution's commitment to substantive justice in the form of civil rights, on the other—could be bridged only if the hegemonic perspective of nonetheless well-meaning whites, with its naive faith in inevitable progress, was converted to a perspective that was sensitive to the fragility of liberty. Whereas the former is characterized by unintentional tone-deafness to the voices of the community's oppressed, the latter is alive to those voices. White people would have to cease seeing civil rights in the way that was natural for them and come to see them from the perspective of the community's most vulnerable and exposed.

The disconnect Powell diagnosed is an enduring feature of American politics and, as Powell suggested, requires explicit statutory guarantees lest it be worsened. Its enduring character is vividly on display in the jurisprudence of the Roberts Court, which in 2015 in the *Shelby County v. Holder* decision gutted the 1965 Voting Rights Act of its "pre-clearance" provisions, which explicitly required states with a history of race-based voter suppression to "pre-clear" changes to their voting laws with the federal government.[56] Repeating the argument of Metcalf, Thomason, and Bolton almost verbatim, Chief Justice Roberts maintained that the pre-clearance provisions were no longer necessary because they had run their course; they could not be justified as necessary bulwarks against a historically recurring problem. Indeed, Roberts maintained that, if left in place, they would constitute a violation of the principle of federalism. Similarly, failing to meet the kind of critique of this argument that Powell had advanced, Roberts had previously, in the *Parents Involved v. Seattle* case, asserted that explicit statutory recognition of race, instead of guaranteeing protections for a historically marginalized class, actually does more harm than good: "The way to stop discrimination on the basis of race is to stop discriminating on the basis of race."[57] Commenting on this particular line, Steven Lubet shrewdly observes (in a remark that vindicates Powell's reasoning): "As with many highly accomplished, affluent white people, Roberts's head start in life is invisible to him."[58] Robert's blindness to the need for substantive guarantees against discrimination is illustrative of the hegemonic perspective Powell undertook to confront.

How to make the invisible visible in a way that honored the Constitution's commitments was, accordingly, the central question Powell faced during his "congressional irritant" phase. Powell believed that submitting to "deliberativeness" as that mode had been defined by whites in Congress would only spell defeat for genuine civil rights reform. He saw that conversion from the hegemonic worldview to a sympathetic worldview would require going outside the channels of "reasonableness" and "deliberation," since fighting a rhetorical battle on the field of "reasonableness" as whites in Congress defined it would mean conceding victory in advance. Conversion by means of reasons—that is, through enumerating why it would be rational to adopt *his* conception of civil rights reform—was doomed because the passions of his audience pointed firmly in the direction of the hegemonic outlook: white people have the emotions of those who are content, and therefore reluctant to change, by virtue of being secure in their rights. Powell saw that conversion would require dislodging, and then redirecting, these passions in the direction of the conception of civil rights he wished to advance. Rather than leading with reasons, then, Powell would lead with appeals to the sub-rational sources of human action. Once their emotions had been redirected, his audience would then be in a position to come to a reasoned appreciation of their new conception.

Powell understood that the real enemy of civil rights progress in America was not an enemy in the strict sense at all but rather a disconnect between two perspectives that had been institutionalized through centuries of reinforcement. Segregationists and active racists were certainly a force, but they were symptomatic of rather than responsible for the regime's racial paradigm. Most whites were wedded to their hegemonic perspective not out of moral corruption—most did not voluntarily choose to bolster racism—but because their day-to-day experience of the regime, together with a sense of complacency and an attachment to what is traditional and familiar, induced them to maintain that perspective. In this sense, Powell's theory of racism falls somewhere between accounts that find it to be the product of institutions (institutional theories) and those that see it more as a matter of personal choice (individual racism theories).[59]

The problem faced by the civil rights reformer—and none was better acquainted with this problem than Powell—is that a story about systemic or structural dysfunction, while truer than any alternative story, is not particularly effective for motivating concerted, aggressive action. Most people need to be angry in order to act, and no one can really be angry at abstract, impersonal forces.[60] The reason is that anger and the other moralistic emotions presuppose agency in the object at which the emotion is being directed; they require an entity that can be held responsible. Powell knew that an accurate assessment of the politics of civil rights—that is, a sophisticated diagnosis of institutional dysfunction—would fail to provoke the kind of attitudinal change necessary to mobilize for strenuous change. In the case of racial equality, there was a trade-off between truth and justice; to use an analogy, there was a gulf between deliberativeness and the common good that only non-deliberative rhetoric could bridge. Powell believed the way to bridge this gulf was by self-consciously injecting the otherwise dry, impersonal story of civil rights in America with moralism. People would be inspired to act, to play an active part, only if that story was brought to life for them by an orator capable of weaving the dreary details into a narrative whose readers felt compelled to take sides. Such a narrative needed to be studded with insults, exaggerations, and deliberate provocations if it was to excite emotion where drier rhetoric had fallen flat. As we have discussed, it was for this kind of rhetoric that Powell became both famous and infamous among his contemporaries.

Powell's tactical uses of demagoguery employed two signature tropes. The first was to characterize committed opponents of civil rights, such as segregationists, as "fascists" and enemies of the American people.[61] The second and more interesting of Powell's tropes was to construe wavering on the part of potential allies as betrayal and cowardice. "Powell," writes John A. David, "had little faith in the temporizing of liberals, most race leaders, and the black bourgeoisie."[62] As this interpretation suggests, Powell directed his animus chiefly at two segments of his potential support base: white liberals who favored civil rights but preferred a conciliatory approach in politics, and Black leaders who believed provocation would do more harm than good. Powell's attacks on the former varied in intensity and vitriol. Some he would chastise for lacking courage and integrity. In July 1945, for example, he spoke before a New York audience about a recently failed attempt at passing a permanent Fair Employment Practices Commission (FEPC) bill. Such a law would have achieved the kind of explicit prohibition against racial discrimination sought by Powell in the legislative debates discussed above. Commenting on the bill's failure, Powell stated that "any American who continues to accept the campaign promises of the Democrats and the Republicans is a gullible fool."[63] Speaking about the broader issue of civil rights at Wilberforce University in Ohio on June 2, 1950, Powell "lashed out at Democrats and Republicans for 'selling the negro down the drain.'"[64] When "a motion of his to end segregation in Washington, D.C., received only nineteen out of 433 votes, he stated . . . 'The time has arrived for the major parties to either set up a bipartisan program of civil rights or give up and acknowledge that it is nothing more than the cheapest political frauds.'"[65] And when President Truman's wife agreed to attend a tea put on by the Daughters of the American Revolution—at the time a segregated organization—Powell, to the outrage of the Truman administration, publicly denounced her as "the last lady."[66]

The latter two interpretations suggest that failure to act on civil rights was the result of deliberate subversion of a just outcome on the part of a malevolent adversary. The first suggests the flip side of the coin—namely, that anyone who continues to accept the promises and reassurances of compromising party members is morally blameworthy for not standing up for what they know to belong to them. This is the same characterization Powell advanced of Black people who, in his view, failed to demand reform with sufficient energy and aggression. As Hamilton observes on multiple occasions, Powell's preferred trope was to label such figures "Uncle Toms."[67] His use of this derogatory term traded on its deep historical connotations.[68] Specifically, Powell used it to signify not only cowardice in the face of the white power structure, but deliberate (and therefore morally corrupt) betrayal of one's allies for the sake of personal aggrandizement by means of obtaining favor with one's oppressor. One of his most memorable and remarkable uses of this term occurred in the wake of the 1952 Democratic National Convention (DNC), whose election platform was regarded by Powell as pathetically weak with respect to civil rights and the FEPC. Accordingly,

> at a rally of three thousand at the Golden State Ballroom in Harlem he attacked the Democratic convention as a "sellout." He particularly singled out his Negro congressional colleague from Chicago, William

> L. Dawson, who was on the platform drafting committee and reportedly argued for a mild, compromising civil rights plank. Dawson, said Powell, was an "Uncle Tom." [Asserted Powell,] "I am not saying that any money had to pass to Dawson, for there always have been men who for a slap on the back are willing to sell their people down the river."[69]

These kinds of appeals mixed invective and chastisement with solicitation of empathy. Those directed at white liberals might be classified as instances of what Pollock was referring to when he observed that "[Powell] did not hesitate to appeal to white guilt feelings."[70] They embody demagogic rhetoric insofar as they presuppose agreement and therefore eschew reason-giving in favor of a direct appeal to (allegedly) shared knowledge of what justice demands—on the one hand, chastisement of those who ought to know better (liberals and "Uncle Toms"); on the other hand, outright dismissal and demonization of unpersuadable enemies (fascists).

One can imagine a significantly more charitable critique of all of these opponents of Powell. Specifically, one can imagine a critique of Dawson's involvement in the DNC platform drafting committee that contested the merits of the platform itself and questioned Dawson's reluctance to bargain more aggressively without implying (as Powell aggressively did) that Dawson had been motivated by a loathsome desire for approval at the expense of the rights of his true friends. Such an interpretation differs radically from the sophisticated diagnosis we have seen Powell articulate in Congress itself, according to which failure to press for civil rights reform was explained by him as a symptom of good-natured ignorance, as opposed to active malevolence, on the part of white people.

Powell's rhetorical strategy was based on the argument that a narrative that highlights the good nature of one's adversary—for example, the rhetorical narratives of Dr. King—will fail to excite the popular passions necessary for conversion because it will render one's adversary in a fundamentally sympathetic light. Ethically, one cannot blame someone for acting out of ignorance if their intentions were just; the disconnect is an informational or cognitive one rather than a moral one. Recognizing this moral perspective, Powell developed an iterative, or multi-stage, rhetorical strategy.[71] He believed it was first necessary to enlist the audience's strong passions in his cause by means of hard demagoguery. Such passions were necessary for conversion. Once conversion had been effected, the merits of the cause could then be elaborated, thought through, and internalized by his audience through a process of reason-giving or rationalization akin to that which Powell himself undertook in his House floor speeches. Converts to Powell's civil rights vision would be impelled to make the arguments in favor of that vision their own once their passions had been attached to its core edifice. Demagoguery was the necessary means to effect that initial attachment.

Senator Joseph McCarthy and Communism

In Adam Clayton Powell Jr., we see a member of a historically marginalized community using demagoguery in a creative and provocative attempt to persuade an oftentimes hostile white audience of a truth they were politically, socially, and economically incentivized to ignore. It is difficult to imagine a more uphill rhetorical battle. And in many respects, the case of Joseph McCarthy presents the very opposite spectacle. McCarthy sought above all to leverage the preexisting prejudices and fears of the public to pursue an outsider to the community whom he accused of actively subverting the integrity of the American regime.

The core of McCarthy's rhetorical position can be summed up in one sentence: the problem of American foreign policy is so obvious that a proportionally obvious solution must exist. As nearly any sample of his rhetoric from his Senate tenure will confirm, McCarthy's diagnosis of that problem was infiltration of the U.S. State Department and military apparatuses by Communists intent on subverting the U.S. government and the American way of life. McCarthy's proposed solution was to expose both the infiltrators and those who abetted them and to remove all of these from their government positions.

In the years leading up to McCarthy, of course, the issue of Communism had been debated at a high level of sophistication by those advocating more and less aggressive American foreign policies toward the Soviet Union and other Communist nations and movements abroad. Historian Robert P. Newman helpfully describes the background psychology of this debate. During the 1950s,

> Americans could not believe that China had made [the choice to become a Communist nation] freely. Its adherence to the "World Communist Conspiracy," many thought, must have been coerced both by Soviet manipulation and by the treasonous actions of American diplomats and politicians. We had "lost" China because some Communist mastermind in the American government had deliberately sabotaged the efforts of Chiang Kai-shek . . . to defeat Mao Tse-tung in the Chinese civil war.[72]

Advocates of a more hawkish stance in this conflict opposed defenders of the Roosevelt and Truman administrations, defenders who had advocated a more pragmatic and in some cases sympathetic approach to Communism.[73] Whereas the practical dimensions of this debate centered around questions of how to deal with Communist nations politically and militarily—of which the strategic disagreement between Truman and General Douglas MacArthur regarding Korea was illustrative—the *theoretical* debate implicated matters of deep principle, such as whether liberalism and Communism shared common aspirations and should therefore work toward an understanding, or whether they were fundamentally irreconcilable in their normative commitments.[74]

McCarthy's own public position on this matter was not just that the hawks had the stronger argument. Many of McCarthy's most thoughtful and politically sophisticated colleagues, such as Senator Robert Taft, California governor Earl Warren, and Representative Richard Nixon, shared his basic substantive concerns, and at various points in his brief career were willing to use McCarthy to fight their uglier rhetorical battles for them.[75] McCarthy stood out among the Republicans on account of the way he constructed arguments around the issue of Communism and presented those arguments to the Senate and the public. McCarthy's rhetoric inside and outside of the Senate chamber drew attention for its aggressive disregard for institutional norms from the outset of his career.[76] "What was remarkable about McCarthy's Senate apprenticeship was not policy positions—liberal or conservative, internationalist or isolationist—but rather his continual violation of the rules, customs, and procedures under which the Senate operates."[77] "By 1952 Joe McCarthy had made his name synonymous with the issue of communism-in-government. . . . [H]is extravagant charges had dramatized the issue as never before."[78] McCarthy was unique in that he used, or exploited, his constitutional office to wage a rhetorical campaign that weaponized the most simplistic version of the most hawkish possible stance on Communism.

> McCarthy's true significance lay in the fact that he brought to [the] thoroughly conventional political issue [of Communism in government] his own thoroughly unconventional personal qualities—a flair for dramatization, a superb sense of press-agentry, and a stubborn unwillingness to back down. He would later recall that Republicans had been yelling "treason" for some time, but that their notices had been buried in the want ads. The way to get action, he declared, was to change "treason" to "traitors."[79]

Traitors, indeed. McCarthy held that no honest citizen could in good conscience choose a less-hawkish alternative to his own view of what American foreign policy should be. By the same token, he maintained that Roosevelt-Truman foreign policy was so patently self-defeating that the only conceivable explanation of it was purposeful and concerted treasonous action on the part of American security forces—that is, a conspiracy. In his telling, then, any person assessing America's situation post–World War II in a spirit of candor would have wished for the very opposite of what was in fact pursued. For this reason, McCarthy felt himself to be under no obligation to lay out, or even to acknowledge, the possible merits of alternative approaches to Communism. Rather, because in his telling there were no merits to those positions, the only possible explanation of the current situation must be a fait accompli on the part of Communist conspirators.

Before discussing and attempting to evaluate McCarthy's rhetorical approach, it is worth acknowledging that his allegations of conspiracy were based on a modicum of plausibility. After all, conspiracies do happen.[80] And from a certain standpoint, America's approach to Communism—many of whose espousers proclaimed their desire to infiltrate and subvert non-Communist governments—was dangerously lenient. Moreover, in the years leading up to McCarthy's rhetorical campaign, several high-ranking Communist infiltrators had been apprehended and prosecuted by U.S. security agencies, resulting in a general sense of uneasiness and suspicion that, at the time, was perhaps not unwarranted.[81] The most plausible elements of the anti-Communist narrative, however, were the actual atrocities that citizens of the Soviet Union had been suffering since the 1920s. Historian Stephen Kotkin has painstakingly detailed these atrocities in his recent biography of Joseph Stalin, showing how, among other things, the Stalin regime managed to foment murderous hatred among the Russian peasants in order to impose collectivization, a scheme the peasants would not have voluntarily adopted. Characteristic of the Stalin regime's tactics, which were also on display in the purges of the 1930s, was the ability to turn ordinary citizens against each other so as to advance the broader aims of the Soviet government. Collectivization and the purges witnessed colleagues, acquaintances, neighbors, and friends voluntarily betraying each other to the regime, in many instances as ways of settling personal resentments and grudges.[82] From this perspective, the Stalin regime does appear to have succeeded in infiltrating the minds of, and weaponizing, ordinary people for its own broader aims. This is not to say that McCarthy's arguments about the proper approach to Communism were true, only that retrospective investigations of Communist regimes reveal that they contained a sliver of truth.

On this score, scholars of rhetoric, Congress, and the Constitution who discuss McCarthy have tended to downplay considerations of the Communist threat in their evaluations of his rhetorical approach, perhaps fearing that by acknowledging that threat they might appear to be exonerating McCarthy himself. Relatedly, these scholars tend to assume that what made McCarthy a demagogue was his willingness to advance false allegations for the sake of his own aggrandizement, as well as his disregard for the nation's welfare. "He was," argues Signer, "a product of his own ambition."[83] Similarly, Rovere speculates that "McCarthy took up the Communist menace in 1950 not with any expectation that it would make him a sovereign of the assemblies, but with the simple hope that it would help him hold his job in 1952."[84]

Considerations like these are important and deserve to be examined by scholars wishing to give the fullest possible account of McCarthy's personal psychology and biography. But they also have their downsides. One of these has been the somewhat unthinking demonization of McCarthy, which in turn has colored our understanding of McCarthy's role as a United States senator. Indeed, a conspiracy theory worthy of McCarthy himself has emerged purporting to explain the origins of his anti-Communist campaign. The theory was first advanced by columnist Drew Pearson, an enemy of McCarthy who claimed that the senator had met with several prominent right-wing Catholic political figures at the Colony Club restaurant in early 1950.[85] As the story goes, these figures conspired with McCarthy as a means to augment their own political influence and to advance a far-right Catholic political agenda. Accordingly, though the meeting has never been corroborated, several well-known (and otherwise credible) scholarly accounts of McCarthy have reported it as if it were known to be a fact—thereby perpetuating the same kind of counter-demagoguery on display in the case of Daniel Shays.[86]

I believe there is a better way to study McCarthy as a demagogue, one that builds on all of these observations but also views them alongside a broader range of political and constitutional considerations. It may be true, as Signer insists, that McCarthy was a product of his own ambition, but this fact alone does not equip us to evaluate the character of his rhetoric; rather, it causes us to reduce and thereby distort his rhetoric by analyzing it in terms of something other than itself—namely, McCarthy's own baser motives. Whatever McCarthy's personal ambitions may have been, forming a political judgment of his conduct requires taking his rhetoric on its own terms, trying to understand the character and quality of the public arguments he ended up making in order to advance his ambitions and seeing them in light of his duties as an officer of the Constitution. As I will argue, the quality of his case as well as the merits of his rhetorical strategy deserve a hearing because there are conceivable situations in which a member of Congress using similarly demagogic tactics might have good reasons for doing so.

Accordingly, this chapter's burden is twofold. First, I argue that McCarthy's rhetoric is illustrative of the core features of demagoguery as I have defined that concept. McCarthy dismissed the very possibility of substantive debate over how America should approach the Communism issue, insisting that American foreign policy under Roosevelt and Truman was itself evidence of a Communist conspiracy in the U.S. government. He refused to supply any verifiable criteria for what it might have meant to be a Communist conspirator, thereby giving himself free rein to accuse any individual he chose. He alleged that the absence of hard evidence of Communist conspiracy was itself evidence of a cover-up by the conspirators. And he used his rhetoric to portray the nature of the Communist threat in a way that justified and necessitated absolute license and power on his part. Nevertheless, I also argue that had McCarthy been correct in his allegations of a Communist conspiracy, his use of demagogic tropes would have been at least defensible. Relatedly, there are ways McCarthy could have, to some extent, justified his demagoguery by anchoring it in a more solid argumentative foundation; he could have elaborated an argument for why a senator in his position would have reason to suspect a Communist conspiracy—an argument he could have deployed together with his demagogic rhetoric. I conclude the chapter by sketching out one such argument that was available to McCarthy but which he failed to make use of.

On February 9, 1950, McCarthy delivered a Lincoln Day speech at a Republican women's club in Wheeling, West Virginia. The Wheeling speech constitutes the theme on which all of McCarthy's subsequent rhetoric concerning Communism is a kind of variation. And though the actual speech he delivered was not recorded, the reporters who were present for the speech concurred regarding his peroration.[87] As he concluded, they reported, "the senator waved aloft a sheet of paper and shouted, 'I have here in my hand a list of 205—a list of names that were made known to the Secretary of State as being members of the Communist Party and who nevertheless are still working and shaping policy in the State Department.' "[88]

McCarthy cabined this specific accusation within a broader argument for more aggressive action toward the Soviet Union and global Communism in general, which was itself derived from a specific characterization of the nature of the threat that Communism posed to the United States. This characterization was based on the axiom that "the real, basic difference" between "our Christian world" and "the atheistic communist world" "lies in the religion of immoralism."[89] According to McCarthy, the real danger presented by Communism could not be measured in terms of better and worse political and economic outcomes. Indeed, the enemy McCarthy sought to depict was itself neither a political nor an economic regime: "This religion of immoralism . . . will more deeply wound and damage mankind than any conceivable economic or political system."[90] The word "religion" is not accidental but rather would seem to be core to McCarthy's understanding. Communism as he interprets it implicates the conscience, the human capacity to tell right from wrong. Communists, as such, share a commitment to moral corruption—choosing to think and do what they know to be wrong and declaring it to be right nonetheless.

Communism so conceived does not just issue in objectively worse outcomes (e.g., war, poverty, or oppression by the state). It renders its victims morally defective, and this is precisely what makes it so dangerous in McCarthy's characterization. A "normal" conflict between nations might be settled in part by answering the question of whose way of life is superior: Which nation promises a better, more prosperous, and freer life for those living in its orbit? But in order for this question to be answered in any satisfactory way, one must trust those whom one is asking to answer it *honestly*; they must actually evaluate the two ways of life according to their own best understandings of what makes life good. And Communism, as an internal moral choice, makes this kind of evaluation impossible, for the reason that Communists choose to deny what they know in their consciences to be morally superior. Communism and those influenced by it therefore cannot be trusted to choose right over wrong. Communists can never be engaged with in a spirit of candor and they will never speak and act in good faith, and it is for this reason that a policy of leaving it for people to decide which system they would prefer to live under is fundamentally flawed: A Communist will deny what any honest individual knows to be the morally superior system. Once Communism has infiltrated a country, the good has no hope of prevailing. As a consequence, "we are now engaged in a show-down fight . . . not the usual war between nations for land areas or other material gains, but a war between two diametrically opposed ideologies."[91]

McCarthy's depiction of Communism is the basis of his allegations of conspiracy. For McCarthy, no moral person would ever choose Communism over the just alternative. The only people who would "choose" Communism are those who have already been corrupted by it. The only possible explanation of its rise, therefore, is neither honest misjudgment nor legitimate disagreement, but subversion. Specifically, Communism has gained victories globally not because American officials acting in a spirit of candor saw reasons to defer to the judgment and sovereignty of other nations, but because the American people were "blinded," deceived by conspirators without themselves being aware of it. "There is still a hope for peace if we finally decide that no longer can we safely blind our eyes and close our ears to those facts which are shaping up more and more clearly," McCarthy claimed. And he knew who was responsible for this blinding:

> The reason why we find ourselves in a position of impotency is not because our only powerful potential enemy has sent men to invade our shores . . . but rather because of the traitorous actions of those who have been treated so well by this Nation. It has not been the less fortunate, or members of minority groups who have been traitorous to this Nation, but rather those who have had all the benefits that the wealthiest Nation on earth has had to offer . . . the finest homes, the finest college education and the finest jobs in government we can give. This is glaringly true in the State Department. There the bright young men who are born with silver spoons in their mouths are the ones who have been most traitorous.[92]

Had those who are responsible for choosing the nation's foreign policy honestly assessed the nation's situation with respect to global Communism, there is no doubt they would have chosen the opposite path. By the same token, the only conceivable explanation for America's current situation was that the nation's affairs had been purposely mishandled. The fact that America had permitted Communism to triumph in Russia and China was evidence not of honest errors in judgment or of alternative legitimate interpretations of what is best for the country and the international order, but of purposeful subversion.

McCarthy's allegations at Wheeling—his claim to possess special knowledge of Communist infiltration—precipitated a flurry of controversy and curiosity.[93] Without making any definitive causal arguments, it is not implausible to suggest that McCarthy was successful in using his rhetoric to provoke the outcome he would seem to have desired: government investigations into Communist infiltration. In response, the State Department "wired him a request for the names he had said he had and promised a prompt investigation of the 205," and the Senate agreed to hear McCarthy's allegations on February 20 in order to ascertain their basis and to discern whether a credible threat to national security existed.[94]

Like those he put into practice at Wheeling, the rhetorical patterns McCarthy displayed at this initial hearing—"one of the maddest spectacles in the history of representative government"—are emblematic of those he would go on to practice for the rest of his career.[95] McCarthy entered the Senate with one hundred "dossiers" of, he claimed, known Communist infiltrators. In fact, the list (which McCarthy "may have received . . . from Robert E. Lee, and House investigator and a friend of McCarthy's") was an assemblage of old reports and information long available to other members of Congress: "There were many copies of the 'Lee list' scattered around Capitol Hill."[96] Nevertheless, McCarthy never admitted "that he was reading to the Senate from a badly outdated committee file. Instead, he told his colleagues that he had 'pierced the iron curtain' of State Department secrecy and with the aid of 'some good, loyal Americans in the State Department' had compiled an alarming picture of espionage and treason."[97]

The picture he was drawing here was a modified version of the one he drew in his Wheeling speech. There existed in the country a fundamental division between, on the one hand, the real, as-of-yet uncorrupted American people whose consciences were clean and who understood Communism for what it was, and, on the other hand, members of the elite who were protected from scrutiny because they controlled the country's information sources, such as the State Department. Though the "Lee list" McCarthy presented was available to many of the senators present, it was invaluable for the rhetorical image he sought to project in the Senate and to the people at large, which was that he was working hand in hand with the few true Americans still inside the State Department who could get him the information he needed. Rhetorically, this assertion seemed to substantiate McCarthy's claim both to possess special information (i.e., the names of infiltrators) and to be the embodiment of commonsense morality shared by the American people he claimed to be representing.

The Senate response to McCarthy's allegations was a mixture of suspicion and enthusiasm, but what characterizes them above all is the way McCarthy was able to insulate his allegations from external verification by means of cognitively closed rhetoric. As Rovere puts it, Senator Brien McMahon of Connecticut "made thirty-four vain attempts to have McCarthy submit to a testing of his claims against reason and evidence—to conduct the debate within the framework of rationality as rationality is codified in the Senate rules. Other Senators tried, too, but it was useless."[98] A prolonged exchange between McCarthy and Senator Scott Lucas from Illinois best captures their tone and substance. Commenting on McCarthy's Wheeling speech, Lucas at one point remarked:

> There is no one in the Senate or in the country who is any more opposed to Communist domination of any nation or Communist infiltration into any country than is the Senator from Illinois. What I am asking the Senator to do—and I hope he will do it, and the country wants him to do it—is to follow through with the speech which he made in Wheeling, W. Va., in which he stated more than 200 persons working in the State Department were known to the Secretary of State to be members of the Communist Party. If the Senator made that statement—and that is what has been reported—I want him to name those Communists. If there are card-carrying Communists in the State Department, the Senator from Illinois will go along with the Senator from Wisconsin in any way possible to remove those Communists from the rolls.[99]

Lucas went on to assure McCarthy that even if he named the 205 individuals and they turned out subsequently not to be Communists as he claimed, McCarthy would still be protected by congressional immunity. McCarthy responded, "I will not say anything on the Senate floor which I will not say off the floor. On the day when I take advantage of the security we have on the Senate floor, on that day I will resign from the Senate. Anything I say on the floor of the Senate at any time will be repeated off the floor."[100] Nevertheless, McCarthy refused to give the names, instead opting to read a modified version of the Wheeling speech into the official record.

In the days following the February 20 exchange, the Senate introduced Resolution 231, launching an investigation of the claims McCarthy had advanced at Wheeling and on the Senate floor:[101]

> *Resolved,* That the Senate Committee on Foreign Relations, or any duly authorized subcommittee thereof, is authorized and directed to conduct a full and complete study and investigation as to whether persons who are disloyal to the United States are employed by the Department of State as charged by the Senator from Wisconsin [McCarthy]. The committee shall report to the Senate at the earliest practicable date the results of its investigation, together with such recommendations as it may deem desirable.

It would appear that McCarthy was again successful in getting what he wanted. His public appeal at Wheeling successfully leveraged both his credibility as a member of the Senate and his claim to possess special knowledge of infiltration and conspiracy in order to precipitate an investigation that, it seems, would not otherwise have happened.[102] Indeed, as Rover speculates, it seems plausible that those who heard McCarthy's accusations "must have felt that a man who made such a precise compilation had surely gone to some lengths to get hold of the facts."[103] Presenting himself this way was one of the distinguishing features of McCarthy's rhetorical style. Specifically, McCarthy marshaled the *trappings* of knowledge and precision—for example, specific numbers, briefcases, "dossiers"—as stage props to create the impression of a thoroughly researched argument. Trappings or mere semblances of knowledge were consequently substituted for real knowledge; in McCarthy's rhetoric, the signifier replaced the signified.[104] Relatedly, his rank and reputation as a senator seemed to ensure that his claims were trustworthy. "The chances were against a United States Senator being *entirely* wrong. Surely he wouldn't dare get up on the Senate floor and make such large claims if he couldn't back up *any* of them."[105] By making him look like the kind of person who would have taken care to verify his assertions before going public with them, these features of his rhetoric insulated McCarthy from having to submit his arguments and allegations to external verification in fact.

Rhetorically, McCarthy found himself in a paradoxical situation in the wake of the February 20 hearing. It was precisely his claim to possess hard evidence of infiltration that had provoked an official Senate investigation. And yet he possessed no such hard evidence, only soft evidence, like the Lee list, already in the possession of many other government officials. As a consequence, McCarthy was operating in the dark as to the plausibility of his diagnosis. On the one hand, the fact that the information he did possess was in no way demonstrative of conspiracy (as he claimed it was) by no means precluded that the Senate would actually expose something of interest in the course of its investigation—say, treason akin to that of the Rosenbergs from the previous decade.[106] In a narrow sense, such an outcome would have vindicated his wager that an investigation would turn up evidence of infiltration.

And yet, recall the second part of McCarthy's rhetorical wager. American foreign policy *itself* was held by McCarthy to be sufficient evidence of conspiracy. According to the senator, since no uncorrupted person would ever tolerate Communism, nothing could explain the toleration of Communism by the State Department except Communist corruption of that department. Yet McCarthy also claimed to possess hard evidence of conspiracy, on the basis of which a Senate investigation looking for further evidence could be justified.

McCarthy, in sum, advanced a *deductive* as well as an *inductive* argument regarding conspiracy. He appears to have made his inductive argument to the Senate—namely, that a conspiracy could be inferred from the hard evidence he claimed to possess—having calculated that an investigation was unlikely to be authorized by the Senate without the promise of obtaining further hard evidence. By the same token, he must have anticipated that using his deductive argument before the Senate—only a corrupt State Department would make the foreign policy choices that had actually been made—would have failed to provoke an actual investigation; after all, no argument on the merits had hitherto persuaded the Senate of this specific conclusion. And McCarthy, for his part, never elaborated a cognitively open argument as to why, in his estimation, the State Department's approach to global Communism under Roosevelt and Truman was beyond contestation. The extent of his "evidence" was the kind of assertion about Communism and moral corruption he advanced in the Wheeling speech.

The Tydings Committee investigations proceeded awkwardly because, as Rovere points out and others contemporaneous with the committee have observed, the nature of their mandate was ambiguous.[107] Was the committee tacitly endorsing McCarthy's allegations, such that the aim of its investigations was to discover *further* evidence of Communist infiltration and conspiracy? Or was its primary objective the more modest one of corroborating the specific allegations McCarthy had *already* leveled, so as to establish their credibility? Senator Millard Tydings, for his part, seemed to believe it was the latter, opening the investigations on March 8 by questioning McCarthy as to the actual identity of a specific dossier. Characteristically, as in his initial presentation on February 20, McCarthy refused to acquiesce in divulging the name—again without offering an argument as to the propriety of withholding the information in question. Indeed, it was the Republican senator Henry Cabot Lodge Jr. who provided McCarthy with a way out, insisting that he "be allowed to present his charges in his own way and in his own order."[108] McCarthy was thereby able to maintain the guise of possessing special knowledge without having to submit the basis of his allegations—that is, the actual name and identity of the accused person in "case 14"—to the scrutiny of a person other than himself.

When McCarthy *did* divulge the identity of those he was accusing, the basis of his accusation turned out to be highly conjectural. The cases of Dorothy Kenyon and Philip C. Jessup are particularly revealing.[109] Jessup was a diplomat (specifically the U.S. ambassador at large); Kenyon, by contrast, was a private citizen who had at one point been part of the United States' delegation to the United Nations Commission on the Status of Women.[110] Nevertheless, McCarthy opened his remarks on Kenyon with the assertion that "this lady has been affiliated with at least 28 Communist-front organizations, all of which have been declared subversive by an official Government agency. Nine of the 28 have been cited as subversive by the Attorney General of the United States."[111] McCarthy knew his allegations were gravely exaggerated. Only six, not nine, of the twenty-eight organizations had been "cited by the Attorney General as communist fronts." In addition, the rest of the organizations had been cited by such "official Government agencies" as a committee of the New York City Council and the California Committee on Un-American Activities. Rhetorically, McCarthy presented the information in a way that both inflated the significance of Kenyon for national security interests and created the false sense that there existed a consensus among trustworthy government officials—"an official Government agency"—as to her status as a Communist. More generally, by means of rhetoric like this he was able to construe ambiguous information in a way that seemed to render it definitive evidence for his broader position.

McCarthy alleged that Kenyon had been "affiliated" with these organizations, an allegation similar in character to McCarthy's claim that Ambassador Jessup had "an unusual affinity" for Communist causes.[112] As noted above, McCarthy routinely employed vague yet sinister-sounding relational expressions, such as "affiliated" and "sympathetic with," in order to cast doubt on an individual's loyalty. His reason for using these designations would appear to be the rhetorical license it afforded him to deem as a Communist whomever *he* wanted to so label, irrespective of how definitive the evidence of those "affiliations" actually was. McCarthy employed his rhetoric to evade articulating verifiable criteria for what it meant to be a Communist, criteria that a person not committed to his particular view of things might have questioned or contested. To be "affiliated with" or "sympathetic to" a group could have signified (at least in the way McCarthy used these designations) so many possible degrees of intimacy as to be useless as a relational classification—that is, unless one had already been primed to see the world as McCarthy wished one to interpret it. Recall that Communism in McCarthy's fictive account was so insidious as to render even the weakest indication of support for it in a government official grounds for investigation. And insidiousness—the quality of being at once very dangerous and very difficult to detect—warrants and necessitates great discretion and wide license on the part of whoever is charged with exposing and combatting it. In the universe of his own fictive account, the nature of the Communist threat as McCarthy portrayed it rendered his own investigative powers warranted and necessary. His fictive narrative of Communism served as the normative justification for his investigations.

McCarthy's denouement during the investigations was his accusation of Owen Lattimore, a government official who had never held an official post in the State Department, of purposely sabotaging American foreign policy and enabling Chinese Communists to defeat the Nationalist forces under Chiang Kai-shek.[113] Specifically, McCarthy asserted that "China had been 'betrayed' by a State Department 'more loyal to the ideals and designs of communism than to those of the free, God-fearing half of the world.'"[114] And it was Lattimore who, according to McCarthy, was "one of the principal architects of our far eastern policy."[115] Accordingly, McCarthy informed the press on March 21 that he was going to announce "the top Russian espionage agent" in the United States, who turned out to be Lattimore. In Senate committee, McCarthy asserted: "When I give you this information it is to the best of my knowledge, and I am absolutely confident that this is the case that you really should find—well, it's explosive. If you crack this case it will be the biggest espionage case in the history of this country."[116]

McCarthy met with considerable resistance on this point. Senator Tydings declared publicly in response to McCarthy's public announcements that " 'it was the universal opinion of all the members of the committee present' that there was nothing in the file to show that Lattimore was or ever had been a Communist."[117] In response, McCarthy pivoted away from the specific, tangible charge that Lattimore was a Soviet spy—"Maybe in the case of Lattimore I have placed too much stress on the question of whether or not he has been an espionage agent"—toward the more nebulous yet still grave allegation that as "the principal architect" for American Far East foreign policy Lattimore bore responsibility for the loss of China.[118] And he continued to press his claim that Lattimore, like Kenyon, was some kind of Communist. In a particularly illustrative exchange, McCarthy began to read selectively from a letter by Lattimore that, McCarthy held, demonstrated Lattimore's pro-Communist inclinations. When other senators demanded that McCarthy place the *whole* letter into the official record, he refused on the grounds that it was classified.[119] His reasons for doing so seem obvious. Had the letter been part of the record, it would have been open to contestation by other senators attempting to evaluate McCarthy's allegations on the basis of the letter's contents rather than what McCarthy *said* about its contents.

Similarly, McCarthy at one point demanded that the Truman administration's "loyalty and security" files be opened on the grounds that they would substantiate his charges against Lattimore.[120] These files "were made up of material gathered by the FBI, the Civil Service Commission, and various other department agencies" during the late 1940s.[121] Tydings agreed and "implored [Truman] to let the Committee see the files, despite an executive order discontinuing the practice of releasing personnel files to congressional committees and despite McCarthy's refusal to place any charges." Remarkably, "the President agreed." However, when the files turned up nothing that supported his allegations, "McCarthy called it 'a phony offer of phony files,'" alleging that the records had been "raped and rifled."[122] McCarthy's response to the Tydings report was characteristic of his overall rhetorical campaign. He denounced it as "'a green light to the Red fifth column in the United States' and 'a signal to the traitors, Communists, and fellow travelers in our Government that they need have no fear of exposure.'"[123] In sum, McCarthy interpreted the outcome of the committee's investigations, which seemed to invalidate the allegations he had begun to make at Wheeling, as evidence themselves of the very conspiracy he had sought to expose. One would be hard pressed to find a better example of demagogic argumentation than that which was on display in these exchanges. If the evidence supported his allegations, held McCarthy, then those allegations were validated. If the evidence did not, then it was further evidence of the truth of those very same accusations. In other words, the very evidence that would have seemed to undermine McCarthy's thesis within a scheme of cognitive openness was interpreted by him as evidence that in fact supported his allegation. Within the rhetorical universe he created, McCarthy could not be wrong; *all* evidence could be interpreted as supporting his ultimate position.

The majority report issued by the Tydings Committee "denounce[ed] McCarthy in terms of harshness rarely used toward fellow senators. They accused him of perpetrating a 'fraud and a hoax' upon the Senate and the American people. They denied his accusations and charged him with deliberate and willful falsehood."[124] This description of the Senate's eventual reaction to McCarthy captures only one aspect of what made that reaction interesting from our perspective, however. As we have seen, initial reactions to McCarthy by his colleagues tended to blend skepticism and optimism, with those who opposed him fervently challenging him on particular details and denouncing him with considerable emotion. Yet in the wake of the Tydings investigation, this story began to change. Senators replaced their initial, truncated responses by evolving a more sophisticated set of arguments about the character of the problem McCarthy posed. By stirring the anger as well as the fear of his Senate colleagues, McCarthy appears to have provoked them into articulating an argument that would not merely counteract each of his discrete accusations (he made so many of these that refuting each one was impossible), but would offer a deeper justification of the Senate's essential functions in the constitutional order—oversight and deliberation—and on this basis diagnose the threat McCarthy's demagoguery posed to the Senate as a constitutional institution. These developments are interesting as illustrations of healthy constitutional politics.[125] They are also emblematic of the kind of evaluative argumentation that we are attempting to apply to McCarthy's rhetoric and to political rhetoric in general, and for this reason they are worth considering.

Though the committee investigations issued in no formal punishment of McCarthy, they provided the basis for the backlash against him that gathered momentum in the months and years following. On Monday, August 6, 1951, Senator William Benton of Connecticut introduced a resolution to the Senate calling upon the Rules Committee to investigate "whether or not it should initiate action with a view toward the expulsion from the United States Senate of . . . Joseph R. McCarthy."[126] In response, McCarthy lashed out at Benton publicly, declaring that he had "established himself as a hero of every Communist and crook in and out of government," an allegation he would repeat subsequently in charging two of his Senate adversaries with trying to thwart his "exposure of Communists in the State Department."[127] Then, two days later, McCarthy went a step further, calling a press conference in which he promised to "name names" of specific Communist infiltrators, thereby refuting the charge that he had misled the Senate with his initial allegations. On August 9, however, McCarthy merely repeated the list of names he had previously made public at his February 20, 1950, presentation to the Senate immediately following his Wheeling speech.[128] In response, Senator Ernest McFarland of Arizona elaborated a detailed and explicit argument against McCarthy's rhetorical tactics:

> If any Senator has evidence that any man has committed a high crime, or if he has evidence that any man serving in the Government is disloyal, he has the solemn duty to place that evidence before a proper tribunal. If a court of justice does not act, he has of course the responsibility of placing the evidence before his colleagues. Mr. President, *our forefathers, when they wrote the Constitution of the United States, granted us certain immunity on the floor of the Senate. Why? Because it was their opinion that the Members of this body could always be relied upon never to charge any individual unfairly or unjustly, never tear down his character, or hurt his good name unless compelling evidence against him was in their possession.* Mr. President, just as it is the duty of a Member of the Senate to lay before the proper tribunal or to lay before a court or before this body evidence, he has a like responsibility never to say one word against the good name of an individual unless he has the evidence to support the charge. If he has such evidence, it is his duty to lay it before the Senate at the time he makes the charge against the individual.[129]

By raising this "why" question, McFarland begins to elucidate the deeper reasons for senatorial immunity and its role in the American constitutional system. On the one hand, the principle of due process seems to require that accusations of the kind leveled by McCarthy be made in a court, where evidence can be weighed. Yet as McFarland well acknowledges, matters of national security are not so easily adjudicated within the normal legal system. It is for this reason that the Senate, a lawmaking institution, also has an oversight function that can overlap with and sometimes contest the constitutional terrain of the courts. In making this argument, McFarland indicates that there are conceivable situations in which a member of the Senate might plausibly circumvent the courts and go directly to his or her chamber, as McCarthy did. Key, however, is McFarland's insistence on the additional duties these senatorial powers entail. Senatorial immunity as an institution is, he explains, justified on the basis of a deeper commitment to informational exchange, which is itself necessary for deliberation and oversight. It is not a power to be exploited with impunity but rather a means to constitutional goals, a means that can be used and abused and, for this reason, one that can be evaluated in terms of the higher-order values of the Senate and the regime. McFarland here was glimpsing the kind of constitutional theory that is elaborated systematically by Sotirios A. Barber: "The founding generation did not grant powers to the government solely for the pleasure of seeing them exercised. . . . [C]onstitutional powers [are] forms of such intrinsically praiseworthy practices or states as autonomy, deliberation, and moderation."[130] It is on this basis that McCarthy's rhetoric as a senator was judged by McFarland to be destructive of the ends of the Senate:

> Mr. President, I have sat on this floor and heard one Senator, by innuendo and insinuation, charge a high official of this Government, a man who had served his country for a lifetime with distinction and honor, with being a traitor or a near traitor. Tragically there seems to be no easy way to cope with a situation like that, since to attempt to refute such charges merely dignifies the assertion. There is only one way to meet that kind of conduct and it is to remind Members of their duty and responsibility.[131]

Similarly, on September 21, Senator Benton testified before a Senate subcommittee, contending that "McCarthy's 'pattern of conduct as a Senator' was unbecoming a member of the nation's highest legislative body."[132] Arguments like these constituted the basis of the Senate's eventual censure of McCarthy, which held that the senator "repeatedly abused the [Subcommittee on Privileges and Elections] and its members who were trying to carry out assigned duties, thereby obstructing the constitutional processes of the Senate, and that this conduct of the Senator from Wisconsin, Mr. McCarthy, is contrary to senatorial traditions and is hereby condemned."[133]

In general, demagoguery is a kind of pale imitation of basic empiricism. Any individual can deny an obvious fact or piece of logic explained by another individual, and there is nothing the latter can do except work harder to persuade the former. At a certain point, the individual who fails to be persuaded might plausibly be accused of lying about what they actually know to be the case. Demagoguery trades on a similar logic. It contends that demonstration of a conclusion's validity is unnecessary because its reasons are readily attainable by everyone, and therefore the only people who could possibly be questioning or denying the conclusion's validity are those arguing out of bad faith—that is, those lying about what they know to be the case. According to this logic, bad faith in one's opponents signals an unwillingness to recognize the merits of any argument; in short, it signifies illegitimate recalcitrance. It therefore justifies additional pressure beyond argumentation if the public interest is at stake.

We can see this logic at work in McCarthy's rhetoric. Because the problem of Communism and its solution were obvious and therefore known to everyone, held McCarthy, any individual who questioned or denied these thereby revealed him- or herself as denying what the American people already knew to be true. They thereby confirmed that they were arguing in bad faith—specifically, that they were objecting to McCarthy not out of a genuine disagreement over the merits of the argument in question but on account of perverseness, pigheadedness, or corruption. It was on this basis that he deduced that Communism itself, in the form of a conspiracy, must have been responsible for America's foreign policy.

McCarthy's explanation of what he claimed were the failings of American foreign policy was less a diagnosis of institutional failure than a conspiracy theory. In his fictive rendering of the situation, no political institution, no matter how well designed, could resist the kind of Communist conspiracy he described. For no set of institutions can survive deliberate and concerted subversion, by the institutions' members, of the political regime of which those institutions are a part. In McCarthy's narrative, then, there was no dysfunction in American institutions *as institutions*; the problem was that they had been captured by the wrong people. If you exposed those people and removed them, you would rectify the entire situation without having to change the institutions themselves. Yet because the institutions were already controlled by the conspirators, they were certain to resist investigation and exposure. Exposing the conspiracy would therefore require an uncorrupted leader with absolute power to decide upon the means he regarded as necessary for rooting out the conspiracy. The narrative McCarthy elaborated in his speeches thus served a fictive purpose: justifying and necessitating the kind of leader he was trying to make himself into.

Part of McCarthy's justification for his rhetorical approach was the urgency of the situation he claimed to be facing. The very members of the federal government in charge of the nation's intelligence were those who were most suspected of betraying the nation's interests. McCarthy supported this argument with the true observation that previous cases of treason and infiltration had been exposed. He went a step further, however, by inducing that these cases had been symptomatic of a broader conspiracy, one that would go some distance in accounting for the broader foreign policy decisions which (in McCarthy's judgment) had been unpardonably accommodating to Communist forces abroad.

One might well fault McCarthy for not trying to gather more genuine evidence of conspiracy before going public with allegations of conspiracy. Indeed, the obvious gamble McCarthy took was pretending to have knowledge initially, in the hope that this bluff would enable him to obtain genuine information subsequently. McCarthy's gambit was no doubt fraught with risks—but can we say there was no basis for it given the risk that he was correct?

The question a politician in this situation must confront is why an argument on the merits is insufficient to persuade the public and the government of the position that seems best to the demagogue. Are they misperceiving what the demagogue is perceiving accurately? Are they denying what they know to be true? Or is the demagogue misconstruing and oversimplifying a matter about which legitimate disagreement is possible? The logic of demagoguery—which Churchill articulated in arguing for "every means"—holds that some *additional* insight about the present state of affairs must be espoused in order to move the public and government toward an opinion they would voluntarily adopt if they saw things the way the demagogue does.

In light of this comparison, consider again McCarthy's rhetoric. The very people who, in McCarthy's telling, should have been pressed for answers were those who were shielded from interrogation on account of their top-secret position, and who knew enough about any potential whistleblower in the government to make themselves utterly formidable. How then would one even *begin* an investigative process if the suspected conspirators were precisely those whose jobs shielded them from questioning by the elected branches? Accordingly, though it is reasonable to ask why McCarthy seemingly went in reverse order—going public and *then* looking for information—it is unlikely that anyone in his place would have acquired information had there existed a concerted attempt to resist his efforts on the part of state officials. In this perspective, using demagoguery to apply public pressure seems defensible.

The dilemma this scenario presents is an obvious one, however. If you have no tangible evidence of conspiracy, then with what justification can you initiate hearings on the basis that you have evidence to go on already, hearings whose purpose will be to extract further evidence? And with what justification can you go to the public purporting to have special knowledge—as McCarthy did on countless occasions after Wheeling—so as to pressure other members of the federal government to comply with your investigations? This was McCarthy's point of departure from his more hesitant colleagues in the House and Senate, such as Nixon and Taft. Whereas the latter two may have disagreed just as vituperatively with Roosevelt-Truman foreign policy as did McCarthy, they did not see such disagreement as *itself* constituting the basis for suspicion of conspiracy.

As Tulis argues, "We cannot know that the statesman is not a demagogue, or whether a leader [using demagogic tactics] is not also a statesman, without an account of the purposes and effects of his or her actions."[134] There are a number of ways McCarthy could have given a plausible justification for his demagoguery by supplying an account of its purposes and effects. He could have elaborated an argument for why a government official viewing the political landscape from his standpoint would have had reason to suspect a Communist conspiracy—an argument in which he could have grounded his demagogic rhetoric. Let me conclude this section by sketching some of the rhetorical alternatives available to McCarthy in light of which we might form an evaluation of the rhetorical decisions he in fact made.

McCarthy could have argued that the broader public policy issue—the proper foreign policy toward Communism and Communist nations—had *not* been debated adequately. To make a plausible case in support of this view, he would have had to answer or at least acknowledge and address several lines of questioning that implicate the functionality of the institutions of government. Had past presidents, as commanders in chief of the armed forces, accurately characterized the nature of Communism as a foreign adversary, both to Congress and the public at large? Had they responded to arguments by Congress, the bureaucracy, and members of their own party about potential inadequacies in their characterization? Had Congress used its oversight powers to seek and obtain information, perhaps secret information, that it deemed necessary to make informed judgments about treaties, legislation, and executive appointments relevant to Communism? The conclusion reached by McCarthy after having answered these questions, together with the supporting arguments he would have had to elaborate in defending the conclusion, would themselves have suggested the appropriate rhetorical approach. If his analysis of past deliberations suggested that those deliberations had not succeeded in canvassing an adequate range of views, he would then have faced a range of alternatives. Answering which of these alternatives was best would have depended in large measure on McCarthy's explanation of why the deliberations had malfunctioned in the first place. If they had malfunctioned because the institutions had failed to induce officeholders to articulate their positions, then McCarthy himself might have undertaken to devise and prescribe a scheme of institutional reform. Alternatively, or perhaps in addition, he might have attempted to provoke the debate that never happened but should have.

Senator Huey P. Long and the Concentration of Wealth

> When HUEY LONG in his "share-our-wealth" reply . . . said that 1 percent of Americans own 59 percent of America's wealth, while 4 percent own between 85 and 95 percent of the wealth, we knew he was a liar. We intimated as much, and added that somebody ought to look into this question and get the true figures on American wealth distribution in order to refute the demagogue LONG. . . . The results of that research are now being published in the News. And to the consternation of many people (including ourselves when we first heard of them), the results of that research show that LONG had essentially the correct dope.
>
> —New York *Daily News*, April 11, 1935

Perhaps more than any so-called demagogue in American political history, Huey P. Long's antics and ethical shortcomings have all but eclipsed the merits of his political vision and his statecraft. Surveying the history of demagoguery and populism in the United States, Levitsky and Ziblatt helpfully tabulate the predominant views of the nature of Long's leadership.[135] According to the consensus expressed in these views, Long was a national dictator-in-the-making, perhaps an aspirational fascist, who was prepared to impose the "totalitarian" regime he had established as governor of Louisiana on the country as a whole.[136] Given the moralistic conception of demagoguery that, as we have seen, dominates American political thinking, this consensus is understandable. Long was unusually brazen in his willingness to exploit whatever rhetorical means he anticipated would advance his goals. Relatedly, he lived a lavish lifestyle and was unafraid to display it.[137] This combination of ostentation and opportunism furnished his political adversaries with a handle to manipulate him as they pleased, contemporaneously and retrospectively.

Long was peculiarly attuned to the ways in which context and form render certain modes of communication more or less compelling. Specifically, he was gifted at judging whether complying with or purposely violating rhetorical norms would get his message across to his audience, regardless of whether they were inclined to agree or disagree. Unlike McCarthy—who, as we have observed, possessed a single rhetorical mode that guaranteed success when the political winds were at his back but precipitated his downfall when the winds shifted—Long was a nimble tactician who could self-consciously toggle between different rhetorical forms based on which of them he judged to be most likely to render his message persuasive. In the Senate, this meant that he tended to lean heavily on affect and gesture, on jokes, banter, and direct provocation—even while he was developing a sophisticated argument in response to his critics. Hence, while his relentlessly flamboyant speaking style made him attractive to those who were receptive to his breezy style, it also prevented his many insights from shining through to those in his audiences, especially party and Senate colleagues, whose sense of decorum frequently chafed at Long's indiscretions even though their political commitments in many ways resonated with his.[138] (Long's floor speeches were legendary for their ability to attract risible crows to the Senate galleries, whom the floor manager frequently had to chastise for laughing.[139]) Long was, as a result, easy to fit into the preexisting demagogic mold that had been prepared for him by his adversaries.[140]

Long's underappreciated sophistication does not simply concern his powers as a strategist, either. Some reflection on his three-year tenure as a U.S. senator, especially his speeches on the Senate floor, reveals that Long worked out an unusually thoughtful critique of the American political system, one that was significantly more robust, even searching, than one might suspect based either on what subsequent commentators have said about him or on a fleeting glance at his rhetorical excesses, which did tend to distract attention away from the sophistication of his arguments. The key to Long's particular form of demagoguery is recognizing that his understanding of the American political system and his rationale for deploying rhetoric the way he did went much deeper than commentators have generally acknowledged—but they did not go as deep as they might have gone. On this score, situating Long alongside Powell and McCarthy is particularly illuminating. McCarthy never even tried to supplement his demagoguery by working out a rationale for it; instead, he relied exclusively on the sources of provocation and motivation that bad demagoguery trades on. McCarthy almost perfectly illustrates bad demagoguery. Powell, in stark contrast, recognized the indispensable—yet fundamentally instrumental—role demagoguery would have to play if his diagnosis was to be translated into concrete political reform.

On the spectrum of demagoguery, then, Long falls somewhere between these two. Unlike McCarthy, he did offer a rationale, one that deepened and broadened in response to challenges by his fellow senators and other public officials. In particular, in responding to the deliberative ethos of the Senate, Long came to take ideas and arguments seriously even though his natural inclination may have been to resist them. At the same time, Long's speeches lack argumentative discipline. Too often they ramble, conflating repetition with rigor. All of this suggests that he failed to think through the deepest implications of the positions he took, and that he failed to recognize the sheer radicalness of his commitments and the extent to which they struck even thoughtful defenders of the regime as a rejection of the basic principles of the American political order.

To this end, the question an assessment of Long's demagoguery necessarily raises is whether Long indicated in his public utterances that he understood the radical principles he espoused to be fundamentally incompatible with the principles of the American regime and, as a result, decided that demagogic rhetoric used to advance his principles was nevertheless necessary to save that regime. Or did Long continue to maintain the compatibility of these principles precisely because he had neglected to think through the ways in which they might reasonably seem to be contradictory in the eyes of those in the Senate and the broader public who were inclined to oppose him? My interpretation is that Long occupies a space between these two poles. Though Long went some distance in developing an argument that would justify his Share Our Wealth program, *and* his rhetorical defense of it, by reference to the principles of the American constitutional order, he failed to articulate an understanding of those principles comprehensive and probing enough to justify his use of demagoguery.

A helpful place to begin analyzing Long's leadership is his account of the origins of the Great Depression and, more generally, the sources of economic disturbances that tended to undermine American prosperity. This account reflects a deep ambivalence. On the one hand, Long argued as though the system itself was fundamentally sound, and that it was the morally corrupt individuals who inhabited and ran the system who were at fault. If only elites would voluntarily comply with the rules that they know justice requires, limiting their own greed and embracing the values of solidarity and charity, the system would deliver desirable outcomes for everyone and individuals could enjoy their private property and individual rights in peace and harmony. On the other hand, Long sometimes seemed to fault the system of individual rights and private property itself, arguing that a more communitarian regime in which property was under public control was the only way to achieve justice. Because self-serving, greedy elites responsible for the Depression were merely responding to the goals the system incentivized them to pursue, it was not their morality that was to blame but rather the incentive structures of the regime itself. After all, who doesn't want to get rich? The way to remedy the problem, therefore, is to design a political regime that does not leave the most economically vulnerable behind. Both of these accounts lend themselves to the kinds of cognitively closed rhetorical appeals that I have argued constitute the core of demagoguery, and Long employed both to this end. The crucial question for us is whether there is evidence in his public rhetoric of a more developed diagnosis that would go some distance in reconciling these contradictory arguments.

In a typical Senate floor speech, for example, Long asserted that the fortunes of wealthy businessmen "have not been regularly and honorably acquired in this country . . . [W]hoever tries to guard the existence of these fortunes becomes a statesman of high repute."[141] A statement like this would seem to presuppose the first position—namely, that the system itself is sound but those who happen to be in power are morally corrupt. Accordingly, in this view America's leaders were corruptly betraying the common good in order to serve the interests of the wealthy, by whom they could profit. Along these lines, Long frequently speculated about a conspiracy between party elites, President Herbert Hoover, and tycoons such as John D. Rockefeller and Bernard Baruch: "It was the Hoover-Baruch régime that caused the great disaster to the great works that been done in the six years preceding."[142]

These ideas were given their initial expression in Long's first extended speech to the Senate, in 1932, in which he developed a lengthy allegation that a shady, unofficial "coalition" had emerged in the House and the Senate whose purpose was to secure a tax bill favorable to the country's financial elites:

> You do not have to eat a whole beef to tell when it is tainted. . . . *[T]here never was a more determined fight than is being waged to-day*—silently, under cover, behind the silken veil, and out in front—to keep this tax bill from going into the field of surtaxes and inheritance taxes, that would give the common man of this country a chance, and to give the wealth of this country an opportunity to be distributed among the people of the United States.[143]

The tainted beef analogy was one of Long's favorite tropes, and it is illustrative of the way he wielded demagoguery.[144] Corruption in the political system could be accurately "sensed"—that is to say, inferred—on the basis of minimal empirical evidence. One does not have to eat the entire piece of tainted meat to know it is fundamentally spoiled; by analogy, one does not have to amass neutrally verifiable evidence, to connect all of the proverbial dots, to know that there is a conspiracy among those in power to direct the country's wealth toward themselves.

The tainted beef analogy is tempting politically because it flatters our belief that political knowledge is akin to sense perception, that we can know what is politically right and wrong without having to demonstrate our conclusions in a rationally verifiable way. But what precisely is it that is wrong, or "tainted," in the picture Long is trying to draw? In the 1932 speech quoted from above, for example, Long initially posited a "coalition" or oligarchic conspiracy between financial elites and government officials acting as "the outer guard of Wall Street."[145] But he fairly quickly abandoned this particular line of attack when pressured by Senate majority leader Joseph Robinson to supply actual evidence in support of his charge. Indeed, Robinson's rebuke bears all the hallmarks of deliberative Senate norms:

> Let us not . . . get some hobgoblins started going around. There is no coalition. . . . There will be no coalitions at work. Men of the same mind and thought and idea will probably vote together when the time comes, and others of different views will have the opportunity to vote their views. . . . Of course, we will differ as to details of the tax measure. . . . One of the great things about American life is that Americans differ and have the courage to express themselves. It is only through exchange of views that we are likely to arrive at the right conclusion.[146]

In Long's modified rhetoric in the weeks that followed, we can see the deliberative norms of the Senate and the constitutional system working. One can see them being enforced even more forcefully in an exchange between Long and the president *pro tempore.* Drawing out the theme that Congress is Wall Street's "outer guard," Long went so far as to suggest that the Senate leadership, and specifically Robinson, were actually in the pay of financial elites whose interests they were protecting, that Robinson as a senator represented "every nefarious corporate interest on the living face of the globe." Indeed,

> it is difficult for one to see the evil of the way by which he profits. The Bible tells us that wherever a man's treasure is there is his heart also, and I say to the Senators . . . that when a man comes into the United States Senate without enough clients as a lawyer to make a corporal's guard and winds up representing every big corporate interest in this country—if that does not mean something, what does?[147]

In response, Long was compelled to take his seat in accordance with Senate Rule XIX, the second paragraph of which states: "No Senator in debate shall, directly or indirectly, by any form of words impute to another Senator or to any other Senators any conduct or motive unworthy or unbecoming a Senator."[148]

Long also described the Great Depression as the consequence of an impersonal system that invariably leads to bad outcomes like wealth concentration and inequality. The question is whether Long, like Powell and unlike McCarthy, recognized the disparity between these two explanations: the one emphasizing moralism, the other impersonal forces. One possible interpretation is that Long, like Powell, was purposely injecting what would otherwise have been a complex, impersonal, systemic account of economic depression with a narrative calculated to stir his audiences to action by assigning blame and demanding retribution. Long demonized capitalists, political parties, and governmental institutions like Congress, and he flattered the virtues of the "people" whom these interests had, in his view, betrayed. Unlike Powell, however, it is far from clear how self-conscious Long's moralism was, because his diagnosis of the American regime is bedeviled with sources of serious incoherence. As a consequence, it seems possible that his moralism was both a cause and a consequence of his incoherence, rather than a deliberately deployed tactic designed to supplement an otherwise coherent political argument.

Sometimes, Long would articulate a philosophy of *raison d'état* that made redistribution sound like a matter of mere prudential calculation designed to prevent class conflict and popular revolution. Wealth becomes concentrated in a few hands, and it is no use chastising those who are able to reap the rewards of the system. What is required is steely resolve on the part of clear-sighted statesmen to periodically redistribute wealth in order to restore equilibrium. As Long put it in a Senate speech following Roosevelt's 1932 landslide election, "We do not need to argue about [wealth decentralization]; we have got everything on earth we need except the matter of mechanics. It is merely a matter of mechanics." Note here Long's emphasis of impersonal process ("mechanics") and his deemphasis of human choice ("We do not need to argue"). His implication is that, left to its own devices, the system will undermine itself and that there is no use deliberating with those whose financial interests are at stake in retaining the status quo; they will always resist reform, and rightly so from their perspective. What is needed, therefore, is raw force coupled with prudential calculation.

It is no accident that Long was a great admirer of Francis Bacon's essay on political economy, which he quoted frequently in his Senate and radio addresses. It might seem that appealing to a philosopher of Bacon's stature in a popular speech amounts to a kind of demagoguery in that it involves an appeal to authority. Yet Long's use of the relevant passages coheres with what we might call the "top-down, impersonal" thread of his political thought. Indeed, Long frequently flattered his audiences' desire to become rich and decried that the system had made it excessively hard to do so. He presented himself as the savior of the wealthy rather than their enemy, insofar as he claimed to be saving the system from its own demise. Consider the following passage from a lengthy exchange between Long and majority leader Robinson:

> Mr. President and Senators, what is the class hatred that has been aroused? I am not appealing to class hatred. If I have ever been the friend of the owners of wealth in this country, I am serving them as the greatest friend I have ever been before. . . . [U]ntil they have awakened some morning and have been surrounded by a crowd of men [the wealthy] will never understand that there is no living for the top unless there is a living for the bottom; and when they have been divested of all their properties it will be too late to cry out for what I now advocate for the abyss is yawning for all.[149]

By the same token, Long—echoing the basic arguments of Marx and his followers—portrayed wealthy capitalists as the unwilling abettors of Communist revolution insofar as their rigid resistance to moderate redistribution augmented wealth centralization, thereby providing further credibility to the idea of regime change and collectivization: "I have not undertaken to persecute the rich, but, on the contrary, I have sought to favor them. Their policy is to load the tip until the bottom caves in. They are the everyday working partners of communism."[150] In this view, the core logic of capitalism is sound but the stewards of the system are unwittingly and irresponsibly disregarding the prudential considerations necessary for safeguarding that system. Deeper still, the internal motivations of the system's inhabitants are not responsible for the bad outcome that the system invariably produces: excessive concentration of wealth. The problem is one of imprudence or ignorance, not of moral depravity. Accordingly, because the players in the capitalist game cannot help themselves, the solution to the system's invariable problems is to periodically redistribute that concentrated wealth, lest the polity divide into factions of haves and have-nots, thereby precipitating outright regime change.

For their part, Long's opponents in the Senate interpreted his speech as stirring up class conflict between rich and poor by drawing attention to disparities in wealth that did in fact exist. As Senator Royal Copeland of New York insisted, "This is no time to create dissen[s]ion between the millionaires and those who are in poverty. . . . I think the Senator from Louisiana [Long] is right when he speaks about the unrest prevailing in the country, but we are not allaying that unrest or that distress by calling attention to those distinctions." For Copeland and his like-minded colleagues, the true state of the regime—unrest and massive inequality—had to be suppressed or at least left unarticulated and opaque if the regime was to survive. The health of the regime depended on a certain degree of deception. In contrast, Long justified his rhetorical strategy on the ground that he was trying to remove the very causes of the conflict that would inevitably obtain if radical measures—redistribution—were not adopted to circumvent it. He was advocating for the rights of property owners in a way that they would embrace if they truly understood their own self-interest.

It is unclear whether Long saw Share Our Wealth as a new, sustainable model of political economy that would make the American regime a better version of itself, or rather as a palliative that could temporarily relieve the system's worst consequences but would never remedy the defects at the system's core. To answer this question we must probe Long's understanding of the American regime: what he believed to constitute the essence of the American constitutional order and what he thought a picture of systemic flourishing looked like.

In response to charges of socialism and Communism, Long frequently reiterated that his vision did not entail a departure from American constitutionalism but rather amounted to a vindication of America's true principles and aspirations. "The great and grand dream of America," he proclaimed, "that all men are created free and equal, endowed with the inalienable right of life and liberty and the pursuit of happiness . . . has almost gone out of sight in this day in time." The American people have endeavored "to save the American country to the ideal and purposes of America."[151] But on what grounds should we believe that America's ideals and purposes demand the kinds of radical redistribution Long proposed, rather than some other, less radical mode of restructuring? The question is how coherent was the picture of the American regime he drew. Were his policies tailored to the needs of that regime, or did he tailor his depiction of that regime to the policies to which he was already committed but which he should have been willing to modify in light of contradicting information?

In response to criticisms that construed his proposals as fundamental departures from American principles, Long gradually developed the argument that the notion of radical wealth redistribution is not as alien to the American regime as such criticisms would suggest. Cleverly, he did this by invoking American historical figures traditionally associated with conservatism in order to contend that Americans have not been as opposed to wealth redistribution as the tradition suggests. In a speech to the Senate on March 13, 1933, he justified his proposed redistribution policies on the grounds that he was "going the way Daniel Webster said to go; that Thomas Jefferson said to go; that Abraham Lincoln said to go."[152] Four days later, in a nationally broadcasted radio address, he quoted passages from the speeches and writings of, among others, Jefferson, Lincoln, Webster, and Theodore Roosevelt, all in an effort to substantiate the assertion that the regime's fundamental principles, as expressed in the Declaration of Independence, did not forbid or proscribe the kind of wealth redistribution he was advocating, but rather demanded it:

> In our Declaration of Independence, our immortal forefathers declared it the right of man that all be created equal, and declared it the inalienable right of everyone to share in a government guaranteeing the life, liberty and pursuit of happiness to all. We have forgotten all about that. We have forgotten those guarantees.[153]

It might well be the case, Long's argument would seem to be, that the reigning interpretation of these guarantees favors a radical protection of private property and right to contract, as expressed in the *Lochner*-era opinions of Justices Rufus Peckham and Stephen Field. But it is essential to understand that these are, after all, interpretations, and that the question of what the regime's core guarantees demand in terms of concrete policy remains contestable. Theorists of laissez-faire are entitled to an equal say, but they do not have a monopoly on constitutional meaning.[154]

To this end, Long was proposing an interpretation of these guarantees that would subject the legitimacy of the current distribution of wealth to radical questioning. Long's premise here would seem to be that the crisis occasioned by the Great Depression had necessitated economic measures that would prevent a regime fundamentally committed to individual freedom from being able to minister to the needs that the enjoyment of those freedoms presupposes. By the same token, that crisis had made it necessary for the government and the public writ large to deliberate on a plane of ideas and principles fundamentally different from the *Lochner* regime, which the nation had become accustomed to deliberating on since Reconstruction and the rise of Republican hegemony. Continuing to deliberate on that regime's *interpretation* of the Declaration's fundamental commitments would lead to the obliteration of the constitutional order as a whole: "I am hoping our leadership in the two Houses of Congress will cease to be enamored of the [economically conservative] ideas and principles that wrecked the last part of the Wilson administration and wrecked the Hoover administration." What was needed was a radical reorientation of priorities in the government's deliberations. As Long put it during a debate over President Hoover's budget proposal during the darkest days of the Depression,

> If we adjourn here with this tax bill before us . . . without providing a means for the redistribution of wealth in the United States to-day, and allow this snowball to go downhill two or three more years as it is now . . . [y]ou will have a problem before you that is a great deal bigger than any problem of the Budget of the Federal Government. . . . Yet we are sitting here talking about balancing the Budget.[155]

Accordingly, even though his ultimate goal was to save private property, Long thought it was necessary to argue *as if* the state has absolute discretion to redistribute wealth and to nullify property rights for the sake of the common good, because even if the thought paradigms of private property and individual rights were truer to the system, those same paradigms would never justify the kinds of radical reforms necessary to decentralize wealth and forestall violent revolution, an outcome he was not reluctant to forecast. Indeed, in classic demagogic fashion, Long appealed to his audience's fears by labeling portions of his speeches with subtitles like "The Abyss Yawns for All."[156] Substantively, he sought to mitigate the radicalness of his proposals by prognosticating the radicalness of the consequences of not adopting his proposals.

> Much talk is indulged in to the effect that the great fortunes of the United States are sacred, that they have been built up by honest and individual initiative, that the funds were honorably acquired by men of genius far-visioned in thought . . . *even if they had been that would not alter the case*. . . . Unless we provide for the redistribution of wealth in this country, the country is doomed; there is going to be no country left here very long.[157]

Indeed, several weeks later Long would go so far as to contend that "the Government of the United States, if it falls and when it falls, will owe its fall to the Congress of the United States."[158]

How should we evaluate such hyperbole? Much hinges on the tenability and persuasiveness of Long's predictions. As the regime's lawmaking body, Congress bears responsibility for creating policies that respond to the nation's needs, but the creation of such policies hinges on the ability of members to communicate those needs to each other in a way that issues in legislation adequate to those needs. Similar to Powell's, Long's diagnosis would seem to be that Congress is continuing to deliberate on a set of assumptions about private property and the role of government that can no longer be taken for granted. Like Tocqueville—albeit in a hazier, less theoretically rigorous way—Long seems, according to this interpretation, to have grasped that the kinds of beliefs and arguments that a political order generates are not always the sort that will sustain that political order. Sometimes a regime needs to be injected with a discourse whose principles are likely to seem inimical to the principles of the regime because it needs to be pushed forcefully in the direction opposite to that in which it naturally tends to veer, lest it collapse in the latter direction.

One way of formulating this insight is that the American regime of democratic capitalism, like all other regimes, suffers from a characteristic pathology: a self-generated series of behaviors and discourses that undermine its own integrity. The regime's fundamental commitment is to individual freedom understood as the right to exercise one's private faculties without being dominated or governed without one's consent. Politically, the United States Constitution translates this abstract value into a concrete regime in which citizens are free to pursue wealth and material acquisition and to possess private property with significant limits being imposed on the state's ability to take or interfere with private property. Provisions of the Constitution giving the state the power to seize property are framed as exchanges in which the property owner must be justly compensated, whether through payment or through political representation.[159] In this respect the Constitution differs fundamentally from regimes in which citizens' property is understood as communally owned or as privately owned by a faction, monarch, or dynasty. In such regimes, the fundamental commitment is not to citizens' private faculties but to the needs of the regime, whether the regime is a party, a movement, or a monarch. State interference with and manipulation of citizens' faculties is warranted insofar as it is needed to perpetuate the regime. Accordingly, the logic of the American regime is that giving the state too much latitude to interfere with private property—so the argument goes—would invite non-consensual interference with the private faculties of citizens.

And yet, by liberating citizens to pursue limitless wealth in accordance with certain rules, and then protecting their right to spend that wealth as they please, the system makes it increasingly difficult for citizens to exercise their liberty because it centralizes wealth in the hands of the most ruthless and shrewd. The system loses legitimacy when citizens no longer feel they have a fighting chance to improve their own conditions through hard work and by complying with the rules of the game. Such loss of legitimacy points us back to the regime's fundamental commitment, which is not to private property as such but rather to private property and the pursuit of wealth as bulwarks against domination and as means for exercising one's private faculties. Madison articulates the self-subverting or pathological character of liberal government in *Federalist* #10:

> The diversity in the faculties of men, from which the rights of property originate, is not less an insuperable obstacle to a uniformity of interests. The protection of these faculties is the first object of government. From the protection of different and unequal faculties of acquiring property, the possession of different degrees and kinds of property immediately results; and from the influence of these on the sentiments and views of the respective proprietors, ensues a division of the society into different interests and parties.

By "protecting" human faculties—that is, providing for their exercise through private property guarantees—the system unleashes unequal abilities, thereby precipitating inequalities in wealth and acquisition. These inequalities in turn make it more difficult for individuals to exercise their faculties in the way the regime promises them they can.[160]

The best case that can be made on Long's behalf is that the national government should be understood as having been invested with all the power necessary to meet a crisis that threatens to obliterate the very conditions necessary for individual liberty. But it is reasonable that Long's opponents would have responded—as they did—that his arguments suppressed or at least failed to acknowledge how much discretion would have to be given to the national government over the affairs of ordinary people. If such discretion was to be made legitimate, proportionate evidence would need to be marshaled demonstrating the reality of the threat Long foresaw as well as the severity of the injustice that Long felt much of the public was currently enduring.

Long did not entirely abandon elements of his initially crude allegations of conspiracy and personal corruption on the part of his fellow congressmen, nor did he abandon his suggestion that the fundamental problem of the American system had not been the morals of its overseers but the tendency of the system itself to issue in destabilizing levels of wealth concentration. On this score, Long complied with the Constitution's logic by searching for a more sophisticated set of reasons that would corroborate his initial position regarding the system's flaws. He was convinced that something was wrong from the outset and continued to grope for a rationale that would validate that initial position.

Thus, Long did not dwell myopically on the hypothesis of personal corruption; rather, we see him working his way toward a systemic argument that hinged not on moral judgments, but rather on a neutral evaluation of the American political system's ability to deliver on its commitments to justice and the general welfare. In this respect, Senate norms successfully induced Long to seek a higher plane of reasoning, and Long revealed himself amenable to the system's logic in a way that McCarthy never did. At the same time, Long never produced a diagnosis of the regime as comprehensive and self-conscious as Powell's. Recall that Powell justified his use of non-deliberative rhetoric on the grounds that the hegemonic position of whites in the regime rendered them tone-deaf and therefore irrationally recalcitrant in the face of his insistence that statutory enforcement of civil rights was necessary. This rhetorical disconnect was in turn responsible for the regime's inability to honor its own basic commitments to civil rights. Accordingly, demagoguery was not merely a helpful addition to Powell's strategy; it was rendered necessary by the very structure of the regime itself, which promised equal rights while subverting their realization in practice.

8

Demagogues in the Presidency

Compared to even normal congressional rhetoric, Justice Chase's and Justice Scalia's outbursts seem tame, even stately. Yet in the context of an institution where one's tenure does not depend on successfully winning reelection, and where one is bound only to write the official Court opinions assigned by the chief justice, every additional public utterance outside the normal channels of institutional communication takes on a significance that it would not take on in a legislative assembly.[1] By the same token, a member of Congress who rarely spoke in public or during legislative session would reasonably be seen as abandoning one of their institutional responsibilities.

The presidents I will discuss in this chapter employed very different rhetorical strategies in the context of very different political circumstances. Like Chase and Long, Franklin Roosevelt was speaking publicly and defending his positions and goals during a national crisis whose existence no reasonable person doubted, the Great Depression, and specifically the Supreme Court's rejection of duly enacted legislation Roosevelt felt to be necessary for economic recovery. One can certainly question the appropriateness of Roosevelt's rhetorical attack on the Court, but no one doubts the gravity of the situation Roosevelt was confronting. In stark contrast, Trump, like Scalia and McCarthy, justified his rhetoric with reference to a crisis *whose very existence as a crisis* was controversial: namely, immigration at the Mexican border. Few would maintain that the current regime for handling immigration in the United States is or has been adequate—hence the legislative white whale of "bipartisan immigration reform" that has long occupied policymakers. Yet a dissatisfying policy situation does not necessarily constitute a national crisis warranting provocative—at some points, utterly unprecedented—demagoguery. This is not to say that crises have sometimes gone unrecognized, and that a statesman is well within their duties to sound the rhetorical alarm when public officials and the broader public seem not to understand the gravity of the threat. It is to say that an official who has decided to depart from normally acceptable rhetorical norms on the grounds that a crisis

Demagogues in American Politics. Charles U. Zug, Oxford University Press. © Oxford University Press 2022.
DOI: 10.1093/oso/9780197651940.003.0008

is in need of being met has the responsibility to make a sufficient effort to establish that the problem they are proposing to solve is, in fact, a threat. In Scalia's case, the threat in question—the corruption of the judiciary—was at best debatable; Scalia argued as if the Court had been acting in a way that was obviously illegitimate when there was nothing obvious about his conclusion. McCarthy, as we have seen, made no effort whatsoever to diagnose the crisis he presented himself as the solution to; he assumed the existence of the crisis was established, and demonized anyone who contradicted him as complicit in that very crisis. How should we situate Roosevelt and Trump within this range of possibilities?

Franklin Delano Roosevelt and the New Deal

Franklin Roosevelt has been simultaneously hailed as one of the greatest American presidents and as the president who routed the American constitutional order. His leadership was controversial during his own time and has remained so, with the result that critics of the New Deal and the "imperial presidency" frequently level against FDR accusations of demagoguery, even authoritarianism. For our purposes, Roosevelt is a particularly helpful case because even his most vehement supporters acknowledge the extraordinary character of some of his leadership tactics, including his rhetoric. As I observed in Chapter 1, Erwin Hargrove, who calls FDR "the exemplar of the good leader of the polity," nevertheless acknowledges that the president "used artifice and misleading demagoguery at times," even though he "was not a demagogue or an abuser of power."[2] Bruce Miroff, who calls FDR's leadership during the Depression "impressive" and "a powerful . . . form of democratic political education," similarly faults Roosevelt for at times lapsing into a personalistic rhetorical form that framed issues demagogically in terms not of the common good but of Roosevelt and his personal enemies.[3] Relatedly, Miroff contends that

> there were limitations in the depth as well as the range of Roosevelt's political education. His New Deal discourse was often too fragmented and underdeveloped to serve as a sophisticated guide to democratic citizens. Strongly evocative of moral hope, it was, as James McGregor Burns laments, too "soft and shapeless" when it came to practical action.[4]

Both authors, who espouse a warm regard for Roosevelt, concede that he made use of tactics that one might traditionally associate with demagoguery: "artifice and misleading demagoguery," according to Hargrove, and an excessive reliance on hope and emotion at the expense of coherent argument, according to Miroff.

The question, then, is not so much whether Roosevelt used demagogic rhetoric but, given the unprecedented character of the challenges he faced and the other merits of his presidency, how best to interpret and analyze the way he used it. Were his tactics substitutes for a more robust form of public argumentation, as Miroff and Burns seem to think? An alternative view, which I will suggest here, is that they amounted to legitimate and necessary tools used to gain the attention and engage the minds of a public held in the grip of an unreasonably recalcitrant elite. Like Powell and to some extent Long, Roosevelt recognized that the prevailing public understanding of constitutionalism as it applied to political economy and individual rights stood in the way of the very measures that would be necessary to save the constitutional order, either from collapse or from hostile takeover by authoritarians. It was therefore necessary to introduce demagoguery into his own public discourse so as to provoke the public to deliberate on a set of principles that would make necessary reform, and legitimation of that reform, possible. As Morton Frisch summarized it:

> [Roosevelt's] rhetoric clearly exaggerated the existing state of danger . . . but his intention was to expose the threat to capitalism by exaggerating it. It seems to be clear that Roosevelt recognized and generally exercised moderation. That he wanted at the same time to appeal to popular prejudice is not at all surprising considering the resistance of powerful moneyed interests to his programs and policies.[5]

Or, to use an analogy, Roosevelt confronted an elite and a public that were leaning too far in one direction and that were likely to collapse; he needed to use more force than normal to stand them up straight. The demagoguery he used was that force.

A helpful place to begin studying FDR's approach to constitutionalism during the Depression is the Court-packing plan of 1937. This event will function here as a reference point from which to survey his rhetoric in defense of the New Deal as a whole. Though the details of the plan are familiar to most, it will be helpful to review its most basic features. Most notably, in *A. L. A. Schechter Poultry Corp. v. United States*, 295 U.S. 495 (1936), the Hughes Court invalidated the National Industrial Recovery Act of 1933 under the Commerce Clause and the "nondelegation doctrine," according to which Congress is forbidden by the Constitution from excessively delegating its powers to another entity, including executive agencies. In so doing, the Court sought to bolster the then-reigning public philosophy according to which the federal government is forbidden by the Constitution both from meddling in purely local matters reserved to the states and from excessive coercion of private property by regulating the market.

Unsurprisingly, Roosevelt strongly disagreed with the Court's rulings, though scholars disagree as to his motivations, and they also draw different pictures of the actions he proceeded to take and the public rationale he proceeded to develop. On March 9, 1937, Roosevelt gave his ninth fireside chat, in which he announced his plans to propose legislation to Congress that would add additional members to the Court. Specifically, new justices would be appointed for every current justice who was seventy years or older.

Scholars critical of the plan regard this decision as both unconstitutional and demagogic. Miroff sees the plan as emblematic of FDR's tendency to demagogically construe political disagreements as personal affronts. He quotes the president's infamous statement, given to an audience at Madison Square Garden on October 31, 1936, that "never before in all our history have [the forces of money] been so united against one candidate as they stand today. They are unanimous in their hate for me—and I welcome their hatred."[6] Several days later, Roosevelt would go on to win reelection, and Miroff faults Roosevelt for displaying the personal vices of egoism and aggression: "It was this triumphant figure who, soon after the election, launched his secretive and devious plan to remove the supreme court as an impediment to the New Deal. The court-packing fiasco was the work of a president whose normal political acumen had been supplanted by the overconfidence of the resplendent ego."[7] Miroff bases his charge of demagoguery on the observation that FDR was displaying motivations that are unacceptable for presidents. Similarly, Knott calls the plan "the most damaging and irresponsible event in [FDR's] presidency," arguing that "Roosevelt believed that the failure of the Supreme Court to uphold his New Deal Agenda represented a failure of democracy."[8]

What both of these interpretations have in common is the dual tendency both to diminish the public arguments FDR advanced about the Court-packing plan and how it fit into his broader diagnosis of the American constitutional order, and, by the same token, to emphasize the reasons they suspect to have been motivating the president. For Miroff, FDR was driven by excessive pride and ambition, whereas for Knott it was a simplistic belief that "the wishes of the majority of the public, as expressed through voting, should guide the decisions of the Supreme Court, not the Constitution."[9] But FDR never made such a simplistic claim regarding the authority of the people, nor did he simply wallow in his own egoism. Rather, he developed a sophisticated defense of his actions that was accompanied by demagogic rhetoric of the kind quoted above.

In stark contrast with Miroff and Knott, Frisch contends that FDR saw and argued publicly that the Court was disrupting reform efforts necessary for preserving the very Constitution that the Court claimed to be enforcing. Indeed,

> [Roosevelt's] statesmanship was able to distinguish between preserving rigidly [the American regime's] practices and flexibly its principles. The "Nine Old Men," as the Hughes Court came to be called, saw only

> preserving rigidly these practices and not flexibly these principles. . . . The Hughes Court had argued that the emergency of the depression did not make a difference. Roosevelt argued that the depression did make a difference, but he went further than that. He wanted the Court to understand the various currents and trends prevailing in the country, not so much to simply reflect the changing wants and wishes of the populace, as to direct it toward the preservation of the principles and institutions of government intended to protect the interests of the society as a whole.[10]

Accordingly, one sees this argument on display in the speeches and fireside chats FDR gave in the years leading up to the plan.

Roosevelt opened his ninth fireside chat by reminding his audience of Executive Order 6102 and related legislation authorizing the federal government to purchase gold from private citizens at a statutory price as well as its authority to void gold contracts.[11] In those cases, the Court held for the government in a 5-4 majority, with Justice James Clark McReynolds arguing in his dissent that the government's actions were unconstitutional violations of private contracts.[12] Insisted McReynolds, "We cannot believe the far-seeing framers, who labored with hope of establishing justice and securing the blessings of liberty, intended that the expected government should have authority to annihilate its own obligations and destroy the very rights which they were endeavoring to protect."[13]

Roosevelt began his ninth chat by reminding the public of this narrow decision and by characterizing the minority's view in the following way: "In effect, four Justices ruled that the right under a private contract to exact a pound of flesh was more sacred than the main objectives of the Constitution to establish an enduring Nation."[14] In the minutes that followed, the president developed this initial demagogic repartee—intended to engage the attention of his audience and to make it clear how pressing the subject before them was—into a fully fledged constitutional argument. By dwelling myopically on the sanctity of contracts during a time universally recognized to be one of emergency, argued Roosevelt, the Court was conflating constitutional ends and means; in Frisch's formulation, it was conflating particular norms—for example, the *Lochner*-era convention that gold contracts are inviolable—with the principles or "main objectives" that the Constitution was created to achieve. Indeed, these objectives could be discerned by the fact that the very people who insisted on rigid government absence from business affairs when it accrued to their benefit nevertheless demanded government assistance when "market forces" alone failed them and they thought the government had a duty to come to their aid. As Roosevelt had explained five years before, in the Commonwealth Club Address:

> Some of my friends tell me that they do not want the Government in business. With this I agree; but I wonder whether they realize the implications of the past. For while it has been American doctrine that the government must not go into business in competition with private enterprises, still it has been traditional particularly in Republican administrations for business urgently to ask the government to put at private disposal all kinds of government assistance. The same man who tells you that he does not want to see the government interfere in business—and he means it, and has plenty of good reasons for saying so—is the first to go to Washington and ask the government for a prohibitory tariff on his product.[15]

Pure economic liberty thus fails on its own terms and points toward the architectonic role of the political.

Accordingly, gold contracts should not rigidly be enforced if doing so is likely to jeopardize the very political system whose functioning is the only way to ensure that property can be safely held. In his fireside chat, Roosevelt is elaborating the same point he made in the Commonwealth Club Address: "The issue of government has always been whether individual men and women will have to serve some system of government of economics, or whether a system of government and economics exists to serve individual men and women."[16] In choosing to obtusely enforce a dated scheme of political economy based on *Lochner*-era conceptions of "right to contract" and laissez-faire in the face of changing economic realities, the Hughes Court signaled that it was opting for the former, whereas Roosevelt was trying to make the case for the latter.[17] Specifically, in voiding gold contracts and exchanging gold for currency, the government under Roosevelt and the New Deal coalition was exercising political judgment as to what system of political economy would best vindicate the regime's basic principles.

Rhetorically, Roosevelt began his ninth fireside chat with this particular example to illustrate for the public the extent to which the Court had used a narrow and inflexible construction of the Contracts Clause as an excuse to abdicate its responsibility to enforce the Constitution's fundamental commitment to justice and the general welfare: "There is no basis for the claim made by some members of the Court that something in the Constitution has compelled them regretfully to thwart the will of the people."[18] In the body of his chat, he elaborated this suggestion with reference to contemporary events:

> I hope that you have re-read the Constitution of the United States in these past few weeks. . . . It is an easy document to understand when you remember that it was called into being because the Articles of

> Confederation under which the original thirteen States tried to operate after the Revolution showed the need of a National Government with power enough to handle national problems. In its Preamble, the Constitution states that it was intended to form a more perfect Union and promote the general welfare; and the powers given to the Congress to carry out those purposes can be best described by saying that they were all the powers needed to meet each and every problem which then had a national character and which could not be met by merely local action.[19]

But the framers went further. Having in mind that in succeeding generations many other problems then undreamed of would become national problems, they gave to Congress the ample broad powers "to levy taxes . . . and provide for the common defense and general welfare of the United States."

> That, my friends, is what I honestly believe to have been the clear and underlying purpose of the patriots who wrote a Federal Constitution to create a National Government with national power, intended as they said, "to form a more perfect union . . . for ourselves and our posterity."[20]

This lengthy passage makes clear Roosevelt's serious engagement with the Constitution. It also makes clear that the president did not argue, as Knott erroneously contends, that "the wishes of the majority of the public, as expressed through voting," and "not the Constitution," "should guide the Supreme Court."[21] Quite the contrary; he is developing a reasoned account of the Constitution's powers and purposes that is meant to *contest* the understanding advanced by the Court, particularly its conservative members. Indeed, he is explaining the interpretation of the Constitution that should guide the Court. Indeed, as this passage makes clear, FDR is hardly bowing to majoritarianism; he is advancing the sophisticated Hamiltonian argument that the Constitution is best construed as a vehicle for accomplishing the objectives which a constitutional majority deems necessary and proper to the preservation of the Union and the realization of its core principles through changing economic circumstances. Far from advocating a "living Constitution" devoid of principle and structure, Roosevelt argued for a conception of the Constitution that would protect the regime's values when new threats to those values emerged. Hence,

> where Jefferson had feared the encroachment of political power on the lives of individuals, Wilson knew that the new power was financial. He saw, in the highly centralized economic system, the depot of the twentieth century, on whom great masses of individuals relied for their

> safety and their livelihood, and whose irresponsibility and greed (if it were not controlled) would reduce them to starvation and penury.[22]

Thus, in accord with the Constitution's deliberative ideal, FDR is engaging the Court on the plane of reason by developing an alternative conception of the Constitution's meaning.

Roosevelt elaborates this constitutional rationale with the tangible circumstances of the Depression and the federal government's attempts to combat it clearly in view. Acknowledging that circumstances were as dire in 1937 as they had been in 1933, he insists that measures are needed to fortify the economy against similar events in the future: "The American people have learned from the depression. For in the last three national elections an overwhelming majority of them voted a mandate that the Congress and the President begin the task of providing [a program of protection from events like the 1929 stock market crash]."[23] Especially in a time of crisis, it is significant that these branches are elected—Roosevelt goes on to emphasize "the elected Congress"—because the public is able to choose to staff the government those figures whom it deems most likely to ameliorate its situation.[24]

In contrast, judges are relatively shielded from crisis conditions because they do not have to seek election or reelection—a fact that counts as their virtue as well as their vice. As we have discussed, this grants them more freedom to exercise independent judgment, but it also undermines their credibility during emergencies, when political decision-makers must be unusually attentive to developing circumstances. Courts certainly have the power to review the constitutionality of state action, but by virtue of their institutional design they are well advised to choose carefully the moments in which they exercise that power. To this end, Roosevelt observes:

> The Court itself admitted that it was an extraordinary power to exercise and through Mr. Justice Washington laid down this limitation upon it: "It is but a decent respect due to the wisdom, the integrity and the patriotism of the legislative body, by which any law is passed, to presume in favor of its validity until its violation of the Constitution is proved beyond all reasonable doubt."[25]

In contrast, Roosevelt goes on to note, the modern Court has increasingly disregarded this principle, which is based on a recognition of the Court's own institutional weaknesses, instead "acting not as a judicial body, but as a policy-making body."[26] Further, Roosevelt quotes dissenting opinions from the Hughes Court in support of this very argument: "In the case holding the Railroad Retirement Act unconstitutional . . . Chief Justice Hughes said . . . the majority opinion was 'a departure from sound principles,' and placed 'an unwarranted limitation upon the commerce clause.' In the case of holding the AAA unconstitutional, Justice Stone said of the majority opinion that it was a 'tortured construction of the Constitution.'"[27]

For these reasons, Roosevelt goes on to contend, the Court's decisions in cases like *Schechter* make it clear that it can no longer be trusted to engage with the arguments and proposals of the political branches, which were better positioned to gauge the conditions of the public during a time of national crisis. The Court was exercising powers in a way that did not accord with its role in the constitutional system, and its conservative members had revealed themselves as unwilling to grapple adequately with competing interpretations of the Constitution they claimed to be enforcing: "The Court in addition to the proper use of its judicial functions has improperly set itself up as a third house of the Congress—a super-legislature, as one of the justices has called it—reading into the Constitution words and implications which are not there, and which were never intended to be there."[28]

In light of this diagnosis of constitutional dysfunction, Roosevelt goes on to explain how his plan would remedy the defects of the current state of affairs. As it is currently operating, the Court is a danger both to the broader regime and to itself, for it is threatening to discredit itself as an institution and to invite a reaction more immoderate than FDR's plan: "We have . . . reached the point as a nation where we must take action to save the Constitution from the Court and the Court from itself."[29] Unusual circumstances had made the Court more resistant than it had previously been to the kinds of reforms necessary to achieve the Constitution's basic commitments, and so a reform was necessary to remedy the Court's defect, which, because it resulted in the stymieing of necessary legislation, was a constitutional defect. In order to be restored to a state of normalcy, a reform of the judiciary was needed that would "bring to the decision of social and economic problems younger men who have had personal experience and contact with modern facts and circumstances under which average men have to live and work. This plan will save our national Constitution from hardening of the judicial arteries."[30]

No doubt the president's words here analyzed were fueled and stoked by adversarial and agonistic feelings toward economic elites and toward certain members of the Court. At the same time—and this, as we have been arguing in this book, is the crucial point—Roosevelt was able to translate these feelings into an argument for why the interests of these same elites were, to an important degree, at odds with the common good as he understood it, and his demagoguery was a tactic designed to attract the attention of those who might otherwise have been inclined to dismiss or ignore that argument. His rhetoric was intended to enlist his audience's passions in a way that would make them more likely to engage the ideas he wanted to propose. However, Miroff and to a greater extent Knott sidestep the rationale FDR actually put forward, instead dwelling myopically on his demagogic tactics and the motives they suspect to have generated them. As I have suggested, this kind of misinterpretation is symptomatic of a moralistic conception of demagoguery that causes scholars to search for evidence of moral vice and to ignore counter-evidence.

President Donald Trump and Immigration

One of the arguments I have tried to advance in this book is that an analysis of demagoguery, its uses and abuses, should concentrate on the public statements of constitutional officers in particular and that it should abstract from other aspects of their political conduct. By virtue of the Constitution's commitment to deliberative politics, public officials have rhetorical responsibilities that are related to their other official responsibilities but that can also be analyzed and evaluated separately from those other aspects of their conduct. As a result, a better or worse public defense of state action can, as we have suggested, make the very same state action more or less legitimate; the better an explanation is—in terms of empirical evidence and argumentative rigor—the more likely it is that the public will be able to evaluate that action on the merits and decide whether the official who ordered or undertook it deserves to continue to hold the public trust.

Like his presidential campaign, Donald Trump's presidency was extraordinary and shocking on multiple levels. Trump broke precedents that most observers had forgotten even existed, and even his staunchest defenders, such as Charles Kesler, readily concede that the president violated norms, though these defenders argue that bad or useless norms deserve to be broken and thereby open up a different set of questions.[31] Regardless of how one answers these questions—and we will contest the answers Kesler gives in due course—Trump poses a unique problem for students of the presidency: of the many lenses one might examine him through, which is the most important and illuminating?

Given the endless ways in which all aspects of his official conduct might be analyzed and evaluated—his impeachments, his nominations, his relations with other parts of the government, his relations with foreign leaders, and so on—focusing on his rhetoric, in particular, promises to narrow the scope of the inquiry and, as a result, to improve the quality of the evaluation. Yet here, too, there are difficulties, for the sheer number of public statements Trump has made poses a problem of its own. By any objective measure, *which* of his public statements—including tweets, rally speeches, and off-the-cuff remarks—are most emblematic of his presidency? Is there a non-arbitrary way to read his discourse as a whole, given his torrential rhetorical output? These questions have presented themselves in each of the cases we have examined so far, and the inquiry on which they are based remains an open-ended one: how do you select public statements to examine in a way that avoids overwhelming one's reader while at the same time bringing out the true character of the rhetoric in question?

In trying to resolve this difficulty with respect to President Trump, I have continuously asked myself: which of Trump's public utterances would his most intelligent defenders point to as most illustrative of his presidential rhetoric as a whole? The question is useful for multiple reasons. First, it helps avoid the very pathology that we have been describing throughout this book—namely, the tendency of scholars operating within a moralistic conception of demagoguery to select only those actions and utterances that serve to damage and discredit the case in question (the pathology of weaponization). In contrast, we have tried to find evidence of a broader rationale accompanying or underlying public statements that, taken on their own and out of their broader discursive context, might seem indefensible. Thus, for example, Antonin Scalia's provocative and demagogic dissents in cases like *Lawrence* and *Obergefell* make more sense, and are more plausible, when read in light of his essay defending his conception of the Court. This is the case even if—as we argued—that essay only goes so far (and perhaps not nearly far enough) in establishing a sufficient justification for those dissents. We have adopted the same approach in the case of Trump.

Second, and more significantly, Trump's intellectual defenders do not dispute the unprecedented character of his rhetoric. Indeed, they embrace it precisely because, according to them, rhetoric like Trump's was the very thing needed for comprehensive reform given the corruption sustained by the American regime.[32] In this view, the state of the country before Trump both justified and necessitated a rejection of traditional presidential norms and, by the same token, an embrace of purposely disruptive discourse.

This argument is all well and good, because it at least establishes a baseline for discussion: Trump's rhetoric is singular, and the question is whether there is a sufficient warrant for it. However, the question I pursue here—which is the question I have pursued in each of the previous case studies—is not whether *someone else* can offer a rationale for the constitutional officers in question (e.g., a public intellectual or a think tank) but whether there is evidence of a coherent defense offered by the officers themselves. Does the official develop a coherent defense of their own use of demagoguery, and if so, what is the character and quality of that defense?

In an insightful review of Victor David Hanson's *The Case for Trump*, John Judis poses a question that many scholars and commentators have asked as well:

> [Trump's] language was brutal, crude and sometimes racist or xenophobic, but in contrast to some of his opponents, he acknowledged the loss of more than two million manufacturing jobs to Chinese competition, the propensity of American companies to move abroad in search of lower wages and the continued difficulty of policing the country's southern border. But the question is: What as president has he done about these things?[33]

This is an important question, but it obscures a more constitutionally significant question and the one we will try to clarify in the pages that remain. Regardless of what President Trump did or tried to do about the problems Judis articulates, how did he explain those problems to the public in a way that might legitimize the actions he judged necessary to solve them? Did he adequately demonstrate them *to be* problems—in the way that Powell demonstrated structural racism to be a problem and Franklin Roosevelt demonstrated the Court's approach to the Great Depression to be a problem? The question is central because those who would defend the part of Trump's rhetoric that was most on display and that attracted the most attention—what Judis calls his "brutal, crude and sometimes racist or xenophobic" language—seem to think that the problems Trump was facing did not just excuse but rather justifies such language. But how was the public to know that Trump's approach was the best one and that a superior, less disruptive and offensive approach could not achieve the same or superior outcomes? What was Trump's own rationale for this language, which everyone—supporters and critics alike—acknowledges to be extraordinary for a sitting president? How could the public know them to be problems warranting such rhetoric, and not just take it on faith (as Joseph McCarthy wished them to do), unless the president himself supplied a rationale that could, in principle, persuade a member of the public not already committed to supporting the president? How, in short, was the public to know that Trump's demagoguery was not simply gratuitous, and that Trump himself was not a bad demagogue entirely lacking a plausible rationale?

Too often, Trump's supporters argue—as did Joseph McCarthy—that the president's demagoguery was clearly justified because of how obviously good and necessary his actions were and would be. Like McCarthy, they speak as if the merits of those actions were not debatable and open to legitimate contending interpretations; instead, they maintain a non-verifiable position according to which the virtues of Trump's actions were understood by everyone in the community who counts and which therefore did not require external validation and scrutiny. Hanson, for example, cites Trump's withdrawal from the Paris climate accords and the Iran nuclear deal, his approach to Europe and China vis-à-vis trade policy, and his decision to move the U.S. embassy to Jerusalem as "*undeniably* impressive."[34] Is there really no room for denying that these were impressive, for suggesting they were problematic, and for making the case for alternatives? Again, as Judis helpfully puts it, "except for detailing Trump's success in boosting the economy, Hanson does not argue these points against obvious objections. . . . [M]any of the things Hanson cites as 'undeniably impressive' need justification, at least if Hanson intended his book to be read by people who don't already agree with its bald assertions."[35]

It is one thing for Trump's supporters to offer demagogic defenses of his actions. After all, as we have argued, private citizens should not be held to the same rhetorical standards as public officials. But for those who actually possess the power of life and death over their fellow citizens, for those who hold the public trust, it is not enough to assume that their election entitles them to do whatever they please during their term, and to speak as though everyone in the community whose opinion counts agrees that his or her actions are the correct ones. They are obligated to present reasoned arguments to the public, framed in terms of the general welfare, for why everyone in the community should, in principle, be persuaded of the merits of their conduct. This is by no means to say that everyone will be persuaded—the state could not act if this were the bar that had to be met. Rather, the standard against which presidential rhetoric must be judged is how far the president goes in developing a case for his or her actions that does not appeal to private, non-verifiable evidence or logic and, relatedly, that does not presuppose consensus.

Immigration and the U.S.-Mexico border implicate some of the most important elements of Trump's presidency. As policy issues, immigration and border security touch upon each of the core elements of Trump's politics: white identity, economic protectionism, national security, foreign isolationism, and sovereignty.[36] In addition, Trump engaged in a lengthy public stand-off with the Democratic Party, the federal government, and elements of his own administration over his handling of asylum seekers and his proposed border wall—a stand-off that witnessed some of his most shocking rhetorical displays. Trump's rhetoric on the southern border is a particularly helpful site for studying his presidential rhetoric generally.

On January 25, 2017, five days after his inauguration, President Trump issued Executive Order 13767, "Border Security and Immigration Enforcement Improvements," which, among other things, directed the Department of Homeland Security to begin building a wall along the U.S.-Mexico border.[37] Of course, Trump had begun publicly demanding a border wall well before his presidency, stating at his June 16, 2015, presidential campaign announcement: "I will build a great wall—and nobody builds walls better than me, believe me—and I'll build them very inexpensively. I will build a great, great wall on our southern border, and I will make Mexico pay for that wall. Mark my words"—a claim he would continue to make in subsequent months. On December 25, 2015, for example, he tweeted: "When will the Democrats, and Hillary in particular, say 'we must build a wall, a great wall, and Mexico is going to pay for it?' Never!"[38] The executive order, however, was the first state action he undertook to put this demand into action as president.

Roughly two years after announcing Executive Order 13767, Trump precipitated a thirty-five-day federal government shutdown by refusing to sign a spending bill unless it appropriated $5.7 billion to fund construction of the wall.[39] Trump's willingness to take this controversial and politically costly action testifies to the centrality of the wall, and immigration generally, in his presidency. Accordingly, Trump's rhetorical campaign for the wall during this time showcased his particular understanding of presidential rhetoric.

Paradoxically, Trump based his case for the border wall on the rationale that a wall was necessary given existential threats posed by immigration to national security and sovereignty, while at the same insisting that building the wall was already authorized by existing statutes. Specifically, Trump asserted in his executive order that

> although Federal immigration law provides a robust framework for Federal-State partnership in enforcing our immigration laws—and the Congress has authorized and provided appropriations to secure our borders—the Federal Government has failed to discharge this basic sovereign responsibility.[40]

This assertion gives the impression that the emergency Trump was describing and purporting to solve in proposing the wall was less a matter of responding to an emerging crisis, one that would justify immediate executive action and subsequent evaluation by Congress and the courts, and more a matter of simply rectifying maladministration—as if the government had simply failed or refused to execute the orders that had been given to it and spend money that had been appropriated for that specific purpose.[41]

Trump appears to have been forced into making this conspiratorial argument because the basic details of the situation he faced failed to line up with the sense of urgency he had brought to bear on it in previous public remarks. He could not plausibly frame border insecurity as a sudden emergency requiring immediate action because the border and immigration more generally had been a policy issue for years preceding his election; legislation funding a border fence—which Trump claimed to be merely enforcing—had been passed a decade earlier by the George W. Bush administration.[42] Because he could not plausibly frame the border as a new problem requiring sudden action, he instead had to argue as if the Obama administration had simply thwarted the public's will as regards border security.

This argument is demagogic on two fronts. It makes it sound as if a further rationale for the dramatic new project being proposed was unnecessary because the government had already deliberated on, and the public had already given its consent to, the wall's construction. Second, it was an attempt to shift blame for the government's failure to pass immigration reform from the fact that immigration was and had been a complex and controversial policy debate onto the Obama administration, which Trump accused of having refused to comply with a policy debate that had in fact been resolved. Trump was trying to radically simplify the causes of the current situation vis-à-vis immigration and border security, both by dismissing the ways in which parties could reasonably disagree over what that situation required and by speaking as if a public consensus already existed—a consensus shared by those among the public who supported him and constituted his "base." By the same token, Trump, like McCarthy, insisted that criticism of his positions and of himself did not need to be contradicted or verified because it was illegitimate, having originated with critics arguing in bad faith. Trump would go on to encapsulate this demagogic approach in a Fox News interview on July 1, 2018, asserting of those who had criticized his immigration policies: "I hope the other side realizes that they better just take it easy. . . . They better just take it easy because some of the languages, some of the words you—even some of the radical ideas, I really think they're very bad for the country."[43] In accord with paradigmatic demagoguery, Trump proceeded to connect his defense of cognitive closure—i.e., that views he identified with himself could not be legitimately verified with reference to competing evidence or arguments—with an attempt to discredit and delegitimate his political adversaries, maintaining that "some of the things said [about me and my policies] are terrible. And, you know, it's our people are so incredible. . . . You know, there's probably never been a base in the history of politics in this country like my base."[44]

Relatedly, by issuing the executive order within several days of his inauguration, Trump appears to have been attempting to capitalize on the impetus he felt his unexpected election had given him, spearheading the wall by means of unilateral executive action so as to avoid becoming stymied in the Congress, courts, and bureaucracy. By issuing an executive order instead of proposing legislation to Congress, Trump was trying to create the impression that the wall neither *required* new legislation nor was a crisis that could *wait* for legislation. The fact that he was acting so precipitously through executive order demonstrated the urgency of the situation. More precisely, the order was a means of artificially expressing, rather than a means of actually addressing, the "emergency" character of border security.

Consider that, like McCarthy, Trump reversed the relationship between symbol and symbolized. As we observed in Chapter 5, McCarthy effected this reversal by means of a purely symbolic and allusive use of evidence—his infamous "dossiers," which, as props in his demagogic pageant, functioned as substitutes for verifiable evidence. Whereas normally the trappings of evidence (dossiers) would be of consequence insofar as they contained genuine evidence—thereby relating to genuine evidence as symbols—McCarthy sought to give the symbols *themselves* purchase. He sought to modify the medium of exchange, with the result that symbolized, non-verifiable evidence would replace genuine, verifiable evidence as the currency in which he traded with his audience. For his part, Trump sought to achieve the same effect by issuing an executive order instead of trying to develop legislation, which would have amounted to a tacit acknowledgment that the situation was normal and non-urgent. According to the normal relationship between symbol and symbolized, the executive order would be symbolic of the situation's genuine urgency, which would have made the order necessary. Instead, Trump had to create a sense of urgency where one did not actually exist; to do this, he used the symbol itself—the order—to create an artificial sense of emergency.

In subsequent days, it became clear that Trump's initial strategy had failed to achieve this because it had failed to persuade those it needed to. His attempt to frame border wall construction as simply a matter of executing existing legislation was undercut by the basic fact that, Trump's executive order notwithstanding, there existed no funds to spend—a fact congressional Republicans immediately raised.[45] Nevertheless, in the days following these objections Trump continued to speak publicly as though the wall were a fait accompli, asserting at the Conservative Political Action Conference, "We're going to build a wall, don't worry about it. We're building the wall. We're building the wall. In fact, it's going to start soon. Way ahead of schedule, way ahead of schedule," and announcing four days later, "President Trump signed an Executive Order to get work started on a southern border wall"—as if the executive order alone, in the absence of a public explanation by the president and congressional action, were sufficient to justify and implement the wall's construction.[46] Relatedly, he continued to release statements to the effect that in building the wall he would simply be enforcing statutes that previous administrations had failed or refused to enforce. On June 28, 2017, for example, he released a statement titled "President Donald J. Trump Taking Action Against Illegal Immigration," which asserted that "for too long, politicians across the country have failed to enforce the immigration laws already on the books."[47]

On October 8, 2017, Trump tacitly acknowledged this failure when he sent a public letter to both houses of Congress—"President Donald J. Trump's Letter to House and Senate Leaders & Immigration Principles and Policies"—discussing new legislation he believed to be necessary to increase border security.[48] Despite his having spent the previous months attempting to construct a border wall without new legislation by means of executive order, Trump accused "the previous Administration" of bypassing "the Congress and grant[ing] DACA benefits unilaterally. These actions threatened Congress's status as a coequal branch of Government and have resulted in a surge of illegal immigration."[49] Two months later, in an effort to reignite a sense of urgency around the immigration debate, Trump began his weekly address with the words "Help me, Dad." Continued the president:

> Those were the last words spoken by Kate Steinle as she lay dying on a San Francisco pier—a precious young American woman killed in the prime of her life. Kate's death is a tragedy that was entirely preventable. She was shot by an illegal alien and a 7-time convicted felon who had been deported five times—but he was free to harm an innocent American because our leaders refused to protect our border.[50]

Trump's message was that the pathos of this particular anecdote rendered his solution to immigration—a border wall—non-debatable and non-negotiable. As he contended near the end of his announcement, "People can have different views on the technical details of budget policy or transportation, but no one who serves in elected office should disagree that our highest priority must be the safety and well-being of our nation's citizens."[51] Taken on its own, there is little to find fault with in this statement. The problem is that Trump conflated his own particular conception of "safety and well-being"—the border wall he was using the above anecdote to advocate for—with the broader idea of safety and well-being that *is* debatable and that does not necessarily entail a wall.

In the months and weeks leading up to the midterm elections and budget deadline of 2018, Trump continued to emphasize that the border remained a crisis in need of an immediate solution. On November 1, he released a statement, "Confronting the Urgent Crisis at Our Border," in which he asserted, "Our country is facing an urgent crisis as illegal aliens stream across our border, including a caravan of thousands heading here at this moment," and that "every single Senate Democrat supports an open-borders bill that would effectively grant amnesty to any alien within 100 miles of the border as long as they arrive with a minor."[52] As the December 20 deadline grew closer, Trump continued to present the border wall as the only tenable solution and therefore non-negotiable, with the result that Senate Appropriations Committee chairman Richard Shelby stated publicly in the first week of December that he had doubts "about ever reaching a compromise on the Department of Homeland Security spending measure, which provides funding for the wall and the Trump administration's immigration enforcement efforts."[53]

In subsequent weeks, Shelby's prognostication was borne out. The government shut down on December 22 because Congress refused to include Trump's requested $5 billion for the border wall. In response, Trump went public trying to exert rhetorical pressure. On January 7, according to an article in the *New York Times*, he claimed that "his predecessors have secretly confided in him that they should have done [built a wall] themselves. The only problem: All of the living presidents [Carter, Clinton, George W. Bush, and Obama] say that's not true."[54] The next day, in a national address, "On the Crisis at the Border," Trump claimed as a justification for building the wall that "every week, 300 of our citizens are killed by heroin alone, 90 percent of which floods across from our southern border"—even though a 2018 report from the DEA states that most of the heroin in the United States enters through legal ports of entry (that is, not the unregulated border).[55] Notwithstanding legitimate criticisms such as these, which would seem to require mollification and moderation on the president's part, Trump proceeded to single out Senate minority leader Chuck Schumer (D-NY) for "repeatedly support[ing] a physical barrier in the past, along with many other Democrats." Nevertheless, Trump asserted, "they changed their mind only after I was elected President." This remark had the effect of reducing the policy debate over the merits of a wall—one about which legitimate disagreement is certainly possible—to a private vendetta that congressional Democrats allegedly held against Trump. While elements of this accusation were certainly true, Trump seemed to be unaware of the consequences that his demagogic campaign for a border wall likely had on his ability to negotiate a settlement favorable to him. Indeed, the very strategy Trump initially adopted—announcing border wall construction via executive order—gave the impression that the president did not require congressional action in the first place. And, as we have seen, rather than calling on Congress to deliberate on a set of principles regarding border security, Trump relentlessly claimed that a border wall as he envisioned it was the only feasible option—a claim unlikely to be welcomed by a legislature whose constitutional responsibility it is to develop the content of legislation.

In attributing personal malice to congressional Democrats, rather than elaborating the merits of his own proposal in contrast with Democratic alternatives, Trump framed the policy disagreement in question in terms of an argument that cannot be contested. In this picture, Democrats are portrayed as being entirely resistant to reason, where in fact it was Trump himself who relentlessly claimed that reasoned debate over border security was no longer possible and that his opponents were denying what everyone already knew—or as he asserted in his address: "This barrier is absolutely critical to border security. It's also what our professionals at the border want and need. This is just common sense."[56]

Donald Trump's defenders have suggested that the president's acknowledged demagoguery was simply the spearhead of a legitimate reform effort based on a comprehensive diagnosis of the American regime. If the president's own public utterances are the basis of this interpretation, I would conclude on the basis of this chapter that this is a significant distortion. Regardless of his personal intentions, Trump's public campaign for a border wall began with the assertion that deliberation of immigration policy was unnecessary and culminated in the claim that Democrats were opposing construction not because they disagreed with the policy, but because they wanted to thwart Trump personally. At no point during this rhetorical campaign did Trump publicly search for deeper sources of potential agreement or acknowledge the possibility of a superior border solution. Far from serving an instrumental and therefore plausibly legitimate role in some broader, debatable program for political change, Trump's demagoguery functioned as a substitute for such a program; he used it to compensate for the absence of a genuine rationale.

Scholars have emphasized Trump's personal character as the most important component of his presidency and rhetorical style. Knott faults Trump for lacking magnanimity, and Alan Wolf contends: "The true tragedy of 2016 may well be not that people were ignorant of what Trump would do once president but that they lacked sufficient people skills to realize what kind of man he really was."[57] This book has attempted to establish the relative importance of public behavior, particularly public explanations and critiques of state action, over the moral dispositions of public officials. Accordingly, I believe that there is more to be gained in terms of political and constitutional evaluation from emphasizing Trump's inability to translate his own motives and ambitions—however low they might have been—into non-demagogic public justifications than there is from trying to discern the character of the motives themselves. At the risk of sounding trite, Trump's rhetoric speaks for itself, and there is no particular need to demonstrate whether his rhetoric is the consequence of moral depravity because the quality of his rhetoric alone is sufficient to confirm his inability to explain his own commitments and to engage those of others. Rather, Trump's character matters insofar as it seemed to prevent him from being able to see outside and beyond the myopic lens of his own demagoguery. This might not be the case; Trump might simply have been choosing to use demagoguery relentlessly, and he might have been voluntarily withholding a sophisticated rationale. But for our purposes, Trump, unlike practitioners of good demagoguery like Powell and FDR, gave no indication that he possessed such a rationale, and this fact is central in our analysis.

To glimpse how this makes Trump unique, consider that other similarly ambitious presidents and public officials from American history—from Richard Nixon to Andrew Johnson—have recognized that their own view of things would be insufficiently persuasive unless they framed it with reference to the common good (that is, in a way that could be corroborated independently of themselves and their own "base").[58] Demagogues like Trump and McCarthy, on the other hand, have appeared either unable or unwilling to do just this. Regardless of their motives for failing to do so, their public speech alone constitutes sufficient evidence for categorizing them as bad demagogues.

9

An American Pathology

When I first began work on this project in 2017, shortly after the election of Donald Trump, I hoped the book I would eventually write could serve to both diagnose and correct a profound misunderstanding of the nature of demagoguery and its role within the American constitutional system. My goal was to help us all, scholars and citizens alike, to think more critically about demagogic leadership, without making any strong claims about its causes or consequences—claims I felt myself unprepared to defend.

In many ways, I still feel myself unprepared to adequately defend claims of this kind. And yet, as I neared completion of the book, I began sensing the importance and urgency of questions that were well beyond its original scope. Having interrogated so many studies of political leadership that I regarded as misguided, even foolish, I began to wonder about the relationship between these studies and their subjects. The anecdote with which I begin this book is a perfect example of the phenomenon I am describing. How could a publication as sophisticated as the *New York Times* run an opinion piece equating the rhetorical style of Theodore Roosevelt with the rhetorical style of Donald Trump? During Trump's second impeachment, how could the president's lawyers argue, straight-faced, that a sitting president deserves the same First Amendment protections as someone who shouts racial epithets at a neo-Nazi protest, or burns a cross on the lawn of an African American family?

In light of ludicrous judgments like these, I came to believe that it was precisely the misunderstanding of demagoguery that I had tried to confront and refute in this book that bears responsibility for some of the worst instances of demagoguery we have been experiencing in recent years. Paradoxically, an understanding of democratic politics that regards demagoguery as necessarily evil, as a practice to be castigated wherever it occurs and ultimately banished from the community, becomes the cause of the very thing it wishes to obliterate. Demagoguery is an American pathology, and we have become a community of demagogues because we claim to hate demagoguery.

Demagogues in American Politics. Charles U. Zug, Oxford University Press. © Oxford University Press 2022.
DOI: 10.1093/oso/9780197651940.003.0009

Defending this thesis adequately would be an undertaking far beyond the scope of the present book, so I will not dwell on it at length here. Instead, I will offer only a brief sketch of my reasons for believing it, in the hopes that others interested in demagoguery—in addition to the constellation of political ideas related to it—will join me in the future, both as collaborators and as interlocutors, in my attempt to better understand these ideas.

As I have tried to show in the preceding pages, today the overwhelmingly predominant view of the American founding and the Constitution it produced is that the American political system is designed to suppress all exercises of popular leadership, regardless of the merits of the political causes those exercises might be used to advance. (Relatedly, many today believe that the Constitution is purely procedural and that it is fundamentally unconcerned with the quality of political outcomes—an assumption that is revealed by those who claim that the Constitution's Preamble is irrelevant to constitutional reasoning.) In this perspective, the American founders were elitists who regarded popular appeals as beneath respectable politicians, and who therefore believed it was possible to create a system of government that was both republican in character and capable of realizing its self-stated goals without involving the public through popular appeals in any meaningful way. Incidentally, many who espouse this view also claim to be great admirers of the American founding. It is all the more bizarre, then, that these self-proclaimed partisans of the founding will readily concede that, with a few notable exceptions, the American political system that the founders produced has never actually operated the way they claim it was originally intended to; almost immediately, American politics became more "popular" than it had been at the time of the founding. In this perspective, Jefferson, Jackson, Teddy Roosevelt, and Franklin Roosevelt—often regarded as some of America's greatest statesmen—are instead depicted as corruptors of the American political tradition, as unprincipled demagogues who flagrantly abandoned their constitutional responsibilities, because they supposedly employed popular leadership that threatens the integrity of the founders' constitution. Calvin Coolidge, scholars of this persuasion tell us, was a greater constitutional statesman than FDR.[1]

For those who hold this view of the American regime, regardless of whether they admire it or loathe it, the implication of their understanding is that the U.S. Constitution is essentially irrelevant to politics as it is practiced today, because demagoguery and popular leadership have become a routine part of ordinary politics. (A similar view is held by those who believe the Constitution is irrelevant for political practice today because the so-called administrative state has all but obliterated the original Constitution.)[2] For those who understand the Constitution this way, the architecture of the American regime offers little, if any, guidance for understanding and assessing political practice today; we have no way to make principled, constitutional judgments in a political world dominated by demagoguery. In short, the Constitution was made for a lost political golden age that vanished as quickly as it appeared. Consequently, either our politics today requires a wholly new set of standards for evaluating political leadership (standards that have yet to be articulated), or it simply defies all evaluation—everything goes.

Paradoxically, then, it is the belief that a public within a regime based on public consent could ever dispense with the need to exercise discretion and judgment in cases of demagoguery that might itself bear responsibility for the proliferation of truly indefensible demagogues. Cultivating a public aversion to demagoguery—teaching the public that demagoguery is evil, that it has no place whatsoever in the system we inhabit—appears at first to be the best way to manage demagoguery's excesses. Instead, by teaching us that everything resembling demagoguery is off-limits and beyond the pale of our politics, it sets us up for failure and fills us with collective hopelessness as we look out into a world marked by demagoguery—the very thing our regime is supposedly incapable of dealing with.

My overarching goal in this book has been to demonstrate that not all cases of demagoguery are equal, that demagogues can become constitutional in that they can be recruited to advance constitutionally enjoined ends. Demagoguery can be good or bad in the same way that democracy can be good or bad, because the same normative force that legitimates democracy also legitimates demagoguery; the two are inextricable, and our only choice is to face demagogues soberly. This book is a model for doing just that.

NOTES

Chapter 1

1. Philip Terzian, "Trump's Rhetoric Has Precedent," *New York Times*, December 10, 2019. I thank Gary Jacobsohn for this reference.
2. Terzian, "Trump's Rhetoric."
3. Terzian, "Trump's Rhetoric."
4. On Trump, see David A. Graham, "The President Who Doesn't Read," *The Atlantic*, January 5, 2018, https://www.theatlantic.com/politics/archive/2018/01/americas-first-post-text-president/549794/. On Roosevelt, see, e.g., "Books by Theodore Roosevelt," Critics Rant, https://criticsrant.com/books-by-theodore-roosevelt/. Roosevelt also wrote numerous essays and kept a lengthy correspondence; some of this has been published in book form: "Books Written by Theodore Roosevelt," Theodore Roosevelt Center at Dickinson University, https://www.theodorerooseveltcenter.org/Research/Digital-Library/Record.aspx?libID=o274790. For an account of Roosevelt's understanding of how his presidential leadership related to American founding principles, see Jeffrey K. Tulis, *The Rhetorical Presidency*, 2nd ed. (Princeton, NJ: Princeton University Press, 2017), 95–116.
5. For examples of this view, see, e.g., James Fenimore Cooper, "On Demagogues," in *The American Democrat* (Indianapolis, IN: Liberty Classics, 1981); Reinhard Luthin, *American Demagogues* (New York: Beacon Press, 1954), 3; Allan Nevins, "Foreword," in Reinhard Luthin, *American Demagogues* (New York: Beacon Press, 1954), xv; V. O. Key, *The Responsible Electorate* (Cambridge, MA: Harvard University Press, 1968), 2 (demagogues, writes Key, are defined as those "who have championed intolerance, who have stirred the passions and hatreds of people, or who have advocated causes known by decent men to be outrageous or dangerous in their long-run consequences. No functionary is more repugnant or more arrogant than the unjust man who asserts, with a color of truth, that he speaks from a pedestal of popular approbation"); Michael Signer, *Demagogue* (New York: Palgrave Macmillan, 2009); Steven Levitsky and Daniel Ziblatt, *How Democracies Die* (New York: Penguin, 2018); William Howell and Terry Moe, *Presidents, Populists, and the Crisis of Democracy* (Chicago: University of Chicago Press, 2019).
6. Consider, for example, Patricia Roberts-Miller's suggestion that demagoguery can be used for the sake of virtuous ends, in *Rhetoric and Demagoguery* (Carbondale: Southern Illinois University Press, 2019), 3–4. Nevertheless, Roberts-Miller chooses to focus exclusively on bad instances of demagoguery in her case studies.
7. Erwin C. Hargrove, *The President as Leader* (Lawrence: University Press of Kansas, 1998), 77.
8. Hargrove, *The President*, 85. Works in which the authors are aware of this tension include James W. Ceaser, *Presidential Selection* (Princeton, NJ: Princeton University Press, 1979); James W. Ceaser, "Demagoguery, Statesmanship, and Presidential Politics," in *The Constitutional Presidency*, edited by Joseph M. Bessette and Jeffrey K. Tulis (Baltimore: Johns Hopkins

University Press, 2009); Tulis, *Rhetorical Presidency*; Jeffrey Tulis, "The Rhetorical Presidency in Retrospect," in *The Rhetorical Presidency in Retrospect*, edited by Jeffrey and Shterna Friedman (London: Routledge, 2012); James Darsey, *The Prophetic Tradition and Radical Rhetoric in America* (New York: New York University Press, 1997); Roberts-Miller, *Rhetoric and Demagoguery*; Steven R. Goldzwig, "A Social Movement Perspective on Demagoguery," *Communication Studies* 40 (1989): 204.

9. A note on the scope of this inquiry: Though I focus on the particulars and peculiarities of the American constitutional experience with demagoguery, my method of analysis—examining rhetoric in light of both the substantive values and the procedural design of a constitutional democracy—could in principle be applied to other political regimes. Accordingly, how to think about demagoguery would differ among regimes insofar as their principles and designs differed from one another.
10. Jan-Werner Müller, *What Is Populism?* (Philadelphia: University of Pennsylvania Press, 2016); Kas Mudde and Cristobal Rivera Kaltwasser, *Populism: A Very Short Introduction* (Oxford: Oxford University Press, 2017); Margaret Canovan, "Trust the People!," *Political Studies* 47, no. 1 (1999); Nadia Urbinati, *Me the People* (Cambridge, MA: Harvard University Press, 2019). Though not scholars of populism per se, Rogers Smith in *This Is* Not *Who We Are!* (New Haven, CT: Yale University Press, 2020) and William Galston in *Anti-Pluralism* (New Haven, CT: Yale University Press, 2017)adopt more or less the same approach to the concept of populism as do the abovementioned authors.
11. Roberts-Miller, *Demagoguery*.
12. For her part, as noted above, Roberts-Miller does hold out the possibility that demagoguery can be good, though her work spends significantly more time describing the deleterious effects of demagoguery on public discourse. She also suggests that human communication and interaction are necessarily (i.e., unavoidably) demagogic insofar as drawing any kind of intelligible distinction between groups and organizations with competing goals and interests requires placing people in "in-groups" and "out-groups." To use a contemporary idiom, it would therefore seem that for Roberts-Miller demagoguery is a feature, not a bug, of political life. Yet for precisely this reason, one begins to question the analytical purchase of a concept that every aspect of politics appears to fit into. For Roberts-Miller, what in the political is *not* demagoguery?

    In contrast, Jennifer Mercieca in *Demagogue for President* (College Station: Texas A&M University Press, 2020) suggests that Donald Trump's rhetoric can and should be studied in an impartial, dispassionate way, even though it strikes many listeners as troubling. I take a similar approach to demagoguery in this work, though whereas Mercieca is interested in explaining the political effectiveness of certain demagogic tropes, my goal is to show how the American constitutional system can be leveraged to evaluate and judge the rhetorical leadership of public officials.
13. Jeffrey K. Tulis and Nicole Mellow, *Legacies of Losing in American Politics* (Chicago: University of Chicago Press, 2018), ch. 2.
14. E.g., Sotirios Barber, *Constitutional Failure* (Lawrence: University Press of Kansas, 2014); Jeffrey K. Tulis, *Congressional Abdication* (forthcoming).
15. Sotirios Barber calls this understanding of the American political system the benefits theory of American constitutionalism. See his *Welfare and the Constitution* (Princeton, NJ: Princeton University Press, 2003).
16. My understanding of the history and development of "party government" out of traditional political practices toward parties is based on Russell Muirhead's *The Promise of Party in a Polarized Age* (Cambridge, MA: Harvard University Press, 2014).
17. There is, of course, a robust scholarly debate about the limits of "the freedom of speech" in the American constitutional context, as well as the meaning of "speech" itself (e.g., Donald Downs, *Nazis in Skokie* [South Bend, IN: University of Notre Dame Press, 1985]). For my purposes here, I lean on the broad scholarly and legal consensus that pure speech (as opposed to symbolic speech) about political issues deserves the strongest constitutional protections.
18. My normative understanding of the American constitutional system sketched here is based on the deliberative-democracy approach to American politics as developed by Joseph Bessette in *The Mild Voice of Reason* (Chicago: University of Chicago Press, 1994) and Amy Gutman

and Dennis Thompson in *Why Deliberative Democracy?* (Princeton, NJ: Princeton University Press, 2004). For an alternative to Bessette's reading of the Constitution, see Jeremy Bailey, *James Madison and Constitutional Imperfection* (New York: Cambridge University Press, 2015).

19. Winston S. Churchill, *The Second World War* (Boston: Houghton Mifflin, 1948), I:231.
20. Churchill, *Second World War*, I:231.
21. Churchill, *Second World War*, I:225–226.
22. Churchill, *Second World War*, I:ix.
23. Barack Obama, *A Promised Land* (New York: Crown, 2020), 240–241.
24. I thank an anonymous reviewer for helping me see this connection.
25. The best summary of this methodology to my knowledge is Mariah Zeisberg's in *War Powers* (Princeton, NJ: Princeton University Press, 2013), 51: "I use comparative case studies not to investigate empirical variation, but to address a methodological dilemma of normative work: setting a standard of assessment."
26. Respectively, Dana Farrington, "Read: Trump's Impeachment Defense Brief," NPR, February 8, 2021, https://www.npr.org/sections/trump-impeachment-trial-live-updates/2021/02/08/965412514/read-trumps-impeachment-defense-brief; "Trial Memorandum of the United States House of Representatives in the Impeachment Trial of President Donald J. Trump," February 2, 2021, https://judiciary.house.gov/uploadedfiles/house_trial_brief_final.pdf.
27. E.g., Bob Bauer, "A President's Words Matter," *Lawfare*, September 27, 2017, https://www.lawfareblog.com/presidents-words-matter-deception-public-and-impeachable-offense.
28. As far as I am aware, relatively little has been written on free speech as it applies to the state as opposed to private individuals. Helen Norton's thought-provoking *The Government's Speech and the Constitution* (New York: Cambridge University Press, 2019)argues that the speech of government officials can constitute a violation of the rights of the public. This claim, while certainly innovative, differs fundamentally from my own, which is that government speech can constitute a violation of the principles and norms that should guide the conduct of public officials. For Norton, the victims are individuals whose liberties have been violated, whereas for me the victim is the whole community as structured and defended by the Constitution.
29. Editorial Board, "Justice Ginsburg's Inappropriate Comments on Donald Trump," *Washington Post*, July 12, 2016.
30. Tulis, *Rhetorical Presidency*, chaps. 1 and 2.
31. Tulis, *Rhetorical Presidency*.
32. Address by Justice Samuel Alito, 2020 National Lawyers Convention, November 12, https://fedsoc.org/conferences/2020-national-lawyers-convention?#agenda-item-address-8.
33. E.g., Barber, *Welfare and the Constitution*.
34. My interpretation of the American regime is inspired by Herbert J. Storing, *What the Anti-Federalists Were For* (Chicago: University of Chicago Press, 1981); Zeisberg, *War Powers*; Tulis, *Rhetorical Presidency*; and Tulis and Mellow, *Legacies*.
35. Bessette, *Mild Voice*.
36. My aim is not to elucidate the political philosophy of the founders per se but rather to understand their reasons for designing the institutions they did, with a view to developing the best possible critique of and rationale for those same institutions (irrespective of how the founders understood them). In this regard, I follow the methodology of Sotirios A. Barber in *On What the Constitution Means* (Baltimore: Johns Hopkins University Press, 1984) rather than that of Thomas Pangle in *The Spirit of Modern Republicanism* (Chicago: University of Chicago Press, 1987).
37. From here on, "American founders" and "founders" refers to those among the founding generation who made the most sophisticated contributions to American political and constitutional thought. For discussion of this methodology, see Storing, *What the Anti-Federalists Were For*; Tulis and Mellow, *Legacies*.
38. See esp. *Federalist* #71.
39. I emphasize "relatively" because there exists a robust debate over the extent to which the American founders cared about the development of moral and civic virtue in citizens.
40. The text of the Massachusetts constitution can be found here: http://www.nhinet.org/ccs/docs/ma-1780.htm.

41. The text of the Pennsylvania constitution can be found here: https://avalon.law.yale.edu/18th_century/pa08.asp.
42. I would like to thank Russ Muirhead for helping me see the relationship between demagoguery and the Constitution in this light.

Chapter 2

1. E.g., Michael Signer, *Demagogue* (New York: Palgrave Macmillan, 2009), chap. 2.
2. To reiterate a point from Chapter 1, I by no means assume that the American founders shared a consensus about demagoguery; rather, there was considerable disagreement within their ranks about this subject, among many others. The aim of this chapter is to highlight those utterances by a certain few founders—most prominently, Madison and Hamilton—that best serve to clarify the difference between classical and modern understandings of, and proposed solutions to, demagoguery. In my reading of then, Hamilton and Madison's writings offer the best guide for understanding the Constitution we actually got in 1787.
3. Consider Aristotle's typology of democracies according to which the worst type, the most participatory (type 5), is also the most beset with demagoguery, whereas the best type is one in which "the best citizens lead" and there is no demagoguery. Aristotle, *Politics*, 1291. See Thomas L. Pangle, *Aristotle's Teaching in the Politics* (Chicago: University of Chicago Press, 2013), 178.
4. For helpful accounts of how classical political theory was designed to shape citizens' capacities for political judgment and thereby educate them for responsible civic engagement, see Jill Frank, "The Political Theory of Classical Greece," in *The Oxford Handbook of Political Theory*, edited by John S. Dryzek, Bonnie Honig, and Anne Phillips. (New York: Oxford University Press, 2008), 175–192); Matthew Landauer, "Democratic Theory and the Athenian Public Sphere," *Polis* 33, no. 1 (2016): 31–51.
5. Xenophon, *Memorabilia* 3.6.1. The translation is my own.
6. E.g., Mogens Herman Hansen, *The Athenian Assembly in the Age of Demosthenes*, translated by J. A. Crook (Norman: University of Oklahoma Press, 1999).
7. For a discussion of this obsession, see Plato, *Gorgias*.
8. See Leo Strauss, *The City and Man* (Chicago: University of Chicago Press, 1964), 23. According to Strauss, Aristotle denounced "the sophists' reduction of politics to rhetoric. So far from being 'Machiavellians,' the sophists—believing in the omnipotence of speech—were blind to the sternness of politics."
9. Jeffrey K. Tulis, *The Rhetorical Presidency*, 2nd ed. (Princeton, NJ: Princeton University Press, 2017), 31–32.
10. Devin Stauffer, *The Unity of Plato's Gorgias* (New York: Cambridge University Press, 2006), 23.
11. Carnes Lord, "Poetry and the City: An Interpretation of Aristotle's *Poetics*," PhD diss., Cornell University, 1972.
12. My aim in the following discussion is not to canvas the full range of classical understandings of rhetoric and demagoguery (an endeavor far beyond the scope of this inquiry), but rather to use carefully chosen examples as a way to spotlight a set of conceptual alternatives that help us understand what the U.S. Constitution's originators were rejecting—both wittingly and unwittingly—when they designed the constitution they did. Relatedly, I do not purport to explain how the American founders understood the classical theorists whose understandings of demagoguery I am describing here, but rather how their approach to demagoguery as embodied in the Constitution differs from classical alternatives on a conceptual level.
13. Strauss, *City and Man*; Aristotle, *Nicomachean Ethics*.
14. This interpretation of ancient philosophy is disputed, of course, some scholars arguing that politics was more central in the classical philosophers' concerns. For an outline of the debate, see Leo Strauss, *The Rebirth of Classical Political Rationalism*, edited by Thomas L. Pangle (Chicago: University of Chicago Press, 1989).
15. Stauffer, *Unity*. Of course, the *Gorgias* is not Plato's only treatment of rhetoric; in the *Republic*, Socrates proposes banning poets and sophists from the city. I choose to highlight the *Gorgias* here because it serves as a helpful illustration of the Socratic approach to rhetoric in the context of real-world politics.

16. Stauffer, *Unity*, 177–179.
17. Stauffer, *Unity*, 181–182.
18. Aristotle, *Nicomachean Ethics*, Book X. See also Plato, *Gorgias*.
19. Aristotle, *Rhetoric*, 1355a 10–15. All translations are quoted from Lord, "Poetry."
20. Aristotle, *Rhetoric*, 1355b 10–15.
21. Lord, "Poetry."
22. Aristotle, *Rhetoric*, 1355b 13–14.
23. Lord, "Poetry."
24. Aristotle, *Rhetoric*, 1354a 27–28.
25. Lord, "Poetry," 54.
26. Aristotle, *Rhetoric*, 1355b 14.
27. Plato, *Gorgias*, translated by W. R. M. Lamb (Cambridge: Harvard University Press, 1967), 452e 1–5.
28. Leo Strauss, *Thoughts on Machiavelli* (Chicago: University of Chicago Press, 1954).
29. Hobbes, *Leviathan*, xv: "The writers of moral philosophy, though they acknowledge the same virtues and vices; yet, not seeing wherein consisted their goodness, nor that they come to be praised as the means of peaceable, sociable, and comfortable living, place them in a mediocrity of passions: as if not the cause, but the degree of daring, made fortitude; or not the cause, but the quantity of a gift, made liberality." See also Devin Stauffer, *Hobbes' Kingdom of Light* (Chicago: University of Chicago Press, 2019).
30. David Lowenthal, "Montesquieu," in *The History of Political Philosophy* (Chicago: University of Chicago Press, 1987).
31. Leo Strauss, *Natural Right and History* (Chicago: University of Chicago Press, 1953), 202–251.
32. Machiavelli, e.g., *The Prince*, chap. 15. For a helpful discussion of how Machiavelli understood professions of good, see Harvey C. Mansfield Jr., "Machiavelli's Enterprise," in *Machiavelli's Legacy* (Philadelphia: University of Pennsylvania Press, 2015).
33. This is by no means to deny that Machiavelli regarded rhetoric as an import tactic within political life that astute leaders will, for this reason, happily avail themselves of for the sake of realizing their goals. Rather, it is to say that from a normative standpoint Machiavelli would advise both princes and members of the public to adopt a skeptical, rather than a credulous, posture toward political rhetoric; and, by the same token, to focus more on what leaders are doing than on the reasons they offer for why they are doing it. I am grateful to Devin Stauffer for urging me to clarify my position on this point.
34. Russell Muirhead, *The Promise of Party in a Polarized Age* (Cambridge, MA: Harvard University Press, 2014), chap. 2. Muirhead's argument is an interpretation and elaboration of Aristotle's in the *Politics*.
35. Machiavelli, *The Prince*, chap. 3; Thomas L. Pangle and Timothy W. Burns, *Key Texts of Political Philosophy* (New York: Cambridge University Press, 2015), 177–179.
36. Perhaps the paradigmatic example of such a figure for Machiavelli is Savonarola, who appears to have possessed enough charismatic magnetism to attract an enthusiastic following and to effect a temporary disruption in Florentine political norms, but insufficient political wherewithal to achieve lasting reform or to preserve his own base of power. Consider *The Prince*, chapter 6: "[Brother Girolamo Savonarola] was ruined in his new orders as soon as the multitude began not to believe in them, and he had no mode for holding firm those who had believed nor for making unbelievers believe." *The Prince*, Harvey C. Mansfield, Jr., trans. (Chicago and London: University of Chicago Press, 1998), 24.
37. Bryan Garsten, *Saving Persuasion* (Cambridge, MA: Harvard University Press, 2006), chapter 1.
38. Normatively, it is important in a constitutional democracy that these alternatives be elucidated by those who actually hold power, and that these individuals not just assume that important arguments about politics will be hashed out in the media and by the general public. Because officeholders have actually been invested by the public with decision-making authority, they owe the public an explanation, not of what is motivating them personally when making a decision (which is ultimately irrelevant) but of why a member of the community ought to feel him- or herself bound by that decision and ought to believe it was the right one.

39. For an elucidation of this conception of the general welfare, see Sotirios A. Barber, *Welfare and the Constitution* (Princeton, NJ: Princeton University Press, 2003).
40. *The Federalist* #1.
41. *The Federalist* #1.
42. *The Federalist* #6.
43. Max Farrand, *The Records of the Federal Convention of 1787*, 3rd ed. (New Haven, CT: Yale University Press, 1911) 1:432. See also James Madison's letter to John G. Jackson from December 28, 1821, suggesting that many members of the convention had been excessively influenced by the idea that Shays and demagogues like him constituted the fundamental threat to the Union. For Madison, the truly fundamental threat was not demagoguery but repressive and unresponsive political institutions that resulted in popular turmoil: "The necessity of such a Constitution was enforced by the gross and disreputable irregularities which had been prominent in the internal administrations of most of the States. Nor was the recent and alarming insurrection headed by Shays in Massachusetts, without a very sensible influence on the public mind . . . This view of the crisis made it natural for many in the Convention to lean to a higher toned system than was perhaps in strictness warranted by a proper distinction between causes temporary as some of them doubtless were, and causes permanently inherent in popular frames of Government." See also Jeremy Bailey, *James Madison and Constitutional Imperfection* (New York: Cambridge University Press, 2015), ix.

Chapter 3

1. For a helpful discussion of Hamilton's understanding of experience and its role in his political science, see Clement Fatovic, "Reason and Experience in Alexander Hamilton's Science of Politics," *American Political Thought* 2, no. 1 (Spring 2013): 1–30.
2. Consider Johann N. Neem, "The Elusive Common Good: Religion and Civil Society in Massachusetts, 1780–1833," *Journal of the Early Republic* 24, no. 3 (Autumn 2004): 381–417. The 1780 Constitution of Massachusetts, Article III, reads: "As the happiness of a people, and the good order and preservation of civil government, essentially depend upon piety, religion and morality; and as these cannot be generally diffused through a community, but by the institution of the public worship of God, and of public instructions in piety, religion and morality: Therefore, to promote their happiness and to secure the good order and preservation of their government, the people of this commonwealth have a right to invest their legislature with power to authorize and require, and the legislature shall, from time to time, authorize and require, the several towns, parishes, precincts, and other bodies politic, or religious societies, to make suitable provision, at their own expense, for the institution of the public worship of God, and for the support and maintenance of public Protestant teachers of piety, religion and morality, in all cases where such provision shall not be made voluntarily. And the people of this commonwealth have also a right to, and do, invest their legislature with authority to enjoin upon all the subjects an attendance upon the instructions of the public teachers aforesaid, at stated times and seasons, if there be any on whose instructions they can conscientiously and conveniently attend." See https://malegislature.gov/laws/constitution.
3. Of course, the most memorable discussion of this phenomenon by the founders is in *Federalist* #10.
4. David Szatmary, *Shays' Rebellion* (Amherst: University of Massachusetts Press, 1980), 66.
5. Consider also Signer's widely read discussions of Donald Trump as demagogue: https://www.michaelsigner.com/articles. Signer also argues that Trump's demagoguery is ultimately responsible for the 2017 Charlottesville violence: see "Michael Signer: The Charlottesville Mayor Who's Now in the National Spotlight," CNN, August 14, 2017, https://www.cnn.com/2017/08/14/politics/who-is-michael-signer-charlottesville-mayor/index.html.
6. Michael Signer, *Demagogue* (New York: Palgrave Macmillan, 2009), 79.
7. Louis Hartz, *The Liberal Tradition in America* (New York: Mariner, 1991), 53, 68, 70–78; Louis Hartz, "The Problem of Political Ideas," in *Approaches to the Study of Politics*, Roland Young, ed. (Evanston, IL: Northwestern University Press, 1958), 82.
8. Leonard D. White, *The Federalists* (New York: Greenwood, 1948), 2.

9. Gore Vidal, *Homage to Daniel Shays: Collected Essays, 1952–1972* (New York: Random House, 1972).
10. Joseph Bessette, *The Mild Voice of Reason* (Chicago: University of Chicago Press, 1994), 14.
11. "Daniel Shays," http://shaysrebellion.stcc.edu/shaysapp/person.do?shortName=daniel_shays.
12. *The Emerging Nation* (Washington, DC: National Historical Publications and Records Commission, 1996), 416n4.
13. Jeffrey K. Tulis, *The Rhetorical Presidency*, 2nd ed. (Princeton, NJ: Princeton University Press, 2017), 28.
14. "Proclamation 5598—Shays' Rebellion Week and Day, 1987," https://www.reaganlibrary.gov/research/speeches/011387b.
15. George R. R. Rivers, *Captain Shays: A Populist of 1786* (New York: Little, Brown & Co., 1897), v–vi.
16. Leonard Richards, *Shays' Rebellion* (Philadelphia: University of Pennsylvania Press, 2002), 163–164.
17. Ray Raphael, *Founding Myths* (New York: New Press, 2004), 82.
18. Robert J. Taylor, *Western Massachusetts in the Revolution* (Providence, RI: Brown University Press, 1954), 157. See also Richards, *Shays*, 26, 164.
19. As Szatmary explains, an older generation of historians located responsibility in economic or class tensions between contending elements in Massachusetts society (consider, e.g., Richard B. Morris, *The Forging of the Union, 1781–1789* [New York: Harper and Row, 1987]; Sidney Kaplan, "Veteran Officers and Politics in Massachusetts, 1783–1787," *The William and Mary Quarterly* 9, 1 [January 1952]: 29–57; Taylor, *Western Massachusetts*). These studies tended to be mostly impersonal in approach, and had little to say about particular figures on either side, such as Daniel Shays. Szatmary, by contrast, sees the insurgency through the lens of clashing social patterns or ways of life: "I will locate the roots of the insurrection in a clash between a traditional, agrarian way of life and an ever-encroaching commercial society" (*Shays*, xiv), which leads him to make interesting though only brief and occasional references to Shays (*Shays*, 92–100). Szatmary's approach suggests that the positions taken and the decisions made by individual leaders of the insurgency is of some though ultimately peripheral significance for understanding the movement. Gross, Richards, and Condon, while attending to all aspects of the movement, pay greater heed than do the aforementioned scholars to the political contestations that were at work in it. Accordingly, they place greater emphasis on the roles of particular leaders. As Gross acknowledges, "The disorders in Massachusetts ought not to be regarded narrowly in political or socioeconomic terms. They can tell us a great deal as well about the changing culture and society of post-Revolutionary New England. To that end, we have to shift the focus from the issues of the insurrection to the diverse personalities who brought it forth." *In Debt to Shays*, Robert A. Gross, ed. (Charlottesville and London: University Press of Virginia, 1993), 298.
20. Szatmary, *Shays*; Sean Condon, *Shays' Rebellion* (Baltimore: Johns Hopkins University Press, 2015).
21. See https://www.law.gmu.edu/assets/files/academics/founders/Mass-Constitution.pdf. See also Richards, *Shays*, 5.
22. Szatmary, *Shays*, 39.
23. Richards, *Shays*, 7; Szatmary, *Shays*, 38–42.
24. Richards, *Shays*, 7.
25. Richards, *Shays*, 6.
26. Richards, *Shays*, 5.
27. Richards, *Shays*, 6; Marion Lena Starkey, *A Little Rebellion* (New York: Knopf, 1955), 74.
28. Szatmary, *Shays*, 39. Condon (*Shays*, 48) says fifty of the *fifty-eight*.
29. A consortium of scholars claim that "it was at this point [July and August 1786] that Daniel Shays emerged as one of the local leaders of the protest movement. Shays met with other local men at Conkey's Tavern in Pelham, where they discussed their situation and what could be done in the face of the government's lack of interest in constitutional reforms or debtor relief policies." Though the latter statement is meant to provide evidence in support of the former, neither would seem to be warranted: no citation of primary or secondary sources is

provided. "Daniel Shays": http://shaysrebellion.stcc.edu/shaysapp/person.do?shortName=daniel_shays

30. Starkey, *Rebellion*, 73.
31. Richars, *Shays*, 4–8. Condon and Szatmary say nothing as to Shays' role in these initial events.
32. Richards, *Shays*, 8. The petition summarized the farmers' criticisms of government economic policy and regressive tax policy, as well as "defects" in the undemocratic state constitution ("Article 19," in George Richards Minot, *The History of the Insurrections in Massachusetts* (Worcester, MA: Isaiah Thomas, 1788), 35. Oddly, Richards says there were twenty-one (*Shays*, 8). The *Essex Journal* of September 13, 1786, listed twenty-five. Additionally, Minot (*Insurrections*, 34–36) lists twenty-five, as does Condon (*Shays*, 49).
33. See Condon, *Shays*, 48–49; Richards, *Shays*, 8–9. Richards notes that "among the delegates present were John Hastings, Hatfield's representative to the state legislature; Benjamin Ely, West Springfield's former state representative; and William Pynchon, the eminent voice of Springfield's most powerful family" (8). Shays is nowhere mentioned.
34. Richards, *Shays*, 8.
35. Richards, *Shays*, 9, 166n8; cf. Condon, *Shays*, 49–50.
36. Condon, *Shays*, 49.
37. Szatmary, *Shays*, 74.
38. Starkey, *Shays*, 74. Parmenter's quote actually says: "I told them it was inconsistent after *what* we had agreed to petition." C. O. Parmenter, *History of Pelham, Mass: From 1738 to 1898, Including the Early History of Prescott* (Amherst, MA: Carpenter & Morehouse, 1898).
39. Starkey, *Shays*, 74.
40. Starkey's quotation is slightly misleading. Taken from C. O. Parmenter, the quotation occurs in a conversation between Daniel Shays and General Rufus Putnam, which the latter subsequently reported to Governor Bowdoin. In context, it is clear that Shays is responding to Putnam's question: "Is it a truth that you did not order the men to march to Springfield the other day?" (Parmenter, *History*, 397, my italics). Shays is justifying his behavior at the second Springfield closing, not at the Northampton closing of August 29. Though Starkey concedes that Shays "said this much later and in a much different context," she nevertheless insists that "the remark explains his inactivity in August" (*Rebellion*, 74). Again, though plausible, Starkey presents as certain what is at best her own inference. Shays might well have agreed with the actions of the selectmen in August but decided to wait to take part for strategic reasons. By the same token, his statements to Putnam in January may have been retrospective justifications that did not accurately reflect what took place at the time. Regardless, the fact is that we simply do not possess sufficient evidence of what took place to say, as Szatmary attempts to do, what Shays' "motives" and "convictions" were. Taken together with the fact that Starkey—author of what *Choice* magazine called "the standard work on" Shays' rebellion—includes neither notes nor in-text citations in her monograph, such unwarranted conclusions regarding Shays illustrate one way in which retrospective inferences and attributions have, even among scholars, sustained unwarranted narratives about Daniel Shays.
41. Richards, *Shays*, 10.
42. Richards, *Shays*, 11.
43. A portion of the proclamation reads as follows: "Whereas this high-handed offence is fraught with the most fatal and pernicious consequences, must tend to subvert all law and government; to dissolve our excellent Constitution, and introduce universal riots, anarchy and confusion, which would probably terminate in absolute despotism, and consequently destroy the fairest prospects of political happiness, that any people was ever favoured with, and which this people will realize, if they do not suffer themselves to be misguided by the machinations of internal real enemies, who treacherously assault the character of their best and most zealous friends." "Hampshire Gazette, September 1786": http://www.historic-northampton.org/members_only/gazette/1786-09.html.
44. As Condon puts it, "For Bowdoin, many of the current disturbances were the result of 'wicked and artful men' who were convincing people either to oppose the government or to not get involved to actively protect it. If such men were allowed to operate, they would continue to weaken and ultimately "destroy all confidence in Government" (*Shays*, 65).

45. "Acts and Resolves Passed by the General Court," https://archive.org/details/actsresolvespass178687mass.
46. Condon, *Shays*, 65.
47. Condon, *Shays*, 54–55, 140n54; Starkey, *Rebellion*, 52–56.
48. Condon, *Shays*, 55.
49. Starkey, *Rebellion*, 76; cf. Condon, *Shays*, 59.
50. Starkey, *Rebellion*, 76–77; Condon, *Shays*, 59.
51. Joseph Parker Warren, "The Confederation and the Shays Rebellion," *The American Historical Review* 11, no. 1 (1905): 42.
52. Historians are unclear as to the circumstances of his arrival. Whereas Minot claims he actually led the regulators to Springfield (*Insurrections*, 47), Condon remarks that he was only "seen as one of the leaders of the regulators" (*Shays*, 60, my italics). On the basis of these facts, the only plausible reason for asserting Shays was perceived as a leader is that he took charge of a meeting with General Shepherd, who had been sent to guard the courthouse. Oddly, the latter cites Richards (*Shays*), who says nothing about how Shays was perceived by his contemporaries at Springfield. Specifically, Condon cites Richards (*Shays*, 5–7); but these pages only discuss the July 18, 1786, meeting at Pelham.
53. Condon, *Shays*, 60; Starkey, *Rebellion*, 81.
54. Condon, *Shays*, 61.
55. Parmenter, *History of Pelham*, 395.
56. Putnam had no personal incentive to distort Shays' statement here. He had been sent to interview Shays by Bowdoin, who, as his above statements make clear, wanted the man blamed and punished. If anything, Putnam's interview weakened Bowdoin's rationale in this regard.
57. *Rebellion*, 75.
58. *Rebellion*, 76–77.
59. An article in the September 30 issue of the *Massachusetts Centinel*, a pro-commerce Boston newspaper, contained the following brief though pejorative report of Shays' role in the Springfield closing: "The insurgents were led on by one Shays, a deranged officer of the late army, a Captain Day, and several others of the same stamp; the desperation of whose circumstances had ripened them for scenes of pell mell havock and confusion." No justification is offered for calling Shays "deranged," nor are any details offered concerning how he exercised leadership. Accordingly, two weeks after the events of September 26, his reputation appears still not to have made itself known to the chief British ambassador in the United States, Consul-General John Temple. On October 4, Temple wrote in an official dispatch: "At this hour, I have undoubted Intelligence that at Springfield . . . more than 1,500 Men in Arms are there assembled to stop the proceedings of the Courts of Justice" (Sir John Temple to Lord Carmarthen, October 4, 1786, in *Emerging Nation*, 325). Similarly, Peter Allaire, a prominent British loyalist from New York, noted the event in the October 5, 1786, entry in his private journal, but said nothing about Shays (Peter Allaire, "Occurrences from 7 September to 4 October 1786," in *Emerging Nation*, 326).
60. Henry Knox, writing to George Washington a month later (October 23) regarding the events in Massachusetts, makes no mention of Shays. See *The Papers of George Washington: Confederation Series*, edited by W. W. Abbot (Charlottesville and London: University Press of Virginia, 1992), 4:299–300.
61. *The Papers of John Adams* (Cambridge, MA: The Belknap Press of Harvard University Press, 2016), 509.
62. Representatives met at Paxton in Worcester County, Dracut in Middlesex, and Plymouth in Bristol.
63. Condon, *Shays*, 65–67.
64. Starkey, *Rebellion*, 83. Though she cites no evidence for this claim, it seems plausible. For the next two months, from the Springfield closing in September until the closing of Worcester Court on December 5, Shays largely drops out of the historical record, though the period was much diversified by event. On October 20, the Confederate Congress officially responded to the developments in Massachusetts by passing a law ostensibly raising troops to fight Native Americans, but actually preparing an army to suppress the Massachusetts insurgents (see

Warren, *Confederation*). And, on November 15, the Massachusetts legislature passed a law indemnifying the insurgents.

65. Condon, *Shays*, 70.
66. "Acts and Resolves Massachusetts. 1786–87," https://ia802605.us.archive.org/20/items/actsresolvespass178687mass/actsresolvespass178687mass_djvu.txt.
67. Condon, *Shays*, 70–71.
68. "Full Text of 'Acts and Resolves Passed by the General Court,'" https://archive.org/stream/actsresolvespass178687mass/actsresolvespass178687mass_djvu.txt.
69. Condon, *Shays*, 74.
70. Condon, *Shays*, 74. A separate squadron failed to capture Wheeler and Gale, but threatened and injured several bystanders in attempting to do so.
71. Richards, *Shays*, 21; see also Condon, *Shays*, 75–76. Indeed, "as with rumors circulating throughout the French countryside during the Great Fear of 1789, reports of government brutality provided yeomen with one more reason for radical action against the state" (Szatmary, *Shays*, 94).
72. Minot, *Insurrections*, 81.
73. *Worcester Magazine*, December 7, 1786, https://f35bcb33-cab5-4e5a-b56e-eb23a5af08e7.filesusr.com/ugd/19c525_b5cd433cfb8a4ca69bcf63c448411e1d.pdf. Condon states that only after the closing did Shays and some of the insurgents encamp at Rutland (*Shays*, 78). Richards and Leonard mention the closing but say nothing about Shays. The question of when Shays occupied the military barracks at Rutland is key to establishing Shays' role in the events leading up to his confrontation with General Shepherd at Springfield.
74. See https://f35bcb33-cab5-4e5a-b56e-eb23a5af08e7.filesusr.com/ugd/19c525_0c59e0c05a2e4579bb30600641 15ada5.pdf.
75. Italics in the original are preserved.
76. Condon, *Shays*, 79.
77. Massachusetts Historical Society, *The Bowdoin and Temple Papers 1783–1790* (Cambridge, MA: Wilson, 1907), 116.
78. Richard Beeman, *Plain, Honest Men* (New York: Random House, 2010), 17.
79. "Bowdoin and Temple," 118.
80. *The Papers of John Adams* (Cambridge, MA: The Belknap Press at Harvard University, 2016), 18: 524.
81. "Bowdoin and Temple," 119.
82. "Bowdoin and Temple," 121.
83. "Bowdoin and Temple," 123–124. Lyman notes that "this expedition of theirs was conducted with as much secrecy & precaution as if it was an enterprize of the greatest magnitude and importance,—not more than one hour before these insurgence arrived in town, the Sheriff told me that he had not the least apprehension that the Court would be interrupted by them."
84. "Bowdoin and Temple," 124. Lyman goes on to explain what he understands to be the significance of Shays: "There would have been no opposition to the setting of the Court had it not been for Shays, as they had pretty universally concluded it was best to stay at home, and make no further opposition to government until Saturday of last week, when they received orders from Shays to meet him in this town on Tuesday morning then next. Shays certainly ought to have an opportunity of seeing his friend Shattuck; I hope the insurgents will never know what I have written to you, for they might possibly kill me if they did."
85. Because the legislative session had ended November 18, however, the governor was forced to personally lobby his circle of Boston oligarchs in order to fund the troops. Bowdoin himself contributed a substantial subscription (Condon, *Shays*, 82).
86. Condon, *Shays*, 85–86.
87. Condon, *Shays*, 89.
88. Condon, *Shays*, 90.
89. Condon, *Shays*, 90–91.
90. Richards, *Shays*, 28–29.
91. Condon, *Shays*, 91.
92. Condon, *Shays*, 91–99.

93. *The Papers of John Marshall*, Charles Hobson, ed. (Charlottesville: University of Virginia Press, 2015), 1:200.
94. See https://f35bcb33-cab5-4e5a-b56e-eb23a5af08e7.filesusr.com/ugd/19c525_08d1e955759648e98cb2405cad8f7828.pdf.
95. See https://f35bcb33-cab5-4e5a-b56e-eb23a5af08e7.filesusr.com/ugd/19c525_5b534f0a2c2a4ebc9e2b8cc26d3e5dfa.pdf.
96. Richards, *Shays*, 117, my italics.
97. Szatmary, *Shays*, 134.
98. Adams Family, *The Adams Family Correspondence*, edited by L. H. Butterfield, Wendell D. Garrett, and Marjorie Sprague (Cambridge, MA: The Belknap Press of Harvard University Press, 2005), 7: 443.
99. Richards, *Shays*, 26.
100. See https://f35bcb33-cab5-4e5a-b56e-eb23a5af08e7.filesusr.com/ugd/19c525_88a2a869b90e42f4bbbb3f0d85750eb7.pdf.
101. See https://f35bcb33-cab5-4e5a-b56e-eb23a5af08e7.filesusr.com/ugd/19c525_5b534f0a2c2a4ebc9e2b8cc26d3e5dfa.pdf.
102. The Worcester court opened January 23 without insurgent protest.
103. John Adams, *Papers*, 18:564.
104. "RESOLVE REPEALING A RESOLVE FOR APPREHENDING DANIEL SHAYS AND OTHERS . . . in Pursuance of the said Resolution, his Excellency has offered a Reward for apprehending Daniel Shays and others. And whereas the Reasons which then operated, for offering such reward, do not now exist."
105. See https://f35bcb33-cab5-4e5a-b56e-eb23a5af08e7.filesusr.com/ugd/19c525_395f07c9262f49289569004c57c155fe.pdf.
106. William Smith, ed., *Dictionary of Greek and Roman Antiquities* (London, 1870) 2:439.
107. Robert T. Conrad, *Jack Cade: A Captain of the Commons* (London: Thomas Hatles Lacy), 15.
108. See https://f35bcb33-cab5-4e5a-b56e-eb23a5af08e7.filesusr.com/ugd/19c525_9608db3dc029416 5abc51fc157b59139.pdf.
109. Quoted in Szatmary, *Shays*, 74, my italics.
110. Jonathan Elliot, ed., *The Debates in the Several States on the Adoption of the Federal constitution, as Recommended by the General Convention at Philadelphia in 1787*, 5 volumes, 2d. Edition. Reprinted from the 1845 edition (Buffalo, NY: William S. Hein & Co., Inc., 1996)2:640.
111. Richards, *Shays*, 127.
112. Library of Congress, Prints and Photographs Division, Washington, D.C., https://www.loc.gov/pictures/item/2008661778/.
113. *Papers of James Madison, Retirement Series* (Charlottesville, VA: The University of Virginia Press, 2013), 2:345.
114. Elliot, *Debates*, 5:136.
115. John Adams, *Papers*, 18:544n3.
116. "Hampshire Gazette, September 1786," http://www.historic-northampton.org/members_only/gazette/1786-09.html; "Acts and Resolves," https://archive.org/details/actsresolvespass178687mass.
117. Bernard Bailyn, ed., *Debate on the Constitution* (New York: Library of America, 1993)2:876.
118. Minot, *Insurrection*, 55.
119. See https://f35bcb33-cab5-4e5a-b56e-eb23a5af08e7.filesusr.com/ugd/19c525_699a95c47a46415fb66f8c9012766ae1.pdf.
120. "Proclamation of John Hancock," June 15, 1787, http://shaysrebellion.stcc.edu/shaysapp/artifact_trans.do?shortName=proclamation_clemency&page=.
121. See https://f35bcb33-cab5-4e5a-b56e-eb23a5af08e7.filesusr.com/ugd/19c525_fd8780e0ac534c958d43661e96233b0d.pdf.
122. No founding-era politician more perfectly embodied this view than did Massachusetts Governor James Bowdoin. Through careful analysis of Bowdoin's public utterances at the time of the insurgency, Sean Condon has shown that while the governor indicated he was aware that the insurgency was in large part precipitated by genuine problems in the Massachusetts polity, he nonetheless insisted publicly on giving no ground to the protestors, instead concentrating all the blame on those who had allowed themselves to be influenced

by demagogues and, most emphatically, on the demagogues themselves. "For Bowdoin, many of the current disturbances were the result of "wicked and artful men," who were convincing the people that either to oppose the government or not to get involved to actively protect it. . . . Bowdoin told the [Massachusetts] legislators that they would try to understand the reasons why people had decided to use force to close the courts, so that they could prevent similar problems in the future. However, he argued that no matter what the causes were, the disturbances themselves could not be justified" (Condon, *Shays,* 65). To use a modern colloquialism, Bowdoin's rhetorical strategy was victim-blaming, as opposed to publicly admitting to the existence of flaws in the system which needed to the rectified. "If only the people worked more diligently," parodies Condon, "they would be able to pay their taxes and get out of debt" (46).

123. On the connection between Hamilton and Machiavelli, see John Lamberton Harper, *American Machiavelli: Alexander Hamilton and the Origins of U.S. Foreign Policy* (Cambridge, UK: Cambridge University Press, 2007). On the connection between Machiavelli and the founders in general, see Harvey C. Mansfield, *Taming the Prince: The Ambivalence of Executive Power* (Baltimore: Johns Hopkins University Press, 1989), 247–278.
124. *The Federalist* #74. Hamilton reiterates his views regarding the need for "the terror of example"—albeit with respect to a rebellion in western Pennsylvania—in his *Letter Concerning the Public Conduct and Character of John Adams, Esq., President of the United States*: "The general opinion of the friends of the Government demanded an example, as indispensable to its security. The opinion was well founded. Two insurrections in the same State . . . demonstrated a spirit of insubordination or disaffection which required a strong corrective," *Alexander Hamilton: Writings,* edited by Joanne B. Freeman (New York: Library of America, 2001), 963–964.
125. Mansfield, *Taming,* 131.
126. See also *Federalist* #28.
127. *Alexander Hamilton: Writings,* 769.

Chapter 4

1. Elsewhere, I have attempted to sketch the kind of work that would need to be done in order to develop such a theory and to undertake the kind of wholistic analysis I am proposing here. I call that analysis "political diagnostics"—see Charles U. Zug, "Could Political Science Become Diagnostic? Recovering a Forgotten Method," *Perspectives on Political Science* 48, no. 1 (2019): 56–63. Generally speaking, political diagnostics aim to furnish theoretical justifications for the assumptions that we invariably bring with us whenever we assess the functionality of institutions and the constitutional systems of which those regimes are a part. For example, as Anthony Ives has demonstrated in "Congressional Health, Congressional Failure" (Ph.D. diss., University of Texas at Austin, 2018), familiar claims about the functionality of Congress—is Congress working or broken?—always have in mind a picture of congressional health, a picture that involves more than simple variables such as the number of bills passed per legislative session. After all, nothing guarantees that a large number of bills will contain good bills; but do we not assume that the quality, not just the quantity, of legislation plays a role in assessing the overall functionality of Congress as a legislative institution?
2. In "Liberty, Metaphor, and Mechanism: 'Checks and Balances' and the Origin of Modern Constitutionalism" (https://constitution.org/1-Education/lg/check_bal.htm), David Wootton does a terrific job of tracing the ideational development of the concept of politics as consisting in mechanistic systems. The idea of the American constitution as "a machine that goes of itself" would seem to be descended from this particular intellectual tradition.
3. Obviously, things are different at the state and local level.
4. James W. Ceaser, *Presidential Selection* (Princeton, NJ: Princeton University Press, 1979), 54–55.
5. Bryan Garsten, *Saving Persuasion* (Cambridge, MA: Harvard University Press, 2006), 209.
6. Bryan Garsten, "The Sorry State of American Debate," *Wall Street Journal,* October 22, 2016, https://humanities.yale.edu/news/professor-bryan-garsten-sorry-state-american-debate-wall-street-journal.

7. Garsten, "American Debate"; Garsten, *Persuasion*, 206–207.
8. Ceaser, *Presidential Selection*, 54–55.
9. For an example of how this could happen in ancient times, consider the anecdote of Cleon the Athenian politician being pressured into leading a commando raid at Pylos—while he was speaking on the floor of the legislature! Thucydides, *War of the Peloponnesians and the Athenians*, 4.27.3–4.
10. In this respect, the American Constitution differs both from the Articles of Confederation, which included a recall provision for state electors, and from classical democracies, which extended political participation in actual governance much more liberally.
11. *U.S. Term Limits, Inc. v. Thornton*, 514 U.S. 779 (1995), 799–800. Among other relevant sources cited by Stevens, see Joseph Story, *Commentaries on the Constitution of the United States* (Boston: Hilliard, Gray and Company, 1833), § 626: "The truth is, that the states can exercise no powers whatsoever, which exclusively spring out of the existence of the national government, which the constitution does not delegate to them. They have just as much right, and no more, to prescribe new qualifications for a representative, as they have for a president. Each is an officer of the Union, deriving his powers and qualifications from the constitution, and neither created by, dependent upon, nor controllable by, the states. It is no original prerogative of state power to appoint a representative, a senator, or president for the Union. Those officers owe their existence and functions to the united voice of the whole, not of a portion, of the people. Before a state can assert the right, it must show, that the constitution has delegated and recognized it. No state can say, that it has reserved, what it never possessed."
12. *U.S. Term Limits*, 804.
13. Justice Marshall emphasizes this point in *McCulloch v. Maryland*, 17 U.S. 316 (1819).
14. Ceaser, *Presidential Selection*, 59.
15. *Federalist* #9.
16. *Federalist* #58.
17. Aristotle, *Nicomachean Ethics*, book VIII.
18. *Federalist* #10.
19. My argument here is slightly different from Garsten's, which focuses (correctly) on the way the Constitution is designed to exclude from the very outset office-seekers whose characters are unamendable from deliberation, as opposed to the way in which its design is meant to extract deliberation from whoever enters office, regardless of character. Madison, for his part, makes both kinds of arguments, as does Garsten. Though they are by no means mutually exclusive—both contribute to the ultimate goal of deliberative government—the argument I develop is distinctive because it reflects the Constitution's relative agnosticism regarding personal character, and its concern with what gets said as opposed to *why* it gets said. This framework makes sense of Garsten's (and Madison's) argument that the Constitution in a way selects for personal character. What the Constitution selects for in office seekers is not so much character in the robust sense (i.e., the motivations for why one does what one does) as character understood more narrowly in terms of the kinds of speech and actions an office-seeker can be induced to display in their official capacity irrespective of their personal motivations. See Garsten, *Persuasion*, 206.
20. Jeffrey K. Tulis, "On Congress and Constitutional Responsibility," *Boston University Law Review* 89, no. 2 (2009): 516.
21. *The Federalist* #51.
22. Tulis, "On Congress," 515.
23. Michael Signer, *Demagogue* (New York: Palgrave Macmillan, 2009).
24. Sotirios Barber, *Welfare and the Constitution* (Princeton, NJ: Princeton University Press, 2003).
25. Barber, *Welfare*. This is a provocative reading of the Constitution, of course—though not one we would be led to dismiss casually were we to take the Constitution on its own terms: the Constitution's own stated purpose in the Preamble is to achieve specific goals. Critics of an instrumental reading of the Constitution point to the historical fact that the Supreme Court does not treat the Preamble as binding. This fact is ultimately irrelevant for this book because my argument is not about the Court's interpretation of the Constitution but about the Constitution itself. The Court's understandings of the Constitution can be useful in this respect (as a resource for understanding the regime—see my discussion of Justice Stevens'

majority in *Thornton* above), but they are not authoritative. After all, the Court is itself a creation of the Constitution, not the other way around; and the Court's decision not to regard the Preamble as legally binding is the result of path-dependency—it does not need to be that way. Had an earlier Court decided differently, the Preamble might be a part of modern-day jurisprudence.

26. The most authoritative statement of this position is Madison's in *Federalist* #10: "As long as the reason of man continues fallible, and he is at liberty to exercise it, different opinions will be formed. As long as the connection subsists between his reason and his self-love, his opinions and his passions will have a reciprocal influence on each other; and the former will be objects to which the latter will attach themselves." The Constitution is fundamentally pluralistic in the sense that it rejects the idea that some individual or party could ever reason infallibly about the common good, and therefore deserve to rule in the classical sense (cf. Madison's statement above with Aristotle's *Politics*, III–IV, and Plato's *Republic*, III).
27. For a helpful discussion of this question, see Walter F. Murphy, *Constitutional Democracy* (Baltimore: Johns Hopkins University Press, 2007), 510–518.
28. E.g., Aristotle, *Nicomachean Ethics*, III.
29. Consider Hamilton's distinction in *Federalist* #71 between the intentions and the desires of the public, a distinction that maps onto the real as opposed to the merely perceived welfare of the public.
30. Muirhead and Rosenblum, *A Lot of People Are Saying*, 147.
31. Barber, *On What the Constitution Means*, 49. Barber's interpretation contrasts with Ackermann's in *We the People* (Cambridge, MA: Belknap Press of Harvard University Press, 1991). Ackermann argues that the high amendment threshold was designed to incentivize supermajorities capable of enacting "constitutional moments." For myself, following Barber, what is key is the distinction between core and peripheral change that the Constitution's amendment feature presupposes. Core changes to the polity ought to require more time and deliberation than peripheral changes, and an amendment procedure requiring significant supermajorities at the state and federal level is likely to incentivize this kind of deliberation.
32. *The Federalist* #10.
33. One thinks of Thucydides III, describing the Athenians' decision to slaughter the rebellious citizens of Mytilene—a decision they were roused to make by the arch-demagogue Cleon, and which they were only just persuaded of reversing by the quasi-miraculous intervention of Diodotus (whose name means literally "the gift of Zeus").
34. *Federalist* #27.
35. See, respectively, Jürgen Habermas, *Between Facts and Norms: Contributions to a Discourse Theory of Democracy*, translated by William Rehg (Cambridge, MA: MIT Press, 1996); Robert A. Dahl, *On Democracy* (New Haven, CT: Yale University Press, 1998). For a helpful critique of the contemporary deliberative democracy model, see Stephen S. Salkever, "The Deliberative Model of Democracy and Aristotle's Ethics of Natural Questions," in *Aristotle and Modern Politics*, edited by Aristide Tessitore (Notre Dame, IN: Notre Dame Press, 2002), chapter 11.
36. Jeffrey K. Tulis, *The Rhetorical Presidency*, 2nd ed. (Princeton, NJ: Princeton University Press, 2017), chapters 5–6.
37. The evaluative threshold of an argument for demagoguery should be plausibility rather than probability. The core question is not the retrospective one of whether the anticipated harm actually obtained; after all, officeholders cannot be expected to predict the future. Rather it is whether the officeholder had sufficient reason to expect that it would; whether they supplied reasons for why it was, in fact, a harm; and whether they explained how, in their judgment, deploying demagoguery would aid in moving the polity toward a more desirable state of affairs. Demagoguery can be connected, by means of a comprehensive argument, to a rational, contestable conception of the common good that the statesman is capable of explaining—a conception in which demagoguery has a defensible place. In demagoguery's ideal use, all of these elements must be in place.

Chapter 5

1. Herbert J. Storing, *Toward a More Perfect Union: Writings of Herbert J. Storing* (Washington, DC: AEI Press, 1995), 408.
2. John Locke, *Second Treatise of Government*, chapter 14; Ben Kleinerman, "Can the Prince Really Be Tamed? Executive Prerogative, Popular Apathy, and the Constitutional Frame in Locke's Second Treatise," *American Political Science Review* 101, no. 2 (2007): 101–102.
3. For articulations of this adversarial conception of the separation-of-powers theory, see Jeffrey K. Tulis and Nicole Mellow, *Legacies of Losing in American Politics* (Chicago: University of Chicago Press, 2018); Thomas R. Bell, "Perverse Politics: Recess Appointments, *Noel Canning*, and the Limits of Law," *Presidential Studies Quarterly* 48, no. 2 (June 2018): 373–386; Mariah Zeisberg, *War Powers* (Princeton, NJ: Princeton University Press, 2013).
4. Article 2, Section 3 states only that the president "shall from time to time give to the Congress Information of the State of the Union, and recommend to their Consideration such Measures as he shall judge necessary and expedient." For over a century, presidents following Jefferson's model, submitted written annual messages to Congress.
5. As statements like these should make apparent, I do not assume that political behavior is determined by institutional constraints and path-dependency to the degree that many social scientists assume. At the same time, I do attempt to understand political decision-making in light of the incentive structures that institutions set up; for me, incentive structures interact with the decision-making power of individuals in complex ways. As a methodology, political diagnostics assumes both that standards for assessing political decisions can be abstracted from institutional and constitutional design and that political actors are free to act in ways that violate those standards—hence the need for assessment.
6. Storing, *Union*, 408.
7. Barack Obama, *A Promised Land* (New York: Crown, 2020), 416.
8. See also *Federalist* #63.
9. Respectively, Editorial Board, "Justice Ginsburg's Inappropriate Comments on Donald Trump," *Washington Post*, July 12, 2016, https://www.washingtonpost.com/opinions/justice-ginsburgs-inappropriate-comments-on-donald-trump/2016/07/12/981df404-4862-11e6-bdb9-701687974517_story.html; Sophie Tatum, "Brett Kavanaugh's Nomination: A Timeline," CNN, https://www.cnn.com/interactive/2018/10/politics/timeline-kavanaugh/.
10. Editorial Board, "Justice Ginsburg."
11. E.g., John Rawls, *A Theory of Justice* (Cambridge, MA: Harvard University Press, 1971); Ronald Dworkin, *Law's Empire* (Cambridge, MA: Belknap Press of Harvard University Press, 1986).
12. Chris Cillizza, "Nancy Pelosi Just Trolled Alexandria Ocasio-Cortez. Again," CNN, April 8, 2019, https://www.cnn.com/2019/04/08/politics/nancy-pelosi-alexandria-ocasio-cortez-twitter/index.html.
13. One of Ocasio-Cortez's responses was: "Having respect for ourselves doesn't mean we lack respect for [Speaker Pelosi]. It means we won't let everyday people be dismissed," Twitter, July 8, 2019, https://twitter.com/AOC/status/1148296121149796352. This formulation, while truncated, acknowledges a tension between the leadership hierarchy of the House and the polity's democratic commitments ("everyday people").
14. Joseph M. Bessette, "Introduction," in *Toward a More Perfect Union: Writings of Herbert J. Storing* (Washington, DC: AEI Press, 1995), 9.
15. For a helpful discussion and critique of this interpretation, see David K. Nichols, *The Myth of the Modern Presidency* (University Park: Pennsylvania State University Press, 1994).
16. E.g., Edward S. Corwin, *The President: Office and Powers*, 5th ed. (New York: New York University Press, 1984).
17. Richard Neustadt, *Presidential Power and the Modern Presidents* (New York: The Free Press, 1990); Samuel Kernell, *Going Public* (New York: Sage, 2007); Terry Moe and William Howell, *Relic* (New York: Basic Books, 2016); Eric Posner and Adrian Vermuele, *The Executive Unbound* (New York: Oxford University Press, 2010).
18. The most recent version of this argument is Stephen F. Knott's, developed in *The Lost Soul of the American Presidency* (Lawrence: University Press of Kansas, 2019).

19. Knott, *Presidency*, chapter 9.
20. Knott, *Presidency*, 18.
21. Knott, *Presidency*, 27, 1.
22. Knott, *Presidency*, chapter 1.
23. Knott, *Presidency*, chapters 2 and 3; quote from 41.
24. Knott, *Presidency*, xv.
25. E.g., Knott, *Presidency*, 8: "The demagogue preys on divisive issues . . . issues fraught with emotion, and seeks to inflame these emotions to banish reason and reflection from the public square."
26. Knott, *Presidency*, 210.
27. Knott, *Presidency*, 56.
28. Knott, *Presidency*, 33; Thomas Jefferson to Levi Lincoln, October 25, 1802, https://founders.archives.gov/documents/Jefferson/01-38-02-0513
29. E.g., Knott, *Presidency*, 51–54. Knott spends considerable time on the "penchant for violence" shared by Jackson and his followers, and cites an anonymous threat letter to John Quincy Adams, possibly written by one of Jackson's advisors, as evidence of Jackson's demagoguery (54).
30. E.g., Knott, *Presidency*, 32–33, discussing the "propaganda campaign" waged by Republicans against the Federalists. Knott gives no evidence of Jefferson having publicly participated in this campaign (through public speeches, for example). Similarly, he tries to paint Jackson as a demagogue by asserting that "the coalition Jackson assembled was, at bottom, a cauldron of boiling partisan, racial, and class resentments, and in Jackson's case, all of those, plus decades of accumulated personal resentments thrown into the mix" (57). Notice the emphasis on Jackson's personal feelings and motives and the absence of any discussion of his public rhetoric.
31. Tulis, *Rhetorical Presidency*, 74.
32. Knott, *Presidency*, 31.
33. Knott, *Presidency*, 40.
34. Knott, *Presidency*, 208.
35. Knott, *Presidency*, 53.
36. Edwin A. Miles, "Andrew Jackson and Senator George Poindexter," *Journal of Southern History* 24, no. 1 (February 1958): 62.
37. "The Baltimore Patriot," http://skinnerfamilypapers.com/?page_id=1207. In a letter to James Madison from August 13, 1824, Munroe declares his firm support for then-candidate John Quincy Adams and his opposition to "the 'blood and carnage' candidate on the one side," presumably referencing then-candidate Jackson. "To James Madison from Isaac Munroe, 13 August 1824," https://founders.archives.gov/documents/Madison/04-03-02-0351.
38. Jeffrey K. Tulis, *The Rhetorical Presidency*, 2nd ed. (Princeton, NJ: Princeton University Press, 2017), 64, 66, 73.
39. Tulis, *Rhetorical Presidency*, esp. 74.
40. E.g., Knott, *Presidency*, 30.
41. Knott, *Presidency*, 24.
42. Knott, *Presidency*, 10.
43. For a helpful discussion of Jackson's deliberative arguments, which were nonetheless rooted in the cruder, more amorphous views held by his electoral supporters (e.g., hostility toward the National Bank), see Tulis, *Rhetorical Presidency*, 74–75.
44. Knott, *Presidency*, 40.
45. Knott, *Presidency*, 10.
46. Knott, *Presidency*, 41.

Chapter 6

1. Quoted in Keith E. Whittington, "Reconstructing the Federal Judiciary: The Chase Impeachment and the Constitution," *Studies in American Political Development* 9 (Spring 1995): 86.
2. Whittington, "Judiciary."

3. Whittington, "Judiciary," 85–86.
4. Whittington, "Judiciary," 60.
5. *Annals of Congress* 8, no. 2 (Washington, D.C.: Gales & Seaton, 1852), 674–675.
6. *Annals*, 669. I thank Jeremy Bailey for pointing out the political motivations of the Jeffersonians who led the charge against Chase. Given that their goal in removing Chase from the bench was to further diminish the strength of the Federalist Party, it is quite reasonable to suspect that Chase's demagoguery was merely an excuse for them to initiate impeachment proceedings, and that they did not really care about demagoguery per se. Yet this observation is perfectly compatible with my suggestion that we set aside speculations about the motivations of political actors in order to analyze their understandings of American politics on the merits—on their own terms. Hence, in my analysis, the fact that the Jeffersonians cared more about replacing Chase with a Republican than about Chase's rhetoric does not undermine their constitutionally sensitive arguments about his rhetoric; those arguments do have weight if taken on their own terms, and they ought to be meaningful to anyone who is not a party in the case in question. They are also useful for thinking about related cases.
7. Raoul Berger, *Impeachment: The Constitutional Problems* (Cambridge, MA: Harvard University Press, 1973), 224–251.
8. Richard Ellis, "The Impeachment of Samuel Chase," in *American Political Trials*, edited by Michal Belknap (Westport, CT: Greenwood Press, 1981), 57–78; William H. Rehnquist, *Grand Inquests* (New York: William Morrow, 1992).
9. Ellis, "Impeachment," 73.
10. U.S. Constitution, Article III, Section 1.
11. Whittington, "Judiciary." For a discussion of the limits of the legalistic view of impeachment, see Jeffrey K. Tulis, "Impeachment in the Constitutional Order," in *The Constitutional Presidency*, edited by Joseph M. Bessette and Jeffrey K. Tulis (Baltimore: Johns Hopkins University Press, 2009), 229–246.
12. Whittington, "Judiciary," 71.
13. *Annals*, 669. For a fuller discussion of why this was the case, see Whittington, "Judiciary," 81.
14. Whittington, "Judiciary," 78.
15. *Annals*, 675.
16. *Annals*, 675.
17. *Annals*, 675.
18. *Annals*, 675.
19. *Annals*, 675.
20. *Annals*, 675.
21. *Annals*, 675.
22. Jeffrey K. Tulis and Nicole Mellow, *Legacies of Losing in American Politics* (Chicago: University of Chicago Press, 2018), chapter 2.
23. *Annals*, 676. On the Anti-Federalist position, see, e.g., Herbert J. Storing, *What the Anti-Federalists Were For* (Chicago: University of Chicago Press, 1981).
24. *Annals*, 676.
25. *Annals*, 675.
26. E.g., Whittington, "Judiciary."
27. See Chapter 2.
28. For an outline of this ideal, see Gary J. Jacobsohn, *Pragmatism, Statesmanship, and the Supreme Court* (Ithaca, NY: Cornell University Press, 1977).
29. "The interest of the man must be connected with the constitutional rights of the place." Madison, *Federalist* #51.
30. E.g., Bruce Allen Murphy, *Scalia* (New York: Simon and Schuster, 2014), chapters 6–7.
31. Richard A. Brisbin Jr., *Justice Scalia and the Conservative Revival* (Baltimore: Johns Hopkins University Press, 1997), 1.
32. Lawrence Tribe, "DOMA, Prop 8, and Justice Scalia's Intemperate Dissent," *SCOTUS Blog*, June 26, 2013: https://www.scotusblog.com/2013/06/doma-prop-8-and-justice-scalias-intemperate-dissent/.
33. *Obergefell v. Hodges*, 576 U.S. ____ (J. Scalia, dissenting), at 5.
34. Scalia, *Obergefell*, at 2.

35. Scalia, *Obergefell*, at 6, 5.
36. Brisbin, *Justice Scalia*, ix.
37. Respectively, *Mistretta v. U.S.*, 488 U.S. 361, 427; *Planned Parenthood of Southeastern Pennsylvania v. Casey*, 112 S.Ct. (quoted in Brisbin, *Scalia*, ix).
38. Scalia, *Obergefell*, at 7.
39. Scalia, *Obergefell*, at 8.
40. Scalia, *Obergefell*, at 8n22.
41. *Lawrence v. Texas*, 539 U.S. 558 (J. Scalia, dissenting), at 18.
42. *Planned Parenthood v. Casey*, 505 U. S. 833 (J. Scalia, dissenting), at 996.
43. John Locke, *Second Treatise of Government*, chapter 14.
44. Antonin Scalia, *A Matter of Interpretation* (Princeton, NJ: Princeton University Press, 1997), 3.
45. Scalia, *Interpretation*.
46. Ronald M. Dworkin, "Comment," in Antonin Scalia, *A Matter of Interpretation* (Princeton, NJ: Princeton University Press, 1997), 116.
47. Dworkin, "Comment," 117.
48. Dworkin, "Comment," 120.
49. Dworkin, "Comment," 120.
50. Dworkin, "Comment," 125–126.
51. Dworkin, "Comment," 126.
52. Antonin Scalia, "Response," in Antonin Scalia, *A Matter of Interpretation* (Princeton, NJ: Princeton University Press, 1997), 145.
53. Scalia, "Response," 145.
54. Scalia, "Response," 146.
55. In response, Scalia might have pointed to the *Dred Scott* case as evidence that the Court should not intervene in controversial political matters, such as questions of substantive or fundamental rights. As Christopher Eisgruber observes, however, the "*Dred* Again" equivalence fails because it refuses to acknowledge the substantive differences between *Dred* and subsequent rights cases like *Roe*: the former argued that the Constitution protects property in human beings, a principle fundamentally at odds with the Constitution's basic commitment to individual freedom. Accordingly, the Taney Court erred not because it struck down the Missouri Compromise but because it enforced an arcane, unjust, implausible reading of the Constitution. See Christopher Eisgruber, "*Dred* Again? Originalism's Forgotten Past," https://conservancy.umn.edu/bitstream/handle/11299/166878/10_01_Eisgruber.pdf;jsessionid=C594E0BB2B6BA9A78C05389E3264E665?sequence=1.
56. Hamilton in *Federalist* #78.
57. Scalia, "Response," 147.
58. Scalia, "Response," 146.
59. Consider Justice Hughes' majority in *Home Building & Loan Association v. Blaisdell*, 290 U.S. 398 (1934).
60. Dworkin, "Comment," 126.
61. Brisbin, *Justice Scalia*, 333.
62. Respectively, Aristotle, *Politics*, II, 1269a 20; *Federalist* #49.

Chapter 7

1. Charles V. Hamilton, *Adam Clayton Powell, Jr.* (New York: Cooper Square Press, 2001), 497n47; see also 134–135.
2. Buckley quoted in Michael L. Kurtz, "New South Demagoguery," in *Plain Folk of the South Revisited*, edited by Samuel C. Hyde Jr. (Baton Rouge: Louisiana State University Press, 1997), 255; James Q. Wilson, "The Flamboyant Mr. Powell," *Commentary*, January 1966, https://www.commentarymagazine.com/articles/james-wilson/the-flamboyant-mr-powell/.
3. Martin Kilson, "The First Congressman from Harlem," *New York Times*, November 7, 1971, https://www.nytimes.com/1971/11/07/archives/adam-by-adam-by-adam-clayton-powell-jr-illustrated-260-pp-new-york.html.

4. Thomas A. Johnson, "A Man of Many Roles," *New York Times*, April 5, 1972, https://www.nytimes.com/1972/04/05/archives/a-man-of-many-roles-adam-clayton-powell-former-harlem.html.
5. Bret Fetzer, review of *Adam Clayton Powell* for Amazon, n.d., https://www.amazon.com/Adam-Clayton-Powell-Richard-Kilberg/dp/B001HBVE8I.
6. See esp. Hamilton, *Powell*.
7. Hamilton, *Powell*, chapters 7–15.
8. John A. Davis, "Review of *Adam Clayton Powell, Jr.* by Charles V. Hamilton," *Political Science Quarterly* 107, no. 2 (Summer 1992): 338.
9. Hamilton, *Powell*, 181.
10. Hamilton, *Powell*, 150. For instance, many of Powell's contemporaries in the NAACP believed that Powell undermined that group's credibility with the Truman administration when he publicly criticized Truman's wife and Truman himself for failing to actively support civil rights reform. See Hamilton, *Powell*, 165, 192.
11. Lee A. Daniels, "The Political Career of Adam Clayton Powell," *Journal of Black Studies* 4, no. 2 (December 1973): 117.
12. Hamilton, *Powell*, 186.
13. Henry Paul Orr, "Reflections on the Pragmatic Way of Adam Clayton Powell, Jr.: A Black American," *Negro History Bulletin* 42, no. 4 (October–December 1979): 91.
14. Daniels, "Political Career," 121.
15. E.g., Hamilton, *Powell*, 217.
16. Art Pollock, "'My Life's Philosophy': Adam Clayton Powell's 'Black Position Paper,'" *Journal of Black Studies* 4, no. 4 (June 1974): 458.
17. Daniels, "Political Career," 134.
18. Orr, "Reflections," 92.
19. Daniels, "Political Career," 134.
20. Hamilton, *Powell*, 8.
21. Davis, "Review of *Powell*," 338.
22. Pollock, "Black Position Paper," 461.
23. Daniels, "Political Career," 115–116.
24. Andre Sobocinski, "A Brief History of African-American Navy Nurses," Navy.mil, February 24, 2014, https://archive.org/details/NavyMedicineHighlightsFirstAfricanAmericansInTheNavyMedicalDepartment.
25. "Army-Navy Nurses Act of 1947," *Public Laws of the United States*, Chapter 38, April 16, 1947, https://www.loc.gov/law/help/statutes-at-large/80th-congress/session-1/c80s1ch38.pdf.
26. As an indication, Powell's proposed amendment failed, 47–187. See *Congressional Record* (hereafter *CR*), March 13, 1947, 2013.
27. *CR*, March 13, 1947, 2004.
28. *CR*, March 13, 1947, 2004.
29. *CR*, March 13, 1947, 2005.
30. E.g., Louis Hartz, *The Liberal Tradition in America* (New York: Mariner, 1991).
31. *CR*, March 13, 1947, 2005.
32. *CR*, March 13, 1947, 2005.
33. *CR*, March 13, 1947, 2005.
34. *CR*, March 13, 1947, 2005 (my italics).
35. *CR*, March 13, 1947, 2005.
36. "Frances Bolton, a moderate isolationist before the war, soon embraced military preparedness. She authored the Bolton Act of 1943, creating the U.S. Cadet Nurse Corps, which was responsible for training nearly 125,000 women as military nurses. Bolton later toured Europe to observe these women at work in field hospitals. After the war, she advocated a greater role for women in the military and even suggested they be made eligible for future drafts." *Women in Congress, 1917–2017*, edited by Gregg Harper and Robert A. Brady (Washington, DC: U.S. Government Publishing Office, 2017), 79.
37. *CR*, March 13, 1947, 2005.

38. Niccolò Machiavelli, *The Prince*, translated by Harvey C. Mansfield Jr. (Chicago: University of Chicago Press, 1998), 61.
39. Here I follow the outlines of hegemony as sketched by Gramsci and elaborated by theorists such as T. J. Jackson Lears in "The Concept of Cultural Hegemony," *American Historical Review* 90, no. 3 (June 1985): 567–593. As far as I am aware, Powell does not discuss Gramsci or the concept of cultural hegemony; rather, the latter maps on quite helpfully to the critique that Powell appears to have discovered on his own.
40. For an articulation of this insight, see Herbert J. Storing, *Toward a More Perfect Union* (Washington, DC: AEI Press, 1997), 207–208: "Black Americans are like a revolutionary or . . . a founding generation. . . . [T]hey are in the difficult but potentially glorious position of not being able to take for granted given political arrangements and values, or having seriously to canvass alternatives, to think through their implications, and to make a deliberate choice."
41. *CR*, March 13, 1947, 2011.
42. *Brown v. Board of Education of Topeka*, 347 U.S. 483.
43. *CR*, January 24, 1956, 1191.
44. *CR*, January 24, 1956, 1191.
45. *CR*, February 6, 1956, 2118.
46. *CR*, February 6, 1956, 2119.
47. *CR*, February 6, 1956, 2119.
48. *CR*, January 24, 1956, 1193.
49. Genuine legislative deliberation requires both engagement with the merits of policy argument as well as informational openness to the realities of contemporary life in the regime. Joseph Bessette, *The Mild Voice of Reason* (Chicago: University of Chicago Press, 1994); Jeremy Waldron, "Principles of Legislation," in *Political Theory* (Cambridge, MA: Harvard University Press, 2016).
50. For discussions of the difference between legalistic and political conceptions of separation of powers, see Jeffrey K. Tulis and Nicole Mellow, *Legacies of Losing in American Politics* (Chicago: University of Chicago Press, 2018), 54–59; Thomas R. Bell, "Perverse Politics: Recess Appointments, *Noel Canning*, and the Limits of Law," *Presidential Studies Quarterly* 48, no. 2 (June 2018): 373–386.
51. Abraham Lincoln, "Speech on the Dred Scott Decision at Springfield, Illinois, June 26, 1857," in *Lincoln: Speeches and Writings 1832–1858* (New York: Library of America, 1989).
52. *CR*, February 2, 1955, 1084.
53. *CR*, February 2, 1955, 1084. See Charles U. Zug, "Support for Nationalization and State Building in the Early American Republic: The Act for the Relief of Sick and Disabled Seamen," *Journal of Law and Courts* 9, no. 2 (Fall 2021): 283–304. Powell reflects a diagnosis of congressional culture similar to that in Jeffrey K. Tulis, "On Congress and Constitutional Responsibility," *Boston University Law Review* 89, no. 2 (2009): 515–524, and Jeffrey K. Tulis, "Constitutional Abdication: The Senate, the President, and Appointments to the Supreme Court," *Case Western Reserve Law Review* 47, no. 4 (1997): 1331–1357. But whereas Tulis views the nineteenth-century Congress as healthy and the twentieth-century Congress as deferential, Powell sees both as lacking in institutional patriotism.
54. *CR*, February 2, 1955, 1084.
55. *CR*, February 2, 1955, 1084.
56. *Shelby County v. Holder*, 570 U.S. 529.
57. *Parents Involved in Community Schools v. Seattle School District No. 1*, 551 U.S. 701.
58. Steven Lubet, "Path-Takers and Way-Makers," *New Rambler Review*, October 7, 2019, https://newramblerreview.com/book-reviews/law/path-takers-and-way-makers.
59. E.g., Shirley Better, *Institutional Racism: A Primer on Theory and Strategies for Social Change*, 2nd ed. (Lanham, MD: Rowman and Littlefield, 2008), 10–14.
60. For discussion of why deliberative rhetoric is sometimes inadequate for mobilization, see James Darsey, *The Prophetic Tradition and Radical Rhetoric in America* (New York: New York University Press, 1997); Patricia Roberts-Miller, "Democracy, Demagoguery, and Critical Rhetoric," *Rhetoric and Public Affairs* 8, no. 3 (Fall 2005): 459–476; Steven R. Goldzwig, "A Social Movement Perspective on Demagoguery," *Communication Studies* 40 (1989): 202–228.
61. Hamilton, *Powell*, 178, 181.

62. Davis, "Review of *Powell*," 337.
63. Hamilton, *Powell*, 182.
64. Hamilton, *Powell*, 193.
65. Hamilton, *Powell*, 194.
66. Hamilton, *Powell*, 165.
67. Hamilton, *Powell*, 153, 197, 219.
68. Michel Martin and Patricia Turner, "Why African-Americans Loathe 'Uncle Tom,'" NPR, July 30, 2008: https://www.npr.org/templates/story/story.php?storyId=93059468.
69. Hamilton, *Powell*, 197.
70. Pollock, "Black Position Paper," 459.
71. For a discussion of iterative rhetoric, see Tulis and Mellow, *Legacies*, chapter 2.
72. Robert P. Newman, *Owen Lattimore and the "Loss" of China* (Berkeley: University of California Press, 1992), ix.
73. E.g., Eugene Lyons, *The Red Decade: The Stalinist Penetration of America* (Indianapolis, IN: Bobbs-Merrill, 1941); Owen Lattimore, *Solution in Asia* (Boston: Little, Brown, 1945).
74. For a helpful summary of this disagreement, see Richard Neustadt, *Presidential Power and the Modern Presidents* (New York: The Free Press, 1990), 12–15.
75. E.g., Robert Griffith, *The Politics of Fear*, 2nd ed. (Amherst: University of Massachusetts Press, 1987), 48: "The Hiss case, declared Richard Nixon, was only 'a small part of the whole shocking story of Communist espionage in the United States.'" For their part, men like Nixon and Taft seemed to have been vindicated in their suspicions as a result of the conviction of Alger Hiss on January 21, 1950, and the convictions of Julius and Ethel Rosenberg several years earlier. See also 46–47, 52–53.
76. Griffith, *Fear*, 16.
77. Griffith, *Fear*, 13.
78. Griffith, *Fear*, 188.
79. Griffith, *Fear*, 53.
80. Consider Muirhead and Rosenblum's distinction between "classic" conspiracy theory, which actually tries to *theorize* a conspiracy on the basis of evidence, and "the new conspiracism," whose only evidence is the fact that the allegation has been frequently repeated. *A Lot of People Are Saying* (Princeton: Princeton University Press, 2019), chapter 1. For a deeper investigation into the possible merits of classic conspiracy theory and what distinguishes it from conspiracism, see Jeffrey K. Tulis, "Responding to Political Fiction," *Contemporary Political Theory* 19 (2020): 142–174.
81. The Rosenbergs were the most well-known example. See Griffith, *Fear*, 47.
82. Stephen Kotkin, *Stalin*, vol. II, *Waiting for Hitler* (New York: Penguin, 2017).
83. Michael Signer, *Demagogue* (New York: Palgrave Macmillan, 2009), 126. See also Bob Bauer, "A President's Words Matter, Part II: Impeachment Standards and the Case of the Demagogue," *Lawfare*, October 11, 2017, https://www.lawfareblog.com/presidents-words-matter-part-ii-impeachment-standards-and-case-demagogue.
84. *McCarthy*, 120.
85. See *Washington Post*, March 14, 1950.
86. E.g., Signer, *Demagogue*, 126; Richard Rovere, *Senator Joe McCarthy* (New York: Harcourt, Brace, Jovanovich: 1959), 122–123. Signer cites Griffith's otherwise fastidious account, which rather hesitantly notes that "McCarthy's championship of the 'Communist-in-government' issue may be traced to a now-famous dinner at Washington's Colony Restaurant" (*Fear*, 29). Griffith, however, includes no citation in support of this claim, and his phrasing—"may be traced"—suggests that the only hard evidence supporting the anecdote is the fact that the anecdote is now "famous." For a very helpful article exposing the flimsiness of the anecdote as well as possible political motivations behind those who put it about, see Richard M. Fried, "The Idea of 'Conspiracy' in McCarthy-Era Politics," *Prologue*, Spring 2002, 43–50, https://www.archives.gov/files/publications/prologue/2002/spring/conspiracy.pdf.
87. This draft is said to differ from the one he actually read into the *Congressional Record*, e.g., Griffith, *Fear*, 49n53; Rovere, *McCarthy*, 127–133.

88. Griffith, *Fear,* 49; Rovere, *McCarthy,* 125. McCarthy did not include this number in the speech he read to the Senate on February 20, 1950. All citations above are to this version: *Congressional Record,* 81st Congress, 2nd Session (February 20, 1950), 1954.
89. *CR,* 81st Congress, 2nd session (February 20, 1950), 1954.
90. *CR,* 81st Congress, 2nd session (February 20, 1950), 1954.
91. *CR,* 81st Congress, 2nd session (February 20, 1950), 1954.
92. *CR,* 81st Congress, 2nd session (February 20, 1950), 1954.
93. Griffith, *Fear,* 50–51, 53; Rovere, *McCarthy,* 129.
94. Rovere, *McCarthy,* 127; Griffith, *Fear,* 54.
95. Rovere, *McCarthy,* 131.
96. Griffith, *Fear,* 54–55.
97. Griffith, *Fear,* 55.
98. Rovere, *McCarthy,* 133.
99. *CR,* 81st Congress, 2nd session (February 20, 1950), 1953.
100. *CR,* 81st Congress, 2nd session (February 20, 1950), 1953.
101. Griffith, *Fear,* 58.
102. For a glimpse of the political culture into which McCarthy had entered, consider the following passage for a book that defended McCarthy's rhetoric and goals:

 "Senator Joseph McCarthy was not the only one who had drawn public attention to the China betrayal. But, being a newcomer to the techniques of Communist disputation here, as everywhere, he assumed that Americans would believe the criticisms he made because they were reasonable and plausible and because most of the proof was there. Communist controversy, however, is not conducted in open debate and logical discussion. Its first weapon always is the smear-abuse and character assassination. Its other weapon is to use the strange power Communist leaders in America attained (which is another unbelievable story) to liquidate writers, publicists, critics and journalists who dared to defend some victim marked by the Communists for liquidation. I think it is a fair assumption that Senator McCarthy, a normal American, a newcomer at the time into the field of controversy with the Reds, must have been astounded at the blows that were immediately dealt him, not by the Communist Party openly, but by the *New York Times,* the *New York Herald Tribune,* various conservative magazines and finally such respectable men in the Senate as Senator Millard Tydings and Senator William Benton." John T. Flynn, *The Lattimore Story* (New York: Devin-Adair Company, 1953), 3–4.
103. Rovere, *McCarthy,* 124.
104. For helpful discussions of how, in political rhetoric, the symbol comes to be conflated with the symbolized, see Michael Rogin, *Ronald Reagan the Movie* (Berkeley: University of California Press, 1983); Diane Rubenstein, *This Is Not a President* (New York: New York University Press, 2009).
105. Rovere, *McCarthy,* 138.
106. E.g., Griffith, *Fear,* 48.
107. Rovere, *McCarthy,* 145; "State Department Employee Loyalty Investigation," https://archive.org/stream/statedepartmente195001unit/statedepartmente195001unit_djvu.txt (hereafter *TCH*).
108. Griffith, *Fear,* 67. The exchange is as follows:

 "SENATOR TYDINGS. What I would like to know is this: Is he one of the cases that you are going to bring before this committee, or is he just incidental in this case. You can certainly tell me that.

 SENATOR MCCARTHY. I will bring his name before the committee and give the committee all the information.

 SENATOR LODGE. I would like to express the hope that Senator McCarthy will get the courtesy everyone gets, of being able to make his own statement in his own way, and then be subject to questioning." *TCH,* 4.

109. Griffith, *Fear,* 67–68.
110. Griffith, *Fear,* 67.
111. *TCH,* 18.
112. *TCH,* 28; Griffith, *Fear,* 69.

113. Griffith, *Fear*, 76.
114. *CR*, 81st Congress (March 30, 1950), 4378–4398 (cited in Griffith, *Fear*, 75n62).
115. Griffith, *Fear*, 77. This assertion was vehemently contested during the investigations. Consider the following excerpt from a letter from George C. Marshall to Senator Tydings: "My Dear Senator Tydings: I have received your letter of April 17 in which you refer to a recent statement, in connection with the hearings of the Subcommittee on Foreign Relations under Senate Resolution 231, that 'Owen Lattimore is the principal architect of our far eastern policy.' Your letter then asks the extent to which, in my opinion, 'Lattimore was the principal architect of our far eastern policy' during the period in which I served as Secretary of State. The statement referred to above is completely without basis in fact. So far as I and my associates can recall, I never even met Mr. Lattimore." *TCH*, 873–874.
116. *TCH*, 278.
117. Griffith, *Fear*, 278.
118. Rovere, *McCarthy*, 153; Griffith, *Fear*, 78–79.
119. Griffith, *Fear*, 79.
120. Griffith, *Fear*, 90.
121. Griffith, *Fear*, 40.
122. Rovere, *McCarthy*, 150.
123. *New York Times*, July 18, 1950, 1, 16 (quoted in Griffith, *Fear*, 101).
124. Griffith, *Fear*, 100.
125. For discussions of what healthy constitutional politics means and looks like, see Tulis, "Deliberation Between Institutions," in *Debating Deliberative Democracy*, James S. Fishkin and Peter Laslett (ed.), (Malden, MA: Blackwell, 2003), 200–211; Jeffrey K. Tulis, *The Rhetorical Presidency*, 2nd ed. (Princeton, NJ: Princeton University Press, 2017), 45–59; Mariah Zeisberg, *War Powers* (Princeton, NJ: Princeton University Press, 2013); Bell, "Perverse Politics"; Charles Zug and Connor Ewing, "What Happened to the State of the Union?," *Washington Post*, January 30, 2018.
126. *CR*, 82nd Congress, 1st Session (August 6, 1951), 9498–9501 (quoted in Griffith, *Fear*, 157).
127. *Washington Post*, August 7 and 13, 1951 (quoted in Griffith, *Fear*, 159); *CR*, 82nd Congress, 1st Session (August 20, 1951), 10319–10337 (quoted in Griffith, *Fear*, 161).
128. Griffith, *Fear*, 160; see also 133.
129. *CR*, 82nd Congress, 1st Session (August 9, 1951), 9711 (my italics).
130. Barber, *On What the Constitution Means*, 73.
131. *CR*, 82nd Congress, 1st Session (August 9, 1951), 9711.
132. Griffith, *Fear*, 163.
133. "Senate Resolution 301, December 2, 1954," SEN 83A-B4, Records of the United States Senate, Record Group 46, National Archives, https://www.ourdocuments.gov/doc.php?flash=false&doc=86.
134. Jeffrey Tulis, "Constitutional Statesmanship," in *The Limits of Constitutional Democracy*, Jeffrey Tulis and Stephen Macedo (ed.), (Princeton: Princeton University Press, 2009), 113.
135. Steven Levitsky and Daniel Ziblatt, *How Democracies Die* (New York: Crown Publishing, 2018), 35.
136. William E. Connolly, *Aspirational Fascism* (Minneapolis: University of Minnesota Press, 2017).
137. E.g., Harry T. Williams, *Huey Long* (New York: Vintage Books, 1981).
138. Williams, *Long*, 564.
139. E.g., Williams, *Long*; *CR*, May 12, 1932, 10065.
140. The sentiment expressed in this section's epigraph is emblematic of this dynamic. For example, consider a cartoon titled "Patriotism vs Communism"—created by supporters of Senate majority leader and Long enemy Joseph Robinson—depicting Long as a demagogue waving a Soviet flag. Williams, *Long*, 561.
141. *CR*, April 4, 1932, 7373.
142. *CR*, April 29, 1932, 9219.
143. *CR*, April 4, 1932, 7372 (my italics).
144. E.g., *CR*, April 29, 1932, 9214. "The people of this country want relief, and they do not have to eat a whole beef to tell when it is tainted."

145. *CR*, April 29, 1932, 9213.
146. *CR*, April 4, 1932, 7378.
147. *CR*, May 12, 1932, 10064.
148. *CR*, May 12, 1932, 10065.
149. *CR*, April 29, 1932, 9219.
150. *CR*, May 12, 1932, 10065.
151. *CR*, April 4, 1932, 7372–7373.
152. *CR*, March 13, 1933, [4 (extract)].
153. *CR*, March 13, 1933, [2 (extract)].
154. One of the best articulations of this approach to American constitutional argumentation can be found in chapter 1 of Gary J. Jacobsohn, *Pragmatism, Statesmanship, and the Supreme Court* (Ithaca, NY: Cornell University Press, 1977).
155. *CR*, April 4, 1932, 7372.
156. *CR*, January 25, 1933, 2493.
157. *CR*, April 4, 1932, 7373 (my italics).
158. *CR*, April 29, 1932, 9213.
159. U.S. Constitution, Amendment V, Clause 5.
160. This interpretation of *Federalist* #10 comes from a talk delivered by Jeffrey K. Tulis at the 2019 Jack Miller Center Summer Institute.

Chapter 8

1. As Justice Clarence Thomas' example has demonstrated, even participation in oral argument is optional for a sitting justice, though it is still worth asking if oral arguments are more than merely performative. From a deliberative standpoint, perhaps robust participation in oral argument should be understood as a requisite for judicial excellence.
2. Erwin C. Hargrove, *The President as Leader* (Lawrence: University Press of Kansas, 1998), 85.
3. Bruce Miroff, *Icons of Democracy* (New York: Basic Books, 1993), 244, 237.
4. Miroff, *Icons*, 248–249.
5. Morton J. Frisch, "Franklin Delano Roosevelt," in *American Political Thought*, edited by Morton J. Frisch and Richard G. Stevens (New York: Charles Scribner's Sons, 1971), 219.
6. Miroff, *Icons*, 237.
7. Miroff, *Icons*, 237.
8. Stephen F. Knott, *The Lost Soul of the American Presidency* (Lawrence: University Press of Kansas, 2019), 132–133.
9. Knott, *Presidency*, 133.
10. Frisch, "Roosevelt," 234.
11. "Fireside Chat on Reorganization of Judiciary," March 9, 1937, *Public Papers and Addresses of Franklin D. Roosevelt* (Ann Arbor: University of Michigan Library, 2005), VI:122–132.
12. *Perry v. United States*, 294 U.S. 330 (1935).
13. *Perry v. United States*, Justice McReynolds, dissent, 363.
14. "Reorganization of Judiciary."
15. "Commonwealth Club Address," September 23, 1932, *Public Papers and Addresses*, I:742–756.
16. "Commonwealth Club Address."
17. Some scholars view Roosevelt as a "pragmatist" because he rejected rigid adherence to preconceived doctrines and opened himself to changing circumstances. However, because he sought to interpret changing circumstances in light of enduring constitutional principles, it makes more sense to understand him as a statesman akin to John Marshall Harlan and Charles Evans Hughes as Gary J. Jacobsohn conceptualizes "statesmanship" in *Pragmatism, Statesmanship, and the Supreme Court* (Ithaca, NY: Cornell University Press, 1977).
18. "Reorganization of Judiciary."
19. "Reorganization of Judiciary."
20. "Reorganization of Judiciary."
21. Knott, *Presidency*, 133.

22. "Commonwealth Club Address."
23. "Reorganization of Judiciary."
24. "Reorganization of Judiciary."
25. "Reorganization of Judiciary." The passage is from *Ogden v. Saunders*, 25 U.S. 213, 270.
26. "Reorganization of Judiciary."
27. "Reorganization of Judiciary."
28. "Reorganization of Judiciary."
29. "Reorganization of Judiciary."
30. "Reorganization of Judiciary."
31. Bob Bauer, "Rules and Norms in the Trump Presidency: The Risks and Rewards of 'Playing It Straight' on the Inside," *Lawfare*, September 19, 2019; Max Boot, "Trump Isn't Just Violating Norms—He's Also Breaking the Law," *Washington Post*, April 25, 2019; Charles R. Kesler, "Breaking Norms Will Renew Democracy, Not Ruin It," *New York Times*, August 23, 2018.
32. The most provocative (thought certainly not the most rigorously argued) version of this contention is Michael Anton's *After the Flight 93 Election* (New York: Encounter Books, 2019).
33. John B. Judis, "Donald Trump, Tragic Hero," *New York Times*, March 5, 2019.
34. Victor Davis Hanson, *The Case for Trump* (New York: Basic Books, 2019).
35. Judis, "Tragic Hero."
36. Arthur Milikh, "Trump and *The Federalist* on National Greatness in a Commercial Republic," in *Trump and Political Philosophy: Leadership, Statesmanship, and Tyranny*, edited by A. Jaramillo Torres and M. B. Sable (Cham, Switzerland: Palgrave Macmillan, 2018), 179–194.
37. "Executive Order [13767]: Border Security and Immigration Enforcement Improvements," January 30, 2017: https://www.federalregister.gov/documents/2017/01/30/2017-02095/border-security-and-immigration-enforcement-improvements.
38. Donald Trump, *Twitter*, Dec 25th 2015—3:45:06 PM EST. Because his account has been suspended, Trump's tweets can no longer be accessed at Twitter.com. His tweets have been archived at thetrumparchive.com.
39. "Government Shutdown 2019," *Politico*, https://www.politico.com/latest-news-updates/government-shutdown-2019.
40. Executive Order [13767].
41. For a discussion of the president's prospective advantages vis-à-vis the other branches, see Jeffrey K. Tulis and Joseph Bessette, "On the Constitution, Politics, and the Presidency," in *The Constitutional Presidency*, edited by Joseph M. Bessette and Jeffrey K. Tulis (Baltimore: Johns Hopkins University Press, 2009), 1–27.
42. Trump's executive order cites, among other statutes, the Secure Fence Act of 2006 (Public Law 109-367).
43. Alexander Mallin, "Trump Says Critics of His Administration 'Better Just Take It Easy' with Language, 'Radical Ideas,'" ABC News, July 1, 2018, https://abcnews.go.com/Politics/trump-critics-administration-easy-language-radical-ideas/story?id=56297174.
44. Mallin, "Trump."
45. Manu Raju, "Hill Republicans Revolt over Trump's Plans to Build Border Wall," CNN, February 6, 2017, https://www.cnn.com/2017/02/03/politics/border-wall-republicans/.
46. Bridget Johnson, "Trump to CPAC: Border Wall 'Way, Way, Way Ahead of Schedule,'" PJ Media, February 24, 2017: https://pjmedia.com/news-and-politics/2017/02/24/trump-to-cpac-border-wall-way-way-way-ahead-of-schedule/; "President Trump Is Delivering on Immigration Enforcement for the American People," February 28, 2017, https://br.usembassy.gov/president-trump-delivering-immigration-enforcement-american-people/.
47. "President Donald J. Trump Taking Action Against Illegal Immigration," June 28, 2017: https://trumpwhitehouse.archives.gov/briefings-statements/president-donald-j-trump-taking-action-illegal-immigration/.
48. "President Donald J. Trump's Letter to House and Senate Leaders & Immigration Principles and Policies," October 8, 2017, https://www.presidency.ucsb.edu/documents/letter-congressional-leaders-transmitting-report-immigration-principles-and-policies.
49. "Trump's Letter."
50. "President Donald J. Trump's Weekly Address," December 9, 2017: https://www.c-span.org/video/?438382-1/weekly-presidential-address.

51. "Weekly Address."
52. "Confronting the Urgent Crisis at Our Border," November 1, 2018: https://trumpwhitehouse.archives.gov/briefings-statements/confronting-urgent-crisis-border/.
53. Summary of Shelby's statement by Caitlin Emma in "Lawmakers sprint to settle spending bills despite border wall hangup," *Politico*, December 6, 2018: https://www.politico.com/news/2019/12/06/congress-spending-bill-government-shutdown-077228.
54. Peter Baker, "Trump Says Predecessors Confessed Support for Wall. Not True, They Say," *New York Times*, January 7, 2019, https://www.nytimes.com/2019/01/07/us/politics/trump-carter-presidents-border-wall.html.
55. "President Donald Trump's Address to the Nation on the Crisis at the Border," January 8, 2019, https://trumpwhitehouse.archives.gov/briefings-statements/president-donald-j-trumps-address-nation-crisis-border/; Meg Kelly, "Most Imported Heroin Comes Through Legal Points of Entry," *Washington Post*, January 11, 2019, https://www.washingtonpost.com/politics/2019/live-updates/trump-white-house/live-fact-checking-and-analysis-of-president-trumps-immigration-speech/most-imported-heroin-comes-through-legal-points-of-entry/; Department of Justice and DEA, "2018 National Drug Threat Assessment," 19, https://www.dea.gov/sites/default/files/2018-11/DIR-032-18 2018 NDTA final low resolution.pdf.
56. "On the Crisis at the Border."
57. Knott, *Presidency*, 210; Alan Wolf, *The Politics of Petulance* (Chicago and London: University of Chicago Press, 2018), 154.
58. Jeffrey K. Tulis and Nicole Mellow, *Legacies of Losing in American Politics* (Chicago: University of Chicago Press, 2018), chapter 3, do a nice job showing how, notwithstanding his later demagoguery, Andrew Johnson was able to translate his low motives—especially his racism—into arguments for states' rights and federalism that, despite being ultimately inadequate, were constitutionally superior to those of some advocates of Reconstruction.

Chapter 9

1. See, e.g., Stephen F. Knott, *The Lost Soul of the American Presidency* (Lawrence: University Press of Kansas, 2019).
2. E.g., Paul Moreno, *Bureaucrat Kings* (New York: Praeger, 2016).

INDEX

For the benefit of digital users, indexed terms that span two pages (e.g., 52–53) may, on occasion, appear on only one of those pages.

Note: Figures are indicated by *f* following the page number